RELEASING THE PRAYER ANOINTING

RELEASING THE PRAYER ANOINTING

DR. LARRY LEA

OLIVER NELSON

THOMAS NELSON PUBLISHERS
Nashville • Atlanta • London • Vancouver

Published in Nashville, Tennessee, by Thomas Nelson, Inc., Publishers, and distributed in Canada by Word Communications, Ltd., Richmond, British Columbia.

Unless otherwise noted, the Bible version used in this publication is THE NEW KING JAMES VERSION. Copyright © 1979, 1980, 1982, Thomas Nelson, Inc., Publishers. Scripture quotations noted AMPLIFIED are from THE AMPLIFIED BIBLE: Old Testament. Copyright © 1962, 1964 by Zondervan Publishing House (used by permission); and from THE AMPLIFIED NEW TESTAMENT. Copyright © 1958 by the Lockman Foundation (used by permission). Scripture quotations noted KJV are from The King James Version of the Holy Bible. Verses marked TLB are taken from *The Living Bible,* copyright 1971 by Tyndale House Publishers, Wheaton, IL. Used by permission.

Library of Congress Cataloging-in-Publication Data

Lea, Larry.
    Releasing the prayer anointing : activating your unique gift of prayer / Larry Lea.
        p.   cm.
    Includes bibliographical references (p.).
    ISBN 0-7852-7712-9 (CB)
      1. Prayer—Christianity. I. Title.
BV210.2.L38 1996
248.3'2—dc20   96–6308
                                                   CIP

Printed in the United States of America.

1 2 3 4 5 6 — 01 00 99 98 97 96

CONTENTS

PART 3
Releasing the Anointing of Prevailing Prayer

INTRODUCTION

—✠—

Air-raid sirens shattered the stillness of the dark night in London, England. It was November 1942, and Hitler's Luftwaffe had invaded English skies, launching a nightly reign of terror as their bombs targeted a fearful populace obscured in the unlit city below.

In the midst of this dark period of British history, Prime Minister Winston Churchill spoke these immortal words on November 10, 1942, reviving the spirit of a despondent nation: "Now this is not the end. It is not even the beginning of the end. But it is, perhaps, the end of the beginning."[1]

We see in Churchill's declaration a natural parallel of a mighty spiritual truth. The church of Jesus Christ is positioned at a similar strategic point in time when evil is being manifested as never before, fulfilling the prophetic declaration that in the last days, "lawlessness will abound" (Matt. 24:12). If you do not believe this is so, just review the headlines of your daily newspaper or compare the crime statistics of your city to those of ten years ago or even five years ago. We stand strategically poised at the end of the beginning and facing the beginning of the end.

As we face the tremendous challenges of these cataclysmic days, there is a powerful declaration coming from the Holy Spirit to revive God's people. It is a summons to which we will either respond or rebel: "Today, if you will hear His voice, do not harden your hearts as in the rebellion" (Heb. 3:7–8).

Our critical spiritual position is reminiscent of that of the nation of Israel when they stood on the banks of the Jordan River surveying its swollen, swirling waters. They had been at the same place once before but because of unbelief had refused to heed the Spirit's call:

> For who, having heard, rebelled? Indeed, was it not all who came out of Egypt, led by Moses? Now with whom was He angry forty years? Was it not with those who sinned, whose corpses fell in the wilderness? And to whom did He swear that they would not enter His rest, but to those who did not obey? So we see that they could not enter in because of unbelief (Heb. 3:16–19).

That time, as the people of Israel stood at Jordan's banks, they responded to the word of the Holy Spirit and advanced into the Promised Land. The enemy attempted to hinder their progress, but the Israelites persevered to claim their rightful inheritance. Because they had an ear to hear what the Spirit said and responded obediently in faith, God's people no longer wandered in the wilderness. They moved into intimate relationship with their heavenly Father, which resulted in a new, powerful dimension of spiritual rest.

Poised at the Borders

As you hold this book, *Releasing the Prayer Anointing*, in your hands, you are poised at the borders of a new, supernatural realm that will totally revolutionize your life. Its pages reflect the clarion call that is coming from the Holy Spirit to the church today, and that is the call to pray. I believe that each person has a certain level of prayer for which he or she is responsible to God. For each of us, the call to pray is unique and distinct.

The purpose of this book is to guide you to the prayer level you seek, explain what it takes to function there, and then release the prayer anointing upon you. Like Israel, if you step out in obedience and battle through the enemy forces that would hinder you from reaching your optimum prayer level, your wilderness journey will end and you will terminate your religious struggles. The Spirit of God will begin to move through you to conquer enemy foes, and you will enter into God's rest as the prayer anointing is released upon you.

Just as the leaders of Israel directed the way through Jordan, the pages of this book will guide you from wilderness wandering to the promised land of an anointed, effective personal prayer life. You will enter into an intimate relationship with your heavenly Father where you will no longer have to struggle in prayer. You will learn to pray as Jesus prayed, with the same powerful anointing and the same dynamic results as you experience the anointings of personal, power, and prevailing prayer.

Right now, you may easily relate to a multitude of believers who equate prayer with the frustration of struggling to communicate with what is perceived as an unseen, distant presence. That is about to change! This book will enable you to break through this barrier and come to know God in the intimacy of a Father-child relationship rather than as an absentee father. In so doing, you will tap into an unlimited reservoir of power that will catapult your personal prayer life from simple desire or rigid discipline to absolute delight.

I believe God has given you a personal prayer capacity, a specific level of intercession for which He has ordained you. *Releasing the Prayer Anointing* will empower you to rise up and fulfill your individual destiny. Today, the Holy Spirit is moving across the world calling men and women to experience the prayer anointing. Will you respond in obedience to the call?

PART 1

Releasing
the Anointing
of Personal
Prayer

1

Searching
for My Father

For seven days and nights I remained by his side. Now, in the gathering shadows of a Mexican hotel room, I knew the end was nearing. The clock was ticking off the final minutes of a life. My dad was dying.

How I came to be on foreign soil sitting beside the man who had been my earthly father was a story intricately interwoven into the fabric of my entire life and ministry. As I sat in the quiet stillness, the voices of memory echoed through the lonely corridors of my mind . . .

"You'll never amount to anything, Larry. I will probably have to support you all my life." They were words of alienation and emotional abuse, hurtful words of estrangement that would mark my life for many years to come, and my own father spoke those words.

By outward appearances, our family lived the American dream. My dad accumulated an estate through butane and oil investments in Texas, and as a child, I was privileged to have my material needs abundantly provided. We owned a 5,000-square-foot house, and the entire second floor was mine with two bedrooms, two baths, and a study. In high school I had a brand-new Oldsmobile convertible and a beautiful girlfriend. I was an all-state golfer and earned a scholarship for college.

But against the backdrop of the perfect family image I endured a continuing cycle of alienation, abandonment, and emotional abuse because my father was a textbook case of the syndrome caused by alcoholism. I don't want to depict my dad as a mean person, for when he was himself, he was a caring, kind, and gracious person. But the alcoholism and unresolved spiritual issues in his life surfaced another side of his personality. While I was growing up, my dad was in and out of the home, but even when he was present, the alcohol dependency resulted in mental and emotional alienation. He was there, but he really wasn't *there* for us.

I was only seventeen years old when the emotional impact of my environment resulted in my being committed to the psychiatric ward of Mother Frances Hospital in Tyler, Texas, due to a deep clinical depression. As I walked through the doors of the hospital, I was begging my daddy to help me, but my dad's heart was as empty as mine. He stared at me for a long moment, and then he declared, "Larry, any kid who has everything you have and is this depressed has got to be on dope." Then he turned and walked out. The heavy hospital doors closed behind him, and I was left alone.

You Will Be My Mouth

For six long weeks I lay in the psychiatric ward under the influence of tranquilizers. Finally, my parents made arrangements at the state mental hospital so I could be committed there. One day before the transfer occurred, I began to cry as I sat in my room in a depressed stupor. I fell to my knees and called out, "Jesus! Merciful Jesus!" It was not a very religious or deeply theological prayer. I really had never been taught how to pray, but that cry came from the depths of my being.

Suddenly, I felt a great peace settle over me, and I heard an inner voice speak in my spirit. God said, "Now you are My son. You will take My message to young people of this generation. You will be My mouth and My minister."

The next day the doctor came in and routinely asked, "How are you doing, Larry?"

"I am fine now," I answered. "I talked with God yesterday." The look on the doctor's face readily reflected his opinion of that answer, but soon afterward, I was discharged because the medical staff acknowledged the dramatic change in my life.

After I was released from the hospital, I determined that, with God's help, I would succeed despite the dire predictions of my dad that I would "never amount to anything." In 1972, I graduated from Dallas Baptist University and married my wife, Melva Jo. I was invited by Rev. Howard Conatser, pastor of Beverly Hills Baptist Church in Dallas, to become his youth minister, and by the end of my second year in the position, the youth group had grown to more than one thousand teenagers.

After Rev. Conatser's death in 1978, I was asked to be the pastor of his three-thousand-member church. It was a tempting offer to a twenty-eight-year-old youth minister, but I knew God was leading me in another direction, so I turned it down and began to travel in youth evangelism.

While conducting a youth revival in Kilgore, Texas, I first crossed paths with Pastor Bob Wilhite. For years, my heart had cried out for the intimacy of a dynamic prayer life. In Pastor Wilhite I found a living model of my desire. Through his mentoring and our praying together, the seeds of the revelation that was later to be called *Could You Not Tarry One Hour?* were impregnated in my spirit. Prayer became my highest priority.

Establish My People

I was in Canada conducting a youth revival when the Lord impressed me to go to Rockwall, Texas, and establish His people there. Rockwall was a small town with a population of slightly more than five thousand people at the time, located in the smallest county of Texas some twenty-five miles east of Dallas. Church on the Rock in Rockwall began in January 1980 with thirteen people. We rapidly outgrew the house where we began the fellowship and moved to the Rockwall Skating Rink. We soon outgrew that facility and held services in the Rockwall High School cafetorium.

Due to the tremendous growth of the church, we were in desperate need of our own building. One Sunday after the service, a Texas cowboy came up to me and said, "I don't like preachers, but I like you. God told me you are to be my pastor." Then he took me out to his truck where he pulled out an old work boot and placed it in my hands.

"I've been on the rodeo circuit for the last couple of years and haven't had a home church. I have just been puttin' my tithes in this boot. Now, God says I should give it to you." There was more than $1,000 inside that old boot. I took the boot to the next service at Church on the Rock and shared the story with the congregation. Spontaneously, the audience began to stream forward and stuff the old boot with money to construct the new building we needed. Week after week, the miracle continued, and the Church on the Rock was built without borrowing any money. We moved in debt-free.

Church records reveal that from its 13 initial members, the Church on the Rock grew to more than 11,000 members with a 32-member pastoral staff and 460 home cell groups. During our time in Rockwall, more than 21,000 people walked down those aisles to receive Jesus Christ as Savior.

One of the most thrilling aspects of those years was that my dad became a born-again Christian. All my life I was on an emotional search for my dad, and I struggled to relate to him. These feelings of alienation and abandonment faded as he was delivered from alcoholism, and we became partners in ministry. My dad began to travel with me and became my best friend and confidant.

In the spring of 1986, Oral Roberts asked me to become vice president of spiritual and theological affairs and the dean of the Signs and Wonders Seminary at Oral Roberts University. The elders of Church on the Rock freed me from the routine administrative and counseling duties that consume a pastor's time and released me to take the positions and to pray, preach in our church, and direct the national prayer revival that God was birthing.

We launched a nationwide television ministry focused on prayer, and some 370,000 prayer warriors from all over the world were raised up through the revelation of *Could You Not Tarry One Hour?* In 1987 when my book by that title was released, it immediately became a best-seller; it was translated into thirteen languages and distributed throughout the world. We were poised on the brink of a national revival of prayer, and the mighty power of God affected entire cities.

But in the midst of the tremendous move of God, tragedy struck.

After forty-four years of marriage, my father claimed he was in love with another woman. He married her after divorcing my mother, learned soon afterward that he had terminal cancer, and traveled to Mexico to live out the few remaining weeks of his life.

Searching for My Dad

For seven days as I sat at my dad's bedside, all the childhood emotions of alienation and abandonment returned to haunt me. I recalled all the abusive words he ever spoke to me. I relived the day when the psychiatric hospital doors closed and my dad left me alone. Then I reviewed the past few years when we ministered together during which I thought I had come to know my dad. But had I ever *really* known him? Was it all a surface relationship without any meaning to him? It seemed I had been searching all my life for my real father. As he lay dying, I felt that I had never really found him.

One day, while I sat by his bed struggling with my emotions, my mind went back to an event in 1972 when I was just starting my ministry. My wife, Melva Jo, and I were living in a little house trailer while I was serving as youth pastor. One morning while I was in prayer, God asked me what I wanted out of life. I responded with Philippians 3:10: "That I may know Him and the power of His resurrection, and the fellowship of His sufferings, being conformed to His death."

During the first years of my ministry, I came to know God in power through a prospering ministry, a best-selling book, a growing church, and the national prayer revival of which I had been a part. Now I was to receive another spiritual disclosure, a revelation that could come only through suffering. It would be birthed in the very shadow of death on foreign soil.

The darkness deepened in the room where I sat at my dad's bedside. I wept as I told him good-bye. A few days later there was one last hesitating breath, a flutter of the eyelids, and my dad was gone. Once again, I had lost my father.

2

—✦—

A New Dimension of Life

The birth of a spiritual vision closely parallels the birth of a child. There are the intimacy of conception, the development, and then the birth. Spiritual vision comes through intimacy. The vision develops within the womb of the spirit until time for its birth. Then spiritual birth comes through travail, or what we commonly call labor pains.

In the natural birth process there is a time during labor known as the transition. It is the most difficult time of travail right before the birth canal opens to permit passage of the child. The transition is also evident in the spiritual birth process. Everything within you cries out for relief from the pain, but in this environment of the "fellowship of His sufferings" the birth occurs and the vision emerges.

In the midst of the deep emotional pain I experienced as I sat with my dying earthly father a new revelation was being birthed from the womb of my spirit. It was a vision whose "embryo" was originally conceived with *Could You Not Tarry One Hour?*—a revelation I received when I asked the Lord to teach me how to pray. God directed me to the instructions Jesus gave His disciples when they came to Him with the same request:

> *In this manner, therefore, pray:*
> *Our Father in heaven,*

Hallowed be Your name.
Your kingdom come.
Your will be done
On earth as it is in heaven.
Give us this day our daily bread.
And forgive us our debts,
As we forgive our debtors.
And do not lead us into temptation,
But deliver us from the evil one.
For Yours is the kingdom and the power and the glory forever.
Amen (Matt. 6:9–13).

I know that most believers are quite familiar with this passage and have recited it from early childhood. But when I placed this familiar passage known as the Lord's Prayer under detailed spiritual analysis, the wonders of its true composition were revealed.

There are two versions of this model prayer, one recorded in Matthew 6:9–13 and one in Luke 11:2–4. Most Bible scholars agree that the similarities between them suggest that we are justified in regarding the two versions as forms of the same prayer rather than different prayers.[1] Matthew's version was taught when Jesus presented the Sermon on the Mount. The passage in the book of Luke was given when the disciples came to Jesus asking Him to teach them to pray.

More than two and a half years had passed between the giving of the prayer during the Sermon on the Mount and the incident recorded in Luke. During the interim, the disciples watched Jesus pray. They witnessed the priority He placed on personal prayer. They saw the power resulting from His prayer experiences and the persistence He evidenced in prayer.

As they observed their Master, they noted that His ministry of teaching, preaching, and demonstrating the power of God flowed from His times of intimate fellowship with His Father. What was revealed to Him in prayer was manifested in His ministry. Intercession births revelation, and revelation always results in manifestation.

Teach Us to Pray

All that created in the disciples a yearning desire to learn to pray, so they asked their Master, "Teach us to pray." Jesus responded with the same model prayer He originally taught in the Sermon on the Mount.

When God led me to what is commonly called the Lord's Prayer in answer to my request to learn how to pray, I questioned how I would ever be able to tarry with God for an hour using the passage. Even using the longer version recorded by Matthew, the words take only twenty-two seconds to repeat.

Then God told me to recite the familiar words slowly. When I began to do that, as soon as each phrase was out of my mouth, the Lord dropped into my heart a series of revelations that planted in my spirit the discipline and delight of prayer. I shared the insights in the form of a six-point outline in the book *Could You Not Tarry One Hour?* I took the title from the question Jesus asked His disciples in the Garden of Gethsemane when they could not pray for even one hour.

When the disciples came to Jesus, they said, "Teach us to pray." They did not say, "Teach us a prayer." Jesus responded to their request by using a method employed by the rabbis who listed certain topics of truth and then expanded each point to provide a complete outline. Jesus used the same teaching pattern in the model prayer. He listed various topics and instructed, "In this manner, therefore, pray."

"In this manner, therefore, pray" (*houtos oun* in the Greek text) means "pray along these lines." The text is not saying to use these exact words. As Taylor Bunch explains, Jesus commanded His followers not to repeat the prayer word for word but to pray "in this manner":

> *This indicates clearly that He intended it only as a model, or pattern, to guide them in making their requests to God, and not as a stereotyped form, a meaningless repetition of set words and phrases. It was to avoid this very danger that Jesus warned against the use of vain repetitions which defeat the very purpose of genuine prayer.*[2]

Many people say this prayer, but saying is not praying. Prior to giving the prayer, in the Sermon on the Mount, Jesus warned against vain repetition. The word *vain* includes thoughtless, formal, religious words or phrases repeated ritualistically, habitually, or in chanting form. Jesus did not say that repetition in prayer was wrong, but that repetition without sincerity and understanding was vain. I believe we are to use the exact words of this prayer because His words are spirit and life, but as we repeat them, we must understand and apply their spiritual meaning.

The Prayer Pattern

We easily learn this model prayer by rote, but we understand it only by revelation. In *Could You Not Tarry One Hour?* I focused on six major topics of the prayer as God revealed them, outlining them as follows:

1. *Promises:* Praying based upon the phrase "Our Father in heaven, hallowed be Your name" by appropriating God's names and promises.
2. *Priorities:* Praying "Your kingdom come. Your will be done on earth as it is in heaven," setting and maintaining priorities in your life, your family, your church, and your nation.
3. *Provision:* "Give us this day our daily bread" where you appropriate God's provision for that day.
4. *Pardon:* "And forgive us our debts, as we forgive our debtors" where you learn to have a right attitude toward everyone all the time.
5. *Power:* "And do not lead us into temptation, but deliver us from the evil one" where you put on God's armor and build a hedge of protection about yourself, your family, and your possessions.
6. *Praise:* Obeying God's most dynamic commandment to praise Him, based on "for Yours is the kingdom and the power and the glory forever. Amen."[3]

As thousands of people around the world began to use this model prayer, they found it possible not only to tarry one hour but also to spend longer periods with the Lord in prayer. Although simple in structure, it is so comprehensive that it covers every spiritual and material need of humankind. Every theological precept encompassed in the Word of God and every biblical message taught, preached, or sung relates to its truths.

The Missing Dimension

As powerful as the revelation of *Could You Not Tarry One Hour?* was, I felt something was lacking when I taught on its six-point outline. On occasion I expressed my feelings to the people to whom I was ministering. The topical outline had six points, but seven was God's perfect number. What was missing in the pattern for prayer?

Sitting by my dying father's side, I never dreamed that the missing dimension for which I had sought all those years would be birthed in such an environment. I felt absolutely alone, betrayed, and abandoned. It seemed to me that even God's presence had totally withdrawn from my life and ministry. I experienced what the patriarch Abraham must have felt when God promised to birth a son through him and then for years he had no further word from God.

But during the long years of silence, God was at work in Abraham preparing him for a new dimension of life, that of fatherhood. In the churning bowels of suffering, God was at work preparing me to receive a new dimension of spiritual life. It was a revelation of fatherhood that would lead to a new, supernatural releasing of the prayer anointing. It was the seventh element missing from the original six-point outline of *Could You Not Tarry One Hour?* It was the number of biblical perfection, the number of God.

3

—✦—

The Revelation of the Father

There was a deep chasm that was never bridged in my relationship with my earthly father. It was not because he did not try to be the best father in the world but because of the dissociative effects of alcohol and a lack of spirituality in our home. I was left with a feeling of abandonment throughout my adolescence. Although my dad was a great provider and one of the most genuinely tender and warm people I have ever known, his inability to communicate with spiritual warmth left me always seeking approval. He really cared, yet his demons kept him darkly distant.

During my childhood, I was never able to communicate my thoughts and feelings to Dad. Underneath our surface problems was a bond of love, but it was incomplete and conditional. We never seemed to connect, despite many long conversations.

Many people are privileged to have wonderful, caring fathers, but a vast multitude of people can relate to the somewhat negative image of fatherhood that I carried in my mind. As Phillip Keller notes, "It is a frightening fact that for many people, the word father does not denote a dear one. It does not conjure up the thought of a happy home. Rather, to them it may well be a repulsive and abhorrent title."[1]

Our Concept of God

To a large extent, our concept of God as Father is shaped by our experience with an earthly father. Traumatic childhood images can become barriers to relating to God in the dimension of fatherhood.

That happened in my life. Because of the negative concepts of my father that lingered from my childhood experiences, I could not perceive the powerful revelation of the fatherhood of God set forth in the model prayer. At the end of Dad's life, through the devastating circumstances that marked his final days and their effects on me, I was forced to confront my damaged emotions and deal with them. Only then could I receive the revelation, and the model prayer took on a totally new meaning. I realized that every request—every portion of the prayer—was intricately linked to the fatherhood of God.

This fatherhood aspect of God's nature is basically a New Testament concept. Throughout the Old Testament, God is referred to as Yahweh, a name that dared not be spoken for fear of offense. The Old Testament has relatively few references to God as Father, and most of them are indirect, revealing Israel as a son or comparing God's actions to those of a human father. Philip Harner states,

> *There does not seem to be a single prayer in the Old Testament in which God is actually addressed as "Father." Several times we find the statements, "Thou art our Father" (Isaiah 63:16; 64:8) or "thou art my Father" (Psalm 89:26; Jeremiah 3:4). Strictly speaking, however, these are probably statements rather than forms of direct address to God.[2]*

Jesus Reveals the Father

At the close of the Old Testament record, some four hundred years of silence elapse in the biblical record. Then, similar to the pattern of revelation after the years of silence in Abraham's life, a birth brings a new dimension to our spiritual understanding. Through the birth, life, and ministry of Jesus Christ, the fatherhood of God is revealed.

The first recorded words of Jesus as a child in the temple reference this new relationship when He calls God His Father. Jesus speaks of God as "Father" numerous times in the New Testament record of His ministry. He prays to the Father, teaches about His Father, and does the will and work of His Father.

When Jesus called God His Father, the form of address was controversial. If God was Father, that meant Jesus was claiming sonship to Yahweh. For the Jewish people who dared not breathe

the Old Testament name of God, it was a revolutionary concept. The claim of sonship actually led to Christ's crucifixion (John 19:7).

When the disciples asked Jesus to teach them to pray, Jesus instructed them to direct their prayers to "our Father in heaven." That was an incredible new concept of God to those men. The Aramaic word for Father, which Jesus used in this prayer, is translated "Abba." It was a word that little children used to speak to their fathers, and because of its meaning in Jewish family life, no Jew of the time would have thought of using "Abba" to address God.

By directing the disciples to use that name in prayer, Jesus was giving them the privilege of entering into a new sonship relationship with God. It was a unique relationship that even the angels could not experience (Heb. 1:5).

During the earthly ministry of Jesus, the crowds saw Him only as Joseph's son (Luke 4:22). But from the beginning, some people grasped the powerful new meaning in the Father-Son relationship claimed by Jesus. When the Lord called Nathanael from under the fig tree, he immediately acknowledged Jesus as the Son of God (John 1:49). Demons recognized the sonship relationship of Jesus with the Father. Christ's encounters with demonic forces evidenced the power of the relationship as demons cried out, "What have we to do with You, Jesus, You Son of God?" (Matt. 8:29).

The Father confirmed the sonship of Jesus at the beginning of His earthly ministry when, during Christ's baptism, God said, "This is My beloved Son" (Matt. 3:17). Satan immediately attacked the sonship relationship during the Temptation when he taunted, "*If* You are the Son of God," make these stones into bread and cast Yourself down from the pinnacle of the temple (Luke 4).

Right up to the conclusion of the ministry of Jesus, Satan continued to target the beloved Son–Father relationship. When Jesus hung on the cross, the crowd cried out, "*If* You are the Son of God, save Yourself!"

When the apostle Peter finally came to understand the Father-Son relationship and acknowledged Christ as "the Son of the living God," Jesus indicated that upon that revelation, He would build a church against whom the gates of hell could not prevail (Matt. 16:16–18).

Tremendous spiritual resources are available to those who, like Peter, recognize the fatherhood of God and the power of relating to

Him as sons and daughters. Satan recognized the power inherent in the Father-Son relationship, and that is why he constantly attacked it in the life of Christ. He will target the fatherhood issue in your life, too, just as he did in mine.

The Revelation of the Father

At the time of Peter's recognition of the sonship of Christ, Jesus declared that the revelation could not come by flesh and blood. That is, if we are to really understand the fatherhood of God, if we are ever to enter into the intimacy of sonship, we must experience a spiritual breakthrough. Many of us must rise above the negative connotations resulting from the flesh-and-blood images of our earthly fathers. We must move beyond how our minds and emotions conceive fatherhood and allow our spirits to receive the revelation of our heavenly Father.

Your father may have been an absentee father who deserted and abandoned you. He may have been insensitive, immature, and emotionally distant. He may have evidenced anger, manipulation, and violence. You may have been physically, sexually, or emotionally abused by the very one who should have been your protector.

Recently, the pastor of a large church spoke to me at the conclusion of a service in which I had ministered. He told me he always prayed to Jesus because he had difficulty relating to God as Father. He had never really experienced sonship with God because of a poor relationship with his earthly father. That night, he received a spiritual breakthrough that brought him into intimate fellowship with God the Father.

Phillip Keller observes, "The tragedy is that in ascribing the title to God as our Father, we sometimes unconsciously transfer to Him all those debasing attributes associated in our minds with our human fathers."[3]

Have you sensed something missing in your relationship with God? Do you long for intimacy with your heavenly Father? Do you want to be able to enter His presence every time you pray with assurance that every petition will be heard? Then you are ready to begin the divine progression that leads to the release of the prayer anointing.

4

—⊹—

The Divine Progression

The cry of money changers, the bleating of sheep, and the bellowing of oxen filled the air. The chief priests and scribes, clothed in their long ceremonial robes, mingled in the crowds of people. Pairs of doves beat their wings against the bars of their wooden cages, and the acrid smoke from the sacrifice of animals hovered over the noisy corridors of the temple in Jerusalem.

Into the midst of the frenzied activity walked Jesus. Within moments, the scene became one of utter chaos. Jesus overthrew the tables of the money changers and the seats of those who sold doves, scattering their merchandise and money, and using a small whip to drive them out of the temple. A shocked hush descended on the crowd as Jesus declared with authority, "It is written, 'My house shall be called a house of prayer,' but you have made it a 'den of thieves'" (Matt. 21:13).

This statement regarding the Father's house not only is applicable to the immediate situation Jesus faced in the Jerusalem temple, but it also contains two powerful spiritual truths that will guide us in our quest for relationship with our heavenly Father.

God's Spiritual Residence

First, this statement reveals that our Father has a spiritual residence. His dwelling place is the house of prayer. Those who were

17

previously spiritual "foreigners" will have a place in this house and will be given a new name:

> *Even to them I will give in My house*
> *And within My walls a place and a name*
> *Better than that of sons and daughters;*
> *I will give them an everlasting name*
> *That shall not be cut off (Isa. 56:5).*

We can enter into a relationship with God that is superior to that of the natural father-child bond, which is often tenuously based on performance and can be broken by misunderstanding and conflict. The relationship that our heavenly Father offers is permanent. It is everlasting, and God declares it cannot be terminated.

God also reveals that these spiritual sons and daughters will be brought to His "holy mountain," which means they will have intimate access to Him. Through this familial relationship, His children receive the prayer anointing, and their offerings and sacrifices are accepted on His altar (Isa. 56:7).

All of us were at one time foreigners spiritually, separated from the Father by our sinful nature. It is God's desire to bring us into intimate relationship with Him and bestow upon us the right of unrestricted access to His presence: "That at that time you were without Christ, being aliens from the commonwealth of Israel and strangers from the covenants of promise, having no hope and without God in the world. But now in Christ Jesus you who once were far off have been brought near by the blood of Christ" (Eph. 2:12–13).

The Father wants to give you a new name and adopt you into His family. The name He longs to bestow upon you is better than that of the father-child relationship in the natural world because it is an everlasting name: "Behold what manner of love the Father has bestowed on us, that we should be called children of God!" (1 John 3:1).

Robbing Thieves

The second truth evident in Jesus' declaration as He cleansed the temple is that there are "thieves" who would rob us of this experience

(Matt. 21:13). In the temple at Jerusalem, the people were being robbed of the true experience of the Father's house by the materialistic money changers, the frenzied activities of business, and the superfluous rituals of religion imposed by the priests and scribes. Jesus called this environment a "den of thieves."

A spiritual parallel of this situation threatens us today. There are thieves who would rob us and prevent us from entering into the prayer anointing. Their identities are the same as those in the Jerusalem temple: the unrelenting pursuit of materialistic goals, frenzied activities, and the rituals of religion. If we are to ever enter into the "house of prayer" experience where true intimacy is developed and the prayer anointing is released, we must drive this den of thieves out of our personal temples and our corporate church fellowships.

Immediately after the dramatic confrontation in the Jerusalem temple, the Scriptures record how people who could not see or walk came into the temple, Jesus healed them, and the children began to sing praises, saying, "Hosanna to the Son of David!" The sonship of Jesus was acknowledged when the temple became a house of prayer and an arena for the demonstration of God's power. Your own sonship relationship with the Father will be revealed to the world only when your spiritual temple is cleansed and you become a house of prayer where God's anointing and power are demonstrated.

Imagine the scene unfolding in the temple as the children were praising God and people were throwing down their crutches, walking, leaping, and praising God. Men with newly received vision looked for the first time upon the faces of their wives and children. Instead of a forum for the merchandising of religion, the temple became what God intended. It was a house of prayer for people who were hurting.

But there, at the fringes of the tremendous spiritual move of God, stood the religious leaders with folded arms and indignant, angry countenances (Matt. 21:15). The leaders were upset because their domineering control of the people was eroding and their power and position were threatened. They angrily confronted Jesus by asking, "Do You hear what these are saying?" Jesus answered, "Yes. Have you never read, 'Out of the mouth of babes and nursing infants you have perfected praise'?" (Matt. 21:16).

The religious leaders demonstrated a spirit of accusation, which always attacks people who enter into the spirit of the intercessor by releasing the prayer anointing. Such accusations are motivated by Satan, who is the accuser of the brethren. He wants to discourage you from becoming a house of prayer and receiving this prayer anointing, for he knows there is inherent spiritual power when you develop intimacy with the Father.

A Divine Progression

For many years I struggled with a lack of intimacy and power in my prayer life. Meaningless religious rituals, time-consuming activities, and materialistic pursuits robbed me spiritually. All that changed when I made what I call the divine progression, which is evident in Matthew 21:12–16.

The divine progression evident in this passage will revolutionize your life when you grasp its truths. It changed my life when it was first revealed to me in 1970 while I was a student at Dallas Baptist University. While I was in prayer one day, the Lord told me that in my lifetime I would witness a progression of His church similar to what occurred in the temple.

First, Jesus cleansed the temple, causing it to become a house of *purity* (v. 12). Jesus then made the declaration that it would be called a house of *prayer* (v. 13). Next, the temple became a house of *power* as people who could not see or walk came to Him and He healed them (v. 14). Finally, the temple became a house of *perfected praise* (vv. 15–16).

This same divine progression must take place individually in the spiritual temple of our lives and corporately in the church today: "Do you not know that you are the temple of God and that the Spirit of God dwells in you?" (1 Cor. 3:16).

When you become a child of God, His Spirit dwells in your spirit just as the genetic makeup of your earthly father resides in your physical body. This new nature is conceived by the Spirit of God when you become a believer in Jesus Christ by confessing and repenting of your sin.

It is our Father's divine purpose to take up residence in each person's spiritual "temple" so that each person becomes a "house of prayer." Instead, many of us have allowed a "den of thieves" to seize control.

We long for the power of God to be demonstrated in our lives and churches, but before this can occur, our spiritual temples must be cleansed. Some of us are caught up in a bedlam of "Christian" activities and secular business while right in the shadow of the temple gates people with disabilities and illnesses wait for deliverance. In many cases, the church has become a social or recreational center instead of an arena for the demonstration of God's power. In the frenzy of our religious activities the cries of people who cannot see or walk, representing the whole of suffering humanity, are muted.

In the midst of this chaotic spiritual environment, Jesus stands ready to cleanse us and make us houses of purity. He longs to change our materialistic focus to a focus on the kingdom of God. He wants to calm our frantic activity, rid us of the rituals of religion, and bestow upon us the prayer anointing.

If you permit Jesus to cleanse your spiritual temple, you will become a house of prayer, a place for intimate relationship with your heavenly Father. You will become a spiritual temple where suffering humanity can come to receive their miracle.

Are You Ready?

Are you ready to make this transition? Are you tired of being robbed of intimacy with your heavenly Father? Do you hunger for the manifestation of God's power in your life and want to become a temple of purity, prayer, power, and perfected praise to God? If your answer is yes to these questions, you are already on your way because desire is the first step in this divine progression.

Any change initially requires desire that must be transformed to discipline and will ultimately result in delight. For example, if you want to change your physical appearance, it involves first the desire to do so, then comes the discipline of diet and exercise. If you are persistent, you will be delighted with the results.

Changing spiritually and receiving the prayer anointing also start with desire. To make desire a reality, however, you must have the discipline to cleanse the temple. You must change your priorities, you must adjust your busy schedule, and you must lay aside the outward trappings of religious traditions. You must become a house of prayer, and praying must become your highest priority.

When Jesus comes to cleanse our temples, He comes to discipline, not to destroy. Biblical discipline is receiving revelation from the Word of God and acting upon it. His purging is not punitive (punishment), but corrective: "He has promised, saying, 'Yet once more I shake not only the earth, but also heaven.' Now this, 'Yet once more,' indicates the removal of those things that are being shaken, as of things that are made, that the things which cannot be shaken may remain" (Heb. 12:26–27).

As we are shaken spiritually, the thieves of our spiritual experience scatter. Our materialistic focus changes to a kingdom mentality, and proper spiritual priorities emerge. Our frenzied activities cease, and our empty religious rituals are cast aside like old, worn-out garments.

Following the same pattern revealed in Matthew 21:12–16, when your spiritual temple is cleansed, it becomes a house of purity. You then become a house of prayer where the intercessor's anointing is released, and God demonstrates His supernatural power. This results in a new dimension of praise and worship as you develop true intimacy with your heavenly Father.

When Jesus completed His cleansing of the Jerusalem temple, there were only two divisions of people. You will enter into the house of prayer with the jubilant people who were healed and the praising children, or you will stand in the shadows of the accusers with an attitude of indignation.

As you read these pages, you may be at the place of purity, and God is drawing you to become a house of prayer. Right now, invite Jesus to walk into the midst of your cluttered spiritual temple. Let Him drive out and overturn anything in your life that is preventing you from becoming a house of prayer. Jesus is present in your temple to set in motion the divine progression that leads to the prayer anointing. Will you let Him?

If your heart answer is, "Yes, come, Lord Jesus," I can assure you that the prayer anointing will be loosed in your life, empowering you to rise up and reach your personal prayer capacity.

5

—✠—

Spiritual Adoption

God reveals His passionate desire to relate to us as a Father, declaring in His Word: "I will be a Father to you, and you shall be My sons and daughters" (2 Cor. 6:18). In a survey of members of six hundred churches, however, 64 percent of the people said that they could not relate to God as Father.[1]

The spiritual strategies for entering into this relationship are found in the Lord's Prayer. In the following pages, I will put this prayer under the microscope of the Holy Spirit, presenting each segment through the light of my revelation of the fatherhood of God. In its inspired verbiage you will learn how to gain access to your heavenly Father's presence and appropriate His promises, pardon, provision, and protection as you come under the mantle of the prayer anointing.

Our Father

From the beginning salutation "our Father," the model prayer confirms that God's desire can become a reality in our lives. When we say "our Father," we not only are proclaiming the paternity of God, but we also are acknowledging the brotherhood and sisterhood of all true believers. These words link us with all others who pray this prayer, bridging denominational and doctrinal differences. We cannot say "our" without eliminating the divisions between us and God and between us and other people.

"Our Father" unites us all in one spiritual family with one Father. We are not spiritual orphans. The entire remaining portion of the prayer outline is based upon and prayed within the context of this union with God and all true believers. The word *our* is the spirit of the intercessor who, like Moses, classes himself with God's people. It is not the spirit of the accuser who, like the Pharisee, prays, "I thank You that I am not as other men."

The salutation "our Father" identifies those who can actually pray this pattern of prayer. Only true children of God can pray "our Father." Others may say it, but saying is not praying. All people are God's children by creation, but not by redemption. When people were first created, they were part of God's royal family. Adam and Eve shared an intimate relationship of spiritual communion with their heavenly Father. This original family tie with God was broken when Adam and Eve sinned. Rebellious humanity then became members of an alien family with Satan as their father (Gen. 3).

No Neutrality

This familial division marks all of humankind. There is no neutrality. We are children of God or children of Satan. Jesus told the Pharisees they were of their father the devil (John 8:44). He spoke of "the sons of the wicked one" (Matt. 13:38) and "children of wrath" (Eph. 2:3). John distinguished between children of God and children of Satan (1 John 3:7–10).

Because of the original sin of Adam and Eve, the Bible teaches that all people subsequently born in the natural world have an inherent sin nature. As we exercise this nature, we are further alienated from God the Father by our personal sins. Only through the spiritual rebirth of the "born again" experience described in John 3 can we become children of God (John 3:6, 16). When we accept the sacrifice of Jesus Christ who died in our place for our sins, we receive power to become the children of God: "But as many as received Him [Jesus], to them He gave the right to become children of God, to those who believe in His name" (John 1:12).

When the apostle Philip said, "Lord, show us the Father, and it is sufficient for us," Jesus explained the intimate union between Father and Son by saying, "I am in the Father, and the Father in Me" (John 14:8–11). The Father is revealed in the person of Jesus Christ. God draws us to Jesus, and Jesus reveals the fatherhood of God to us (Luke 10:22). When Jesus taught us to pray to "our Father in heaven," He invited us to share in a sonship relationship with the Father: "But when the fullness of the time had come, God sent forth His Son, born of a woman, born under the law, to redeem those who were under the law, that we might receive the adoption as sons. And because you are sons, God has sent forth the Spirit of His Son into your hearts, crying out, 'Abba, Father!'" (Gal. 4:4–6).

Jesus was the only begotten Son, but we are adopted sons and daughters of God through the death of Jesus Christ for our sins. The Spirit of the Son, the Holy Spirit, enables us to cry, "Abba, Father," a term denoting all the intimacy of a little child who cries, "Daddy." Spiritual adoption restores us to sonship. Regeneration gives us the new nature enabling us to live as sons and daughters because as believers we become partakers of the divine nature of our heavenly Father (2 Peter 1:4).

When we say "our Father" as we begin to pray, we release ourselves from the bondage of fear resulting from the curse of sin and death. We allow the Holy Spirit to speak through our lips and bear witness that we are truly the children of God:

> For you did not receive the spirit of bondage again to fear, but you received the Spirit of adoption by whom we cry out, "Abba, Father." The Spirit Himself bears witness with our spirit that we are children of God, and if children, then heirs—heirs of God and joint heirs with Christ, if indeed we suffer with Him, that we may also be glorified together (Rom. 8:15–17).

As heirs of God and joint heirs with Christ, we have the same access to and attention of our heavenly Father as Jesus had. Once this revelation is birthed in your spirit, you will pray with the same authority and expectancy as Jesus prayed.

A Revelation Birthed Through Suffering

The full understanding of this spiritual Father-son relationship is birthed only through suffering, however. That happened in Abraham's life as God prepared him to receive the revelation of fatherhood in the birth of Isaac. That happened in the life of Jesus who, as a Son, learned obedience through suffering.

We also see this pattern in the lives of Christ's disciples. Jesus taught them the model prayer before the Gethsemane experience, yet they still could not tarry with Him in prayer for even one hour in the Garden. In the Upper Room, however, we find these same disciples tarrying for days in prayer *prior* to the experience of Pentecost recorded in Acts 2. What made the tremendous difference in their prayer life? The revelation of the Father-Son relationship that came through the suffering and death of Jesus. When Jesus died, the vision and dreams of the disciples died with Him. When Jesus appeared in resurrected form, the disciples finally grasped the reality that He was truly the Son of God.

Suffering prepares us to receive a new revelation of the fatherhood of God. It is the process that brings us into intimate fellowship with Him (Phil. 3:10). The resulting impact of this revelation of spiritual adoption accomplishes the same thing in our lives as it did in the lives of the disciples. It takes men and women who cannot tarry for even one hour and turns us into intercessors who can wait before God for days at a time. Prayer becomes a way of life, for we realize that the continuing revelation of God's fatherhood is essential not only to answered prayer but also to the sustenance and strength that make victorious living a reality. Do you seek such a transforming relationship with God? Then let us continue our spiritual quest for the personal prayer anointing.

6

✢

Our Father in Heaven

Over a period of several years, a Christian counselor questioned hundreds of women seeking counseling about the positive traits that should be evidenced by a good father. A summary of these results revealed an emphasis on the importance of love, responsiveness, compassion, tenderness, communication, patience, care, provision, gentleness, and understanding.[1]

These qualities are evidenced in the nature of our heavenly Father, but for some of us to fully comprehend this, we must make a major adjustment in our view of God. Some of us can readily relate to a young man who summarized his feelings about his absentee father in an article entitled "No Father, No Answers": "I realized the gravity of the void he had left in my life had influenced my relationships and my perspectives like an uncharted planet affects the bodies around it."[2]

We must permit the Word of God to transform such negative conceptions to a proper biblical perspective. The Scriptures reveal a compassionate Father (Heb. 2:16–18). He is not a stern, angry disciplinarian who accepts His children conditionally based on performance. Our Father is depicted as gentle and merciful (Ps. 103:13). In our heavenly Father there are security and unconditional acceptance, for we are assured that the "son abides forever" in the Father's house (John 8:35).

"Our Father" indicates nearness, but "in heaven" implies distance. Psalm 139 reveals, however, that God is everywhere:

Where can I go from Your Spirit?
Or where can I flee from Your presence?
If I ascend into heaven, You are there;
If I make my bed in hell, behold, You are there.
If I take the wings of the morning,
And dwell in the uttermost parts of the sea,
Even there Your hand shall lead me,
And Your right hand shall hold me (vv. 7–10).

God is not an absentee Father. He is pictured as a Father who is present to guide us so that we do not stumble:

I will cause them to walk by the rivers of waters,
In a straight way in which they shall not stumble;
For I am a Father to Israel (Jer. 31:9).

When we pray to "our Father in heaven," our words do not emphasize the distance between us and the Father; they immediately bring us from the natural world to a powerful spiritual plane. They assure us that God has at His disposal the entire resources of the supernatural realm with which to respond to the requests we present in the remainder of the model prayer. When we pray "Our Father in heaven," we are immediately linked through Christ with a supernatural God with unlimited supernatural resources (Phil. 4:19). The Father knows our needs (Matt. 6:8), and He listens when we present our petitions to Him (John 16:23).

The Prodigal Son

Our heavenly Father is a God of love, and the Father-child relationship demonstrates the true measure of that love. Perhaps the greatest biblical picture of the true nature of our heavenly Father appears in the story of the prodigal son (Luke 15:11–32). A father had two sons who were his only heirs. One day, the man's younger son came to him wanting his inheritance, and the father graciously complied. The young man then left the father's house, traveled to a far land, and consumed all his inheritance in a wicked lifestyle.

When the prodigal son lost his fortune, he was compelled to tend pigs. While he was sitting in the pigpen, the Bible records that the young man "came to himself," realized his shameful condition, and decided to return to his father's house.

We see a portrayal of our heavenly Father's unconditional love in the account of the prodigal son's return. Seeing his wayward son coming down the road to home, the father ran to meet him while he was still a great way off.

The father readily received his son into the home. He did not disown or disinherit him, nor did he try to reestablish relationship by shaming him in any way. The young man was a son not conditionally based on performance but unconditionally based on relationship. This story reflects the character of our heavenly Father, who does not manipulate us into obedience through shame.

The father placed his signet ring on the son's hand as a symbol of the special union between them. In those days, the signet ring was used to seal letters and important communications with authority similar to that of a corporate seal or a notary's stamp as used today. By placing the ring on his son's finger, the father made available to the boy the resources of his entire estate. The father also removed the son's ragged garments and clothed him in a beautiful robe, representative of the righteousness of Christ. He placed shoes on his feet, which confirmed his position as a son. Only sons wore shoes. Slaves went barefoot.

The saddest image in this parable is that of the older son who remained at home, but never really got to know his father. The young man related to his dad in the same way many of us do to our fathers. He saw him as demanding, and he perceived the relationship with him to be based on performance.

When the younger son returned home, bitterness was evident in the elder son's attitude. He refused to enter the house, and he accused his brother of devouring the father's livelihood with harlots (Luke 15:28–30). Just as the scribes and priests spoke against Jesus in the Jerusalem temple, the spirit of accusation surfaced. It was directed toward the one claiming his rightful relationship of sonship with the father.

The *actions* of the younger son separated him from his father. The *attitude* of the older son alienated him from a loving relationship with his dad. If we are to experience the true nature of our Father's love, we must eliminate the actions and attitudes that prevent us from entering our Father's house of prayer. We must foster a new understanding of our heavenly Father's nature, unaffected by haunting images that might remain from relationships with our earthly fathers.

The positive experience of a loving earthly father will enable many to readily grasp this mental image of our heavenly Father racing down the road to receive them as sons and daughters. A loving relationship with an earthly parent majestically enhances the spiritual relationship with God the Father.

Conversely, those whose lives have been indelibly marked by a poor father image will find it more difficult to grasp the divine nature of the heavenly Father. That was true for a young woman we will call Marie. She was raped by her father, and she conceived his child at age twelve. After the baby girl was born, her father sold it to a childless couple. Years of physical and emotional abuse eventually influenced her to lead a life of crime. Incarcerated in a county jail while awaiting a lengthy sentence at the state prison, Marie returned to her cell one day to find a Bible open on her bed. Her eyes fell on these words: "For God so loved the world that He gave His only begotten Son, that whoever believes in Him should not perish but have everlasting life. For God did not send His Son into the world to condemn the world, but that the world through Him might be saved" (John 3:16–17).

As Marie accepted the supernatural revelation of the love of her heavenly Father through these verses, the horrible memories left by her earthly father were healed. She entered into relationship with a heavenly Father who viewed her through eyes of love rather than condemnation. The impact of this experience revolutionized her whole life. She was later released from prison and graduated from a Bible college with a bachelor's degree in Christian education.

Three Keys to Intimacy

Three dynamic spiritual keys will enable you to develop this intimacy with your heavenly Father, regardless of the nature of your relationship with your earthly father.

First, you must develop an attitude of thankfulness for your earthly father, even though he may have hurt you deeply. William Gaultiere advises,

> Take a realistic look at your father's influence upon you. Sort out the good from the bad in your relationship with him. Thank him and God for the good that you received from your father. Acknowledge the bad too by confessing the sins of your father against you, sins of commission and sins of omission.[3]

Paul learned this secret of thankfulness when he prayed three times about the painful thorn in his flesh, only to still carry its wounds. Finally, Paul began to glory in the infirmity, recognizing that in his weakness God's power was manifested:

> Concerning this thing I pleaded with the Lord three times that it might depart from me. And He said to me, "My grace is sufficient for you, for My strength is made perfect in weakness." Therefore most gladly I will rather boast in my infirmities, that the power of Christ may rest upon me. Therefore I take pleasure in infirmities, in reproaches, in needs, in persecutions, in distresses, for Christ's sake. For when I am weak, then I am strong (2 Cor. 12:8–10).

Despite the failures of your earthly father, thank God for him. You may not feel like doing this because of your past experiences, but remember what Jesus told Peter. This revelation of sonship does not come through "flesh and blood." It comes only by a spiritual experience, and to receive it, you must permit your spirit to overrule your mind and emotions.

As you begin to glory in your infirmity, God will give you a revelation of His fatherhood. Carry your pain with dignity to the cross and confess, "You are my Father!" If you will praise God in the midst of your pain, the resulting revelation of fatherhood will be even greater because of what you missed in the relationship with your biological father because God's power is perfected in weakness.

Second, believe the testimony of the blood of Jesus Christ instead of the feelings generated by your emotions. Hebrews 12:24 indicates that the blood of Jesus "speaks" for us spiritually. The witness of the blood of Jesus is that God is your heavenly Father and you are His child. It is an eternal testimony, and it is always speaking.

Third, as you thank God for your earthly father and acknowledge, "You are my Father," let your faith rise to confess the testimony of the blood of Jesus until you feel your spirit begin to override the mental images and emotions triggered by your earthly father-child relationship. As you confess the Father, the spirit of adoption will work in you to release you from the bondages of the past: "For you did not receive the spirit of bondage again to fear, but you received the Spirit of adoption by whom we cry out, 'Abba, Father'" (Rom. 8:15). Continue to confess, "You are my Father," until you reach a point that from your innermost spirit you can cry out, "Abba, Father."

A Powerful Truth

The concept of God's fatherhood is a powerful theological truth. When we say, "Our Father in heaven," we are brought into the very presence of God Himself. As an unknown Christian noted many years ago, "If you stopped at 'Our Father' you would have uttered the chief part of the prayer. You would have put your life in God's hands."[4]

Satan will do all in his power to prevent you from entering into this experience. He wants to prevent you from tapping into the power inherent in recognizing you are a child of God and an heir to the resources of your heavenly Father.

The words *our Father* acknowledge God as Father of all believers from every people group, tribe, and nation and eliminate national, racial, societal, and personal barriers. These powerful words join us together spiritually as Siamese twins are joined at birth in the natural world, sharing the life force of our spiritual Father.

This confession of the paternity of God is the first dimension of the model prayer and basic to experiencing the personal prayer anointing. Acknowledging God as Father releases us into a cycle of receptivity for His person, programs, provision, and plans as they are revealed in the remainder of the prayer. It adds the seventh element of completeness to the original pattern I detailed in *Could You Not Tarry One Hour?*

The seven steps in this prayer plan are like seven arteries carrying life to your spiritual body and keeping your spiritual blood system functioning properly. As soon as you cry out, "Our Father in heaven," and mean it from the depths of your spirit, you have tapped into this life flow. God has put it in my heart to pray that you will receive this wonderful revelation as we proceed into the supernatural realm of the prayer anointing.

7

—✠—

How to Enter Your Father's Presence Every Time You Pray

Have you ever felt that your prayers were echoing off the walls around you and going no higher than the ceiling? Do you have trouble feeling the presence of an invisible heavenly Father when you pray? You are not alone in these feelings. The psalmist David addressed this problem of accessing God's presence when he questioned, "Who may ascend into the hill of the LORD? Or who may stand in His holy place?" (Ps. 24:3). Then David answered the query he posed:

> *He who has clean hands and a pure heart,*
> *Who has not lifted up his soul to an idol,*
> *Nor sworn deceitfully (Ps. 24:4).*

This passage seems to set impossible standards for our approach to God. It indicates that only those with clean hands and pure hearts and souls can approach His holy place. Does that mean God is like some earthly fathers who set impossible standards of achievement upon which acceptance of their children is conditionally based?

George Dorn comments that this passage is black with despair:

> *For who is there whose hands are clean? Who is there whose heart is pure? . . . If we have to wait until our hands are clean and our hearts*

34

pure we shall never, never ascend unto the hill of the Lord or stand in His holy place. What warrant have I to pray? What right have I to come boldly to the throne of grace?[1]

Accessing God's Presence

I struggled with this issue of access to God's presence for years until the Father revealed to my spirit the pattern of the model prayer. As soon as I uttered, "Our Father in heaven," I received a new perspective of how we are assured access to the presence of God every time we pray.

This understanding came through a vision in which I saw Jesus with a large basin in His hands. He was walking toward a huge rock altar illuminated by the backdrop of a great light. Then the Lord emptied the contents of the basin on the altar, and I recognized it as the living liquid of His blood. While I watched the blood flow down over the altar, I realized that it testified that through its power, I have access to God the Father:

> *Therefore, brethren, having boldness to enter the Holiest by the blood of Jesus, by a new and living way which He consecrated for us, through the veil, that is, His flesh, and having a High Priest over the house of God, let us draw near with a true heart in full assurance of faith, having our hearts sprinkled from an evil conscience and our bodies washed with pure water. Let us hold fast the confession of our hope without wavering, for He who promised is faithful (Heb. 10:19–23).*

The "Holiest" is the place were God dwells. We access it by the blood of Jesus Christ.

A Scarlet Thread

The subject of blood is a scarlet thread that runs throughout the entire Bible, from Genesis to Revelation. The Bible teaches that the life of people and animals is in the blood (Lev. 17:11, 14). Because the penalty for sin is death (Rom. 6:23), and since life is in the blood, God established the principle that forgiveness of sins comes only through the shedding of blood: "And according to the law almost all things are purified with blood, and without shedding of blood there is no remission [from sin]" (Heb. 9:22).

God made the first blood sacrifice in the Garden of Eden after the sin of Adam and Eve when He killed animals and clothed the couple in skins that were representative of the righteousness of Christ. The blood sacrifice is emphasized through the story of Cain and Abel, the covenant of circumcision with the Israelites, and the Levitical ceremonies in the tabernacle. In the Old Testament, the blood of animals was offered as a sacrifice for sin. Hebrews 8 details this process and describes it as the old covenant.

God sent Jesus to shed His blood for sin once and for all. In the New Testament, His blood is described as the "new covenant" (Mark 14:24), and Jesus is the mediator of this new covenant (Heb. 8:6). This made the old covenant obsolete; it is no longer necessary for the blood of animals to be offered as a sacrifice for sin (Heb. 9:12).

The Bible declares that life is in the blood, and as Andrew Murray states, "the value of the blood corresponds to the value of the life that is in it."[2] The blood of Jesus is "precious" because of its tremendous spiritual benefits (1 Peter 1:18–19), and for this reason, we must comprehend its true meaning. To do this, we must listen to what the blood says to us. Hebrews 12:24 indicates that the blood of Jesus speaks for us, and what it confesses provides eternal benefits. It is interesting that a machine can now record a sound emitting from dying blood.[3]

The direction to "hold fast the confession" (Heb. 10:23) relates to the previous verses indicating we have the right to draw near to the Holiest. Hebrews 3:1 directs us to "consider" or meditate on the "High Priest of our confession, Christ Jesus." When we meditate on, confess, and hold fast to what the blood declares, our High Priest takes this confession and acts on the basis of it.

Biblical confession is a declaration of what the blood declares. The blood provides a new and living way to enter the presence of God. We gain access on the basis of its testimony.

You enter God's presence in prayer the same way you are saved: "If you confess with your mouth the Lord Jesus and believe in your heart that God has raised Him from the dead, you will be saved. For with the heart one believes unto righteousness, and with the mouth confession is made unto salvation" (Rom. 10:9–10). God acts in response to your confession that has authority because it is based on the testimony of the blood of Jesus. As in the salvation experience, aimless confession is not sufficient.

You must have faith and believe in the testimony of the blood: "Being justified freely by his grace through the redemption that is in Christ Jesus: Whom God hath set forth to be a propitiation through faith in his blood, to declare his righteousness for the remission of sins that are past, through the forbearance of God" (Rom. 3:24–25 KJV). When you begin to spiritually apply the blood through your confession of faith, the anointing of God is placed upon that blood, and where the anointing is, God's presence resides.

Leviticus 14:15–18 explains how the blood was applied for the cleansing of leprosy, which is a spiritual type of sin. (A *type* is a person, place, or act that foreshadows a spiritual truth, a pattern by which later events are interpreted.) The blood was applied to the finger, the ear, the toe, and the head. Then the priest took the anointing oil and applied it on top of the blood. The anointing of God was applied only where the blood was. Where there was no blood, there was no anointing. Benny Hinn observes, "It is essential to recognize that God anoints what the blood has covered."[4]

When the death angel passed through Egypt to slay the firstborn in every family, God's people were spared only if they applied the blood to the doorposts of their homes. The firstborn could not see that the blood covered them because it was on the outside of the door. They accepted by faith that their fathers completed the sacrifice for them. In similar manner, you must apply the blood to your life spiritually with faith that your heavenly Father has completed the sacrifice for you.

The Importance of Faith

The New Testament emphasizes the importance of faith by using three different words to relate this concept. The word translated "believe" (*pisteuo*) is a verb describing an action we must take to appropriate God's promises. The adjective translated "faithful" or "believing" (*pistos*) describes the attitude we must possess. The word translated "faith" (*pistis*) is a noun, and it is defined as "the substance of things hoped for, the evidence of things not seen" (Heb. 11:1).

These New Testament words for faith—a verb, an adjective, and a noun—document that faith is an act, an attitude, and a fact.

When Jesus explained the new covenant of His blood, He invited His disciples to "drink" of it. "Drinking" of blood in the natural body is done automatically as it flows ceaselessly carrying life to every member of the body. If you are cut off from the blood in your natural body, gangrene sets in and death follows. This is a natural analogy of a profound spiritual truth. The drinking of Christ's blood should be automatic. It should flow ceaselessly within our spiritual beings because if we are cut off from its life-giving flow, spiritual gangrene and death result. Andrew Murray comments, "Each member of a healthy body ceaselessly and abundantly drinks in the blood. So the Spirit of Life in Christ Jesus who unites us to Him, will make this drinking of the blood the natural action of the inner life."[5]

The Blood Speaks for You

In my vision of Jesus with the basin of blood, as I looked on the blood He poured over the altar, it became a living, swirling liquid that testified of its powerful truths. The blood spoke that our past sins are forgiven: "For this is My blood of the new covenant, which is shed for many for the remission of sins" (Matt. 26:28). It testified that there is a continuing atonement for sin in the blood of "Him who loved us and washed us from our sins in His own blood" (Rev. 1:5).

The blood witnessed that we are redeemed from the "aimless conduct" of a sinful lifestyle: "Knowing that you were not redeemed with corruptible things, like silver or gold, from your aimless conduct received by tradition from your fathers, but with the precious blood of Christ, as of a lamb without blemish and without spot" (1 Peter 1:18–19). *Redemption* means "deliverance from slavery by emancipation or purchase." Sin no longer has dominion over us: "For sin shall not have dominion over you, for you are not under law but under grace" (Rom. 6:14).

By the blood of Jesus Christ, we are reconciled to God, and we "who once were far off have been brought near by the blood of Christ" (Eph. 2:13). The guilt and shame associated with sin are removed as we are justified by the blood of Jesus:

Being justified freely by His grace through the redemption that is in Christ Jesus, whom God set forth as a propitiation by His blood, through faith, to demonstrate His righteousness, because in His forbearance God had passed over the sins that were previously committed, to demonstrate at the present time His righteousness, that He might be just and the justifier of the one who has faith in Jesus (Rom. 3:24–26).

The blood cleanses the conscience: "How much more shall the blood of Christ, who through the eternal Spirit offered Himself without spot to God, cleanse your conscience from dead works to serve the living God" (Heb. 9:14). We are sanctified by the blood, which means we are separated from evil and consecrated to the Lord for His purposes: "Therefore Jesus also, that He might sanctify the people with His own blood, suffered outside the gate" (Heb. 13:12).

The blood testifies of both spiritual and physical healing because

He was wounded for our transgressions,
He was bruised for our iniquities;
The chastisement for our peace was upon Him,
And by His stripes we are healed (Isa. 53:5).

The blood positions us to be able to do God's will: "Now may the God of peace who brought up our Lord Jesus from the dead, that great Shepherd of the sheep, through the blood of the everlasting covenant, make you complete in every good work to do His will, working in you what is well pleasing in His sight, through Jesus Christ" (Heb. 13:20–21).

Through the blood of Jesus and our confession of its power, we overcome the evil strategies of our enemy, Satan, for the Word declares, "they overcame him by the blood of the Lamb and by the word of their testimony" (Rev. 12:11).

The blood provides protection: "For the LORD will pass through to strike the Egyptians; and when He sees the blood on the lintel and on the two doorposts, the LORD will pass over the door and not allow the destroyer to come into your houses to strike you" (Ex. 12:23).

The blood of Jesus is the life flow of your spirit. Without it, spiritual death ensues: "Then Jesus said to them, 'Most assuredly, I say to you, unless you eat the flesh of the Son of Man and drink His blood, you have no life in you. . . . He who eats My flesh and drinks My blood abides in Me, and I in him'" (John 6:53–56). When Jesus took the cup of wine and declared it to be the new covenant in His blood, He was saying that every promise of that covenant would be kept at the cost of His life blood.

As we have seen, from the beginning of the biblical record God's dealings with humanity have been through the blood. If we are to access our heavenly Father's presence, we must place the same importance on the blood as He does.

Reaching Your Destination

James 3:4–5 compares the human tongue to the rudder of a ship. James indicates that if the rudder of a ship is properly guided, it will reach its desired destination. If you properly set the confession of your mouth, you will reach your spiritual destination. Begin your prayer on the basis of the blood because faith plus the blood equals the presence of God every time!

Make your declaration on the basis of faith, not facts. The accuser says we stand before God carnal and condemned. The blood says we stand before Him redeemed and righteous. Feeling may indicate we are sick, but faith declares we are healed. Our circumstances might give the appearance of defeat, but the blood says we are victorious.

Grasping the reality of what the blood of Jesus has done for me enables me to enter God's presence with confidence. The blood of Jesus assures my access to the heavenly Father. I need not approach God fearfully; I can approach Him with boldness. I am not accepted conditionally based on my performance as I was with my earthly father; I am accepted unconditionally based on the blood that speaks for me. This revelation enables me to cry from my innermost being, "Abba, Father," as I enter into the Holy of Holies where my Father dwells.

The blood declares that you can enter right now into the most holy place. Let its resounding message increase in intensity in your spirit until it drowns out every other voice of fear and doubt. You don't have to wait until you are "good enough." You don't have to enter burdened down with the guilt and shame of your past. The blood speaks for you, assuring your access to the presence of your Father every time you pray and continually releasing the prayer anointing in your life.

I pray that as you finish this chapter, this revelation of the blood will literally implode into your spirit and you will experience it as impartation, not just as dissemination of information. At whatever level you need the blood applied to your life—redemption, sanctification, protection, or justification—pray this prayer with me believing that right now, the blood is speaking over your life:

Heavenly Father, I believe the blood shed by Jesus Christ on the cross of Calvary is speaking over my life today. That blood says I am redeemed, justified, and sanctified. The stream of its life frees me from the shackles of shame and the spirit of the accuser that would rise up against me. Through the power of that blood, I can boldly enter into the throne room of God, knowing I will be received in the manner that a loving father welcomes his children. I thank You that the blood speaks for me right now and that because the blood covers me, Your anointing rests on me! In Jesus' name, Amen.

8

—✛—

Appropriating Your
Father's Name

The delicate perfume of spring flowers mingled with the romantic fragrance emanating from flickering candles. The church was filled with friends and relatives, and an expectant silence hovered over the waiting assembly. In a few moments Melva Jo Bryant would become Melva Jo Lea as she assumed my name during our marriage ceremony.

When Melva took the name of Lea on our wedding day, it was more than just a ceremonial ritual. It signified our commitment of love for each other, my willingness to protect and provide for her, and her access to all the rights and resources that my family name represented. From that day on, Melva began to appropriate the legal authority of that name.

A similar transaction occurs when you are adopted into your heavenly Father's family and made an heir to the resources of His spiritual kingdom. Assuming your position as a child of God involves rights and responsibilities, both of which are realized only when you learn to appropriate the spiritual authority of your Father's name.

The Importance of a Name

In many modern cultures, a name is used only as a personal label. In Bible times, however, great significance was attached to a person's name. The Hebrews thought of a person's name as revelatory, disclosing some attribute or characteristic of the personality. A name was determined by some circumstance at the time of birth, or it expressed a hope or prophecy.

Because of their significance in Bible times, names were sometimes changed by God. He changed the name of Abram to Abraham, Sarai to Sara, Jacob to Israel, Simon to Peter, and Saul to Paul—all to reflect either their new personality or their special purpose in His plan. William Barclay writes: "In Biblical times the name stood for much more than the name by which a person is called in the modern sense of the term. The name stood for the whole character of that person as it was known, manifested, or revealed."[1]

Although today we generally place less emphasis on the actual meaning of a name, a man's name is important because it comes to represent the man himself: "When the name of a man whom you know is mentioned, he is at once made present to your mind, although he may be far way. You conjure him up before you and visualize him. You see his face, and form, and character."[2]

Hallowing God's Name

Speaking the name of God brings to mind only what we know about Him, so we need to gain a biblical perspective on the true meaning of His name. When we follow the model prayer Jesus gave and say to our Father in heaven, "Hallowed be Your name," it is actually a petition that means "may Your name be sanctified or made holy." The word *hallow* means "to set apart, sanctify, praise, and adore." The Hebrew idiom "to sanctify the name" is also understood to mean "to give one's life for his faith."[3] We demonstrate the hallowedness of God's name not only through our prayer and praise but also through our commitment to a righteous lifestyle. We can hallow our Father's name by our walk with, our work for, and our worship of God.

God's name is sacred, and the mere repetition of the phrase "hallowed be Your name" does not mean we add to its sacredness. Our conduct as sons and daughters of God, however, will either hallow or disgrace our heavenly Father's name:

> *Does it hallow God's name when we murmur at His dealings with us? When we complain of our lot, of His guidance, His provision, His*

providence? Does it hallow the name of our Father when we point out all the faults and failings that we think we see in others of His children? What earthly father would sit and listen to us while we detailed the wrongdoing of his children? . . . Shall we do the Devil's work and become "accusers of the brethren"; and then after slandering the children who bear His name, kneel down and meekly say, "Hallowed be thy name?"[4]

Our heavenly Father's reputation is in our hands. William Barclay comments, "The name of God can only be hallowed when every action of our life is a witness to our faith in him and when we continuously bring credit to the name we bear."[5]

This first petition of the model prayer, "Hallowed be Your name," is the most necessary one, for it is concerned with the greatest need, and that is God's need. As Gerhard Ebeling notes, we pray to God on behalf of God "that He would reveal Himself, that He would arise as God, that He would in every truth become God. . . . Hallowed be thy name is as much as to say, 'Holy One, become holy; God become God.'"[6]

Jesus manifested the name of God during His earthly ministry (John 17:6). When we manifest God's name, we reveal to the world the nature and character of the heavenly Father. When we properly manifest our heavenly Father's name to the world through righteousness, those who have "erred in spirit" (those lost in sin) will come to a knowledge of God through what they see demonstrated in our lives:

> *But when he sees his children,*
> *The work of My hands, in his midst,*
> *They will hallow My name,*
> *And hallow the Holy One of Jacob,*
> *And fear the God of Israel.*
> *These also who erred in spirit will come to understanding,*
> *And those who complained will learn doctrine (Isa. 29:23–24).*

Phillip Keller notes that we may call ourselves children of God, Christians, God's people, or any other such title, "but the point remains that we carry His name. His name is vested in us. Therefore His name, reputation, person, and character are at stake in us. . . .

The personal life and language of any person who says he is related to God comes in for close and continuous examination by an onlooking world."[7]

The Primary Names of God

God's name is not just an identification label. It is an expression of His nature and identity. When we say, "Hallowed be Your name," it "implies the title, person, power, authority, character, and the very reputation of God."[8]

All of these are reflected in the three primary names of God used in the Old Testament: Elohim, Adonai, and Jehovah (or Yahweh). *Elohim* means "God" or the "strong Creator." This title reveals our Father as the source of all that exists, and in its plural form it represents Him as three-in-one, reflecting the Trinity. This name for God appears first in Genesis 1:1, it is one of the most frequently used names throughout the biblical record, and it is the final name used in Revelation 22:19.

Adonai means "Lord and master," and it expresses the personal relationship that exists between a master and a slave. "Master" indicates relationship, while "Lord" points to ownership. Concerning this Adonai relationship, Elmer Towns writes,

> *When Americans try to illustrate the master/slave relationship, it is tempting to think of the book* Uncle Tom's Cabin. *But this would not accurately illustrate God's relationship to us because of the abuse of black slaves portrayed in the book. The relationship of slave and master in the Bible was more often one of love and allegiance. In the Jewish relationship, a slave had more privileges than the hired help.*[9]

In Bible times, the master of slaves gave them a place to sleep, food, clothing, and all basic necessities. He provided training and direction and required accountability. As our heavenly Father, God provides our basic spiritual and material necessities and requires accountability from us.

The names Elohim and Adonai reveal much regarding the nature and character of God, but the name Jehovah is richest in meaning in our quest to relate to God as Father. *Jehovah,* or *Yahweh,* is the personal, intimate name of God. Through this name, we enter into intimate relationship with Him.

Jehovah means "to be" or "to become." When translated into the first person, it becomes "I am." When God called Moses to deliver Israel from Egyptian bondage, God revealed this intimate title to him (Ex. 3:14). *Jehovah* means "I am . . . I will not change," which means God will be what you want Him to be when you need Him to be it. The name Jehovah reveals what God is really like and reflects the attributes of His personality. They include the qualities of holiness, love, and goodness, His omniscience (He is all-knowing), omnipresence (He is present everywhere), and omnipotence (He is all-powerful).

The Compound Names of God

In the Old Testament, the name Jehovah is combined with other descriptive titles to form what are called compound names, which reveal even more to us of the character and nature of our heavenly Father. When I received the revelation of the blood of Jesus described in the previous chapter, I began to cry out, "Our Father in heaven, hallowed be Your name!" As I was speaking these words from the depths of my spirit, God began to reveal to me how eight compound names of Jehovah revealed in the Old Testament correspond with the benefits of the new covenant secured by the blood of Jesus. The blood underwrites what the name represents.

All the benefits we learned about in chapter 7 are spiritual parallels of the provisions of a father for his biological children. They can be grouped in five major categories. To make them easier to remember, I will describe each with a word starting with the letter *s*.

Sin—Benefit 1: Forgiveness of sin and deliverance from sin's dominion

The first benefit of the new covenant is the forgiveness of sin and deliverance from its contamination. This is reflected in two compound names of God, Jehovah-tsidkenu (sid-kay'-noo) and Jehovah-m'kaddesh (ma-kah'-desh).

Jehovah-tsidkenu means "Jehovah our righteousness." God revealed this name to the prophet Jeremiah (Jer. 23:5–6), and it indicates the facet of God's character that transacts the redemption by which we are fully restored to Him. This came through the blood of Jesus Christ who was our Jehovah-tsidkenu: "For He made Him who knew no sin to be sin for us, that we might become the righteousness of God in Him" (2 Cor. 5:21).

When you pray, "Hallowed be Your name," and meditate on the name of Jehovah-tsidkenu, you confess that God has already made a decision about your sins. He elected to forgive them because you bear His name. All you have to do is access that forgiveness by appropriating it, even as the blood applied in Old Testament times released its saving power.

Your heavenly Father's name guarantees more than forgiveness of sins, however. It also offers deliverance from the dominion of sin. When you hallow God's name as Jehovah-m'kaddesh, you confess Him as "the LORD who sanctifies" (Lev. 20:8). The name was revealed when God's people, Israel, were coming into a new land promised to them by God, a region full of wicked nations whose people worshiped other gods.

Many of us work each day alongside similar ungodly people. We live next door to them, we interact with them in the streets of our cities, and their wickedness routinely blazes across the headlines of the morning newspaper. When you hallow God's name in prayer, you confess that through His name and by the blood of Jesus Christ, you will live unaffected by this evil. The power of sin is broken in your life (Rom. 6:17–18).

Spirit—Benefit 2: The fullness of the Holy Spirit

Because God is your Father, the second benefit you enjoy in the new covenant is the fullness of the Holy Spirit. The two compound names of God that reflect this are Jehovah-shalom (sha-lom′) and Jehovah-shammah (sham′-mah).

The name *Jehovah-shalom* appears as the result of a revelation Gideon received. During a time of moral and spiritual decay in Israel, the young man was hiding in a winepress and threshing wheat salvaged from the last attack of an enemy. Suddenly, the angel of the Lord appeared to him, saying, "The LORD is with you, you mighty man of valor!" (Judg. 6:12).

Now remember where Gideon was—hiding in a winepress,

threshing scraps of wheat left by the enemy. But God did not view him as he appeared to be. God saw him as a "mighty man of valor."

When the angel of the Lord greeted him, Gideon responded, "O my lord, if the LORD is with us, why then has all this happened to us? And where are all His miracles which our fathers told us about, saying, 'Did not the LORD bring us up from Egypt?' But now the LORD has forsaken us and delivered us into the hands of the Midianites" (Judg. 6:13).

When you are in a difficult situation, do you sometimes feel like Gideon? Do you question, "If my heavenly Father is really with me, why has this happened to me? Where are all His miracles that I have heard about?" When you feel like that, get ready! You are about to receive a new revelation from God.

Without offering any answers to Gideon's questions, the angel of the Lord commissioned him to deliver Israel from the enemy. The challenge concerned Gideon, for he viewed himself differently from the way the Lord did. His clan was the smallest in his tribe, and he was the youngest in his father's house. How could he possibly deliver Israel from the Midianites? But God promised Gideon, "Surely I will be with you, and you shall defeat the Midianites as one man" (Judg. 6:16).

Gideon then prepared a sacrifice, and the angel of the Lord caused fire to rise from the altar and consume it. Gideon realized that he had spoken with the Lord, and he said, "Alas, O Lord GOD! For I have seen the Angel of the LORD face to face" (Judg. 6:22). The Lord said to him, "Peace be with you; do not fear, you shall not die" (Judg. 6:23).

Then Gideon built an altar to the Lord and called it *The-Lord-Shalom* which means "Jehovah is peace" (Judg. 6:24). The Hebrew word *shalom* is most often translated "peace" and represents wholeness and harmony with God and contentment and satisfaction in life. The blood of Jesus Christ secured these benefits for us.

A basic spiritual truth is revealed in the story of Gideon. When you are in a time of difficulty, you must bring all of your unanswered questions, lay them on the altar of prayer, and sacrifice to God by hallowing His name in praise. If you do all this, the fears and insecure feelings of your spirit will be quieted. God will become your Jehovah-shalom, and the peace of the Holy Spirit will replace your anxiety.

When the true power of the Holy Spirit is experienced, it transforms cowardly men like Gideon into mighty warriors for God. Prior to the Upper Room prayer meeting recorded in Acts 2, the disciples of Jesus failed, scattered, deserted, and denied the Lord. After they experienced the power of the Holy Spirit, they became powerful men of God.

God does not see you in hiding, as the "least of your tribe," a deserter, or a failure. He does not view you as you are, but He sees through the eyes of the Holy Spirit what you will become. You are a "mighty man of valor" from His perspective.

Another compound name of God relates to the fullness of the Holy Spirit. It is the title *Jehovah-shammah,* which means "the Lord who is there." The Lord promised to be present with His people, Israel, from their inception as a nation. The presence set them apart from other peoples of the world (Ex. 33:15–16).

God's presence was first manifested in the tabernacle of Moses and later evidenced in the beautiful temple built by King Solomon. When Israel began to worship false gods and turn away from their heavenly Father, His presence withdrew, and the people were conquered and captured by their enemies.

At that time, the prophet Ezekiel saw a vision of the future when the presence of God would return and God's name of Jehovah-shammah was revealed to him (Ezek. 48:35). When God sent Jesus to this earth He was called *Immanuel,* meaning "God with us," and once again Jehovah-shammah lived among humankind. After Jesus died, rose, and ascended to heaven, He sent the Holy Spirit, and God's presence now dwells in your spiritual temple (John 14:16–17).

God is not an absentee Father, and He has not abandoned you to face the crises of life alone, "for He Himself has said, 'I will never leave you nor forsake you'" (Heb. 13:5). God is Jehovah-shammah, "the Lord who is there." The power of His presence sets us apart from the world. Jehovah-shalom and Jehovah-shammah reveal God as a Father who brings both supernatural peace and divine presence through His Holy Spirit.

Soundness—Benefit 3: Health and healing

Jehovah-rapha (rah-phah') means "Jehovah heals." The name was revealed in an incident recorded in Exodus 15:22–27. After the Israelites escaped the slavery of Egypt, they were traveling through the wilderness of Shur and went for three days with no water. They finally arrived at a stream called Marah, but they could not drink from it because the waters were bitter or poisonous.

The people began to murmur against Moses and ask, "What shall we drink?" God showed Moses a tree on the bank of the waters and told him to cut it down and throw it into the waters to make them sweet or drinkable.

When Moses did that, God revealed Himself as Jehovah-rapha. He said, "If you diligently heed the voice of the LORD your God and do what is right in His sight, give ear to His commandments and keep all His statutes, I will put none of the diseases on you which I have brought on the Egyptians. For I am the LORD who heals you" (Ex. 15:26).

During the traumatic desert experience, Israel received a new revelation of the heavenly Father, which is exactly what God wants to do for us in our own "wilderness" experiences. The tree that Moses cut down and cast into the waters represents the Lord Jesus Christ. Your soul may be embittered by sin and your body polluted by sickness and disease, but when God puts His Son Jesus (the tree) into the bitter waters of your life, you will be healed.

Matthew recorded that "He [Jesus] Himself took our infirmities and bore our sicknesses" (Matt. 8:17), and the prophet Isaiah declared, "By His stripes we are healed" (Isa. 53:5). The apostle Peter also confirmed the healing benefits available to us through the blood of Jesus when he confirmed that Christ "Himself bore our sins in His own body on the tree, that we, having died to sins, might live for righteousness—by whose stripes you were healed" (1 Peter 2:24).

God sees your healing as already done: "By whose stripes you *were* healed." When you appropriate the name Jehovah-rapha, you can claim the physical, mental, emotional, and spiritual healing guaranteed by your heavenly Father's name.

Success—Benefit 4: The promise of freedom from the curse of the law

The fourth benefit you enjoy because of your relationship with your Father is freedom from the curse of the law. This benefit, which assures your success, is reflected in the name *Jehovah-jireh* (ji'-rah), which means "Jehovah my Provider."

The name was revealed to Abraham in an event recorded in Genesis 22. God commanded Abraham to offer his son, Isaac, as a burnt sacrifice on Mount Moriah. Abraham knew it was not God's nature to require human sacrifice as other heathen nations did, but he proceeded to fulfill God's command. He rose early in the morning and made a three-day journey to comply with the directive.

When Abraham arrived at Mount Moriah, he built an altar and placed Isaac on it. Just as Abraham raised the knife to sacrifice the young man, God commanded Abraham to stop. The Lord provided a ram, caught by its horns in the bushes, as a substitute for Isaac. Through that incident Abraham received a new revelation of God, which was reflected as he named the place "The-LORD-Will-Provide," or Jehovah-jireh (Gen. 22:14).

Although my earthly dad had a kind and loving heart, due to the alcohol-induced words he spoke to me while I was growing up, I was programmed for failure. I didn't really expect to succeed in life because his words brought me under a "curse" instead of a "blessing." Gary Smalley and John Trent deal with this issue extensively in a book entitled *The Blessing.* They identify five elements of what they call the blessing that parents should provide for a child: (1) meaningful touch, (2) communication of a proper spoken message, (3) attaching high value to the child, (4) declaring a special future for him, and (5) active commitment to see that their blessing comes to pass.[10]

In reviewing this list, you may discover, as I did, that these elements are exactly opposite of what you received from your dad. Even though your dad—like mine—might have cared for you deep inside, abusive words, lack of communication, low self-image, hopelessness, and alienation may have been the curse you received that has marked your life and destiny to this point.

Without God, all people are cursed to failure—not because of what a parent might have declared but because all have sinned (Rom.

51

3:23). Paul indicated that "cursed is everyone who does not continue in all things which are written in the book of the law, to do them" (Gal. 3:10). But Paul shared the good news that "the law of the Spirit of life in Christ Jesus has made me free from the law of sin and death" (Rom. 8:2).

Through the blood of Jesus, we can be redeemed from the curse of the law: "Christ has redeemed us from the curse of the law, having become a curse for us (for it is written, 'Cursed is everyone who hangs on a tree'), that the *blessing of Abraham* might come upon the Gentiles in Christ Jesus" (Gal. 3:13–14, emphasis added).

You can be delivered from sin and freed from any curse spoken over you by your dad or any other person.

God blessed everything Abraham did because Jehovah-jireh became his provider. The blood of Jesus made provision for us, the curse is removed, and we are heirs of the same promises of success given to Abraham (Rom. 8:32). God promises success if we base our lives on scriptural principles: "This Book of the Law shall not depart from your mouth, but you shall meditate in it day and night, that you may observe to do according to all that is written in it. For then you will make your way prosperous, and then you will have good success" (Josh. 1:8). In Deuteronomy 28, God promised that blessings would "overtake" us if we obey Him. If we do not choose to obey, the curses of Egypt (a spiritual type of sin) will be upon us.

The blood of Jesus releases you from the curse of failure in this world and destines you for success. God sees your needs beforehand and makes provision. While you are going up one side of the mountain as Abraham did, God is sending your ram of provision up the other side!

Security—Benefit 5: Freedom from fear

The fifth benefit you enjoy as a child of your heavenly Father is freedom from fear. This is reflected in two compound names of God, Jehovah-nissi and Jehovah-raah.

In the name *Jehovah-nissi* (nis'-see), or "Jehovah my Banner," the word for banner is translated as "pole, ensign, or standard" and also means "miracle." In Old Testament times, a banner or standard was a signal to Israel that their conflicts were actually God's battles and He would deliver them.

The name Jehovah-nissi was revealed through an incident recorded in Exodus 17:8-15. God's people, Israel, were engaged in heavy battle with their enemies, the Amalekites. While they were fighting, Moses viewed the warfare from the top of a hill, and an interesting phenomenon occurred. As long as Moses held up his hands, Israel prevailed in the conflict. When he grew weary and let down his hands, the Amalekites prevailed. Because the battle was lengthy, Moses' hands became so weary that Aaron and Hur came alongside to support his arms until Israel defeated the enemy. After the victory, Moses built an altar and called its name "The-LORD-Is-My-Banner" (Ex. 17:15).

The prophet Isaiah predicted that someday a "banner" would be raised for God's people (Isa. 11:10). That banner is Jesus Christ who was lifted above all our battles on the cross of Calvary. He is our eternal standard, and through Him, we are freed from the fear of death, hell, and all the power of the enemy. As you and I fight our own "Amalekites" in our valleys of battle, we are assured of victory because this standard was raised over us once and for all on the hill of Calvary. He is raised up over every problem and circumstance in your life. When you get in trouble, don't look to yourself. Look to the Banner raised high above you!

Isaiah 11:12–16, which depicts Jesus as the Banner, has spiritual parallels with the account we studied in Matthew 21:12-16 where Jesus cleansed the temple. When Jesus is lifted up, *purity* results; Isaiah 11:12–13 indicates there are no more petty envy and harassment between Israel and Judah (representative of God's people). Then God's *power* is manifested as outcasts are drawn to this Banner (Isa. 11:12), just as people who could not see or walk went to Jesus in the temple. The power of the enemy is broken over their lives as their adversary is "cut off" (Isa. 11:13). As a result, *perfected praise* erupts in Isaiah 12.

One other compound name of God provides freedom from fear. It is *Jehovah-raah* (rah-ah′), which means "Jehovah my Shepherd." This name occurs in Psalm 23 where David declares, "The LORD is my shepherd." The primary meaning of *raah* is "to feed or lead to pasture" as a shepherd does his flock. It is also translated "friend" or "companion."

In the New Testament, Jesus declared concerning Himself, "I am the good shepherd" (John 10:11). He is our spiritual Shepherd because of the blood of His "everlasting covenant" (Heb. 13:20). Because He is your Shepherd, you do not have to fear evil, you can feed in spiritually green pastures, and you can rest beside the cool waters of the Word of God. Your Shepherd makes every provision for your righteousness and your material and spiritual needs. You do not have to fear in the "valley of the shadow of death" or in the presence of your enemies. The anointing of God rests upon you, and your eternal destiny is assured (Ps. 23).

How to Appropriate the Names of God

All the names of God we have discussed are included in the name Father to whom we address our prayers. When you repeat the phrase "hallowed be Your name" with understanding, you appropriate the five major benefits of the new covenant that are contained in the compound names of God we have studied. All these provisions that God performs in our behalf are scriptural parallels of fatherly functions that should be provided by a loving earthly dad.

In too many churches our Father's name is not hallowed in this way. Phillip Keller notes that often the program, special music, social function, architecture of the building, and/or the preacher's personality are considered more important than the person and presence of God Himself: "His name is not honored in these places. . . . It is not altogether surprising, therefore, that many churches are little more than another social organization in the community. For where our Heavenly Father's name is not held high, the church loses its impact and power upon the lives of its people."[11]

We must learn to hallow God's name and appropriate the benefits of His name personally. We are empowered to do this as we act in obedience and use the model prayer each day.

When you start your prayer time, hallow the Father's name and relate His compound names to the five major benefits of the blood of Jesus. Use the following chart, which summarizes these names and benefits we have discussed:

Name	Meaning	Benefit	Reference
Jehovah-tsidkenu	Jehovah our righteousness	Forgiveness of sin	Jeremiah 23:6
Jehovah-m'kaddesh	Jehovah who sanctifies	Forgiveness of sin	Exodus 31:13
Jehovah-shalom	Jehovah is peace	Spirit	Judges 6:24
Jehovah-shammah	Jehovah is there	Spirit	Ezekiel 48:35
Jehovah-rapha	Jehovah heals	Soundness	Exodus 15:26
Jehovah-jireh	Jehovah my Provider	Success	Genesis 22:14
Jehovah-nissi	Jehovah my Banner	Security	Exodus 17:15
Jehovah-raah	Jehovah my Shepherd	Security	Psalm 23:1

When you boldly make these confessions, you will enter the presence of your heavenly Father every time—I guarantee it! Something supernatural happens when you begin to pray by faith. A channel of divine presence and provision is opened to you, and the mantle of the prayer anointing descends to remain with you throughout the day. It happens because you are approaching your Father on the basis of the blood and its covenant benefits revealed in His name.

The anointing of personal prayer is intricately related to the hallowing of the names of God, recognizing that your Father really is all of these names manifested in your personal life. Until this revelation of divine fatherhood is locked into your spirit, you will not be able to proceed with confidence, assurance, and success in your prayer life.

Agree with me right now as we pray this prayer together:

Heavenly Father, You are Jehovah-tsidkenu, my righteousness, and Jehovah-m'kaddesh, the God who sanctifies me. I thank You that I am forgiven for sins of the past and freed from the power of sin in the present. I claim Your peace, Jehovah-shalom. I acknowledge You as Jehovah-shammah, the God who is always there for me. I receive the benefit of healing provided through Your name Jehovah-rapha, for I know that by the stripes laid upon Jesus I am healed. I acknowledge Your provision for my every need through the power in Your name as Jehovah-jireh. You are the Banner of Jehovah-nissi, which is lifted over my life, and as Jehovah-raah, You are the Shepherd who will bring me safely to my eternal destiny. Because of this, I have the authority to ask You to release the anointing of personal prayer in my life, and I believe it is released right now. In Jesus' name, Amen.

9

—✠—

Living in Your
Father's Kingdom

Airline Hijackers Kill Two"
"Teacher Shot to Death"
"Murder Victim's Body Found"

These are a few of the headlines in just one section of my daily
newspaper this morning. The evening television news hour will be
even worse as it relays graphic images in live satellite reports of these
terrible events.

As you are barraged daily with the negative feedback of this sinful
world, you may question the title of this chapter, "Living in Your
Father's Kingdom." Is it really possible, in the midst of all this insanity,
murder, and mayhem, to live in the kingdom of God right now? Is it
possible, in spite of your difficult problems, to dwell in a spiritual realm
that somehow lifts you above the natural circumstances of life?

Part of the model prayer Jesus taught us to pray includes this
declaration: "Your kingdom come." In this chapter you will learn that
by making this confession, you can live in our heavenly Father's kingdom
right now! I will also share new revelation of how declaring God's
kingdom guarantees that you will be able to know and do His will.

What Is the Kingdom of God?

If we are to pray about it, we must know about the kingdom of
God. Every household has its rules, and the whole meaning of life

for us as children of God is summed up in these three words: *Thy kingdom come.*

The Bible identifies three types of kingdoms. There are the natural kingdoms of this world (Matt. 4:8–9), Satan's kingdom (Matt. 12:26), and the kingdom of God, which is our Father's kingdom. In Greek, Hebrew, and Aramaic the "kingdom" of God refers to the kingship, sovereignty, reign, or ruling activity of God. It is the expression of God's nature in action. Philip Harner writes, "The 'kingdom' or reign of God refers to His activity as King. Since His innermost nature finds expression in His activity, it is appropriate for the petition concerning God's name to precede the petition concerning His Kingdom."[1]

The kingdom of God refers not only to the nature of God in action; its meaning encompasses people who are residents of this kingdom, the spiritual body of all true believers who put themselves under the authority of our heavenly Father. God's realm of operation can be viewed in terms of its inclusive universal organization as the kingdom of God, its local visible organization as the church through which the kingdom is extended, and individuals of which the kingdom is composed, that is, all true believers born into this kingdom. We are related to our Father in this realm as both citizens (by the law of God) and children (through the bloodline of Christ).

When John the Baptist began his ministry by declaring, "The kingdom of heaven is at hand," he was using terms common to his day. The nation of Israel easily understood those words, for the hope of the promised kingdom and its King burned in the heart of every Jew (Matt. 3:1–3). When Jesus began His ministry, He reiterated John's message (Mark 1:14–15). The declaration that the kingdom of God was "at hand" meant it had arrived, although it had not come in visible form (Luke 17:20–21).

Rejecting the King

The Jewish people thought Jesus would establish the visible kingdom with Jerusalem as its capital as prophesied since Old Testament times. Because of that, they rejoiced and honored Him as King as He entered the city (Mark 11:10). But when the kingdom did not manifest itself in visible form, they quickly turned against Jesus: "The Jews did not understand that there were two phases of God's Kingdom. The teaching that the Kingdom of God is first established by the enthronement of the King in the individual heart was entirely contrary to their ideas and teachings concerning the Messianic kingdom."[2]

Even John the Baptist somehow failed to fully grasp what Christ meant by the kingdom of God. From the depths of despair in Herod's dungeon, he sent his disciples to ask whether Jesus was actually the coming King whom he had announced.

The Jewish people rejected both the kingdom and the King because the kingdom of God did not come as they expected. Because of Israel's rejection, Jesus announced that the kingdom was taken from them and given to the gentile nations (all nations other than Israel) who were ready to receive it (Matt. 21:42–43).

Sometime in the future the kingdom of God will be established in visible form. We do not know the exact timing (Acts 1:7), but according to the Word of God, it is certain. All the "kingdoms of this world" will become the property of God, the evil kingdom of Satan will be defeated, and our King will reign forever (Rev. 11:15). God's kingdom in its final, visible form, shall be

an everlasting dominion,
Which shall not pass away,
And His kingdom the one
Which shall not be destroyed (Dan. 7:14).

As an heir of your heavenly Father, you will reign with Him in this kingdom (Rev. 3:21).

Jesus said that our Father's kingdom was not of this world (John 18:36) and that at the present time it is "within you" (Luke 17:20–21). It is a kingdom that is declared not just by word, but by action through the demonstration of supernatural power (1 Cor. 4:20). Because it is a spiritual kingdom, it is based on spiritual principles. The apostle Paul declared that the kingdom is "righteousness and peace and joy in the Holy Spirit" (Rom. 14:17). Taylor Bunch summarizes it this way:

The Kingdom would first manifest itself in inward holiness rather than in outward show. It meant a transformed heart rather than a reformed nation. The basis of heavenly citizenship is a change of character and not a reorganization of the governments and institutions of men. The Kingdom within must precede the Kingdom without.[3]

The centrality of the kingdom message is clear in the New Testament record. Jesus began His earthly ministry by declaring the arrival of the kingdom (Matt. 4:17). He ended His earthly ministry by speaking of things pertaining to the kingdom (Acts 1:3). In between the beginning and ending of His earthly ministry, the emphasis was always on the kingdom. He was constantly declaring He must preach its message in other places (Luke 4:43). Every parable of Jesus related to the kingdom, and His life patterned its principles.

Jesus indicated that we, as believers, are to give similar emphasis to the kingdom: "But seek first the kingdom of God and His righteousness, and all these things shall be added to you" (Matt. 6:33). We should focus our praying, preaching, teaching, and living on the kingdom of God. The King sends us into this world to represent and transact the business of the kingdom on behalf of our Father. Seeking "first the kingdom" assures the answer to the other petitions that follow in the model prayer.

Declaring Your Father's Kingdom

The kingdom of God has come to some dimension, as evidenced in passages like Luke 9:27 and Luke 11:20, but many other passages speak of the kingdom still to come (Luke 19:11; 22:18). Because the kingdom is not yet in its final, visible form, Jesus taught us to pray, "Your kingdom come." An axiom from the ancient school of the rabbis states, "That prayer wherein there is not mention of the Kingdom of God is not a prayer."[4]

George Dorn points out, "So long as there is in the world one man who has not yielded his heart to Christ, so long as there is a single department of life which is not brought into subjection of the law of Christ, so long will the kingdom be unrealized, so long shall we need to pray—Thy Kingdom come."[5]

Because the kingdom of God is a spiritual kingdom, it must be advanced by spiritual means, and that means is prayer. Our prayers should focus on the kingdom of God, not our individual, organizational, or denominational "kingdoms." We are to call on God to fulfill His plans rather than ours.

Praying "Your kingdom come" is more than a prayer for the return of Jesus and the establishment of the kingdom in its final form, however. When we pray, "Your kingdom come," we actually declare that our Father will reign in the lives of believers, unbelievers, and the entire earth. When you say these words, it is a faith declaration similar to spiritually putting your foot down and saying emphatically, "Thy kingdom come!" The Greek verb tense used here is one of declaration meaning, "Come, Thy kingdom!"

Setting Proper Priorities

When your heavenly Father's kingdom is established in your life, it will automatically follow that His will is done. To accomplish this, however, you must establish proper priorities. God first revealed this to me in the early years of my ministry when Melva and I were in the process of earning our master's degrees while pastoring one thousand young people at the same time. God was calling me to prayer, but I was busy struggling to make good grades at seminary, do my job at the church, and try to be a good husband. I questioned, "How in this world can Your kingdom be revealed in my chaotic life under my present circumstances?"

God told me to start declaring, "Your kingdom come," in four prioritized areas of my life. He revealed that when I did this, it would be like setting the rudder of a ship in the proper direction; I would reach my destination every time. When we set the rudder of our lives (our confession) in order with God's Word by declaring, "Your kingdom come," we will reach the destination God has for us in every area of our lives.

Prioritize your personal prayer time to establish God's kingdom in these four areas: (1) your own personal life, (2) your primary relationships, (3) the people of God, and (4) the political entities of this world, including your community, your nation, and other countries.

1. Personal Life

In declaring, "Your kingdom come," *you* are the first priority. If you are not right with God, all the other areas of your life will not come under the authority of the kingdom. When you say, "Your kingdom come," you ask God to remove anything in you that is in rebellion against His kingdom, including words, attitudes, desires, behavior, and so on.

Declare your will, emotions, mind, and body under the control of your Father's kingdom. Claim the kingdom of God to reign in your life with righteousness, joy, and peace. Ask God to empower you with divine wisdom, revelation, efficiency, and might for your tasks that day. Declare God's kingdom to reign over every negative circumstance you face. Ask God to prioritize your responsibilities for the day. Keep a pad of paper and pencil handy while you pray. Many times God will reveal the order in which you are to do things or exactly how to solve problems.

2. Primary Relationships

Now you are ready to make similar declarations in your primary relationships, in behalf of your mate, family, and friends. These relationships are your second responsibility in prayer.

Your mate. Ask God to give you the right kind of love for your mate (or person to whom you're engaged). The Bible identifies three kinds of love. *Agape* love is uniquely Christian, and it reflects a committed, covenant relationship. It is loving because you choose to do so, regardless of what someone does to you. This type of love is the foundation for the other types of love that should be in a marriage. *Phileo* love is a friendship love, while *eros* is the physical expression of the agape and phileo types of love. Ask God to put the commitment of agape love in your marriage upon which you can build phileo and eros love.

Satan has targeted Christian marriages, and no one is exempt from his attacks. As I mentioned earlier, after forty-four years of marriage, my dad divorced my mother and married another woman. This will not happen in your family if you and your mate agree to declare God's kingdom over your marriage and make an agape commitment to each other.

Pray that the kingdom of God will reign in your mate's life with righteousness, joy, and peace. Declare the unity and harmony of kingdom peace between you and your mate. Pray for God's will to be done in every area of your mate's life, and declare God's kingdom to reign sovereignly in your marriage relationship.

Your children. Household salvation is taught in the Old Testament story of Rahab, whose family was saved through her confession of faith evidenced by the scarlet rope hung from the window of her home (Josh. 2). It is reiterated in the New Testament account of the Philippian jailer to whom Paul declared, "Believe on the Lord Jesus Christ, and you will be saved, you and your household" (Acts 16:31). "Your household" means everyone in your bloodline.

If you have children, release them to their heavenly Father. Get them out of your care and into His care. Pray with heartfelt passion for your children. With passion so great that she could not even verbalize it, Hannah prayed for God to give her a son (1 Sam. 1:9–18). Your emotions are God-given, so use them to declare with passion that your Father's kingdom will be established in the lives of your children.

Pray that the kingdom of God will be manifested in each child's life in righteousness, joy, and peace. Ask God to help you train each child in the way he or she should go. Declare your children to be sons and daughters of the Lord who will walk in His ways. Claim this verse: "All your children shall be taught by the LORD, and great shall be the peace of your children" (Isa. 54:13).

Release ministering angels in behalf of your unsaved children (Heb. 1:14). Ask God to bring specific problems and needs of your children to your mind and then pray about each issue. Pray for kingdom peace to reign in your household between siblings. From the time of your child's birth, begin to pray for his or her future mate, declaring God's kingdom to reign in that person's life, also.

Other family members and friends. Claim "household salvation" in behalf of all your relatives. Declare that your Father's kingdom will reign in the lives of your extended family and friends in righteousness, joy, and peace. Pray about specific problems and needs as God brings them to your mind. Do not rush through some prayer formula. Be sensitive to the Holy Spirit. Sometimes God may give you a word of encouragement or a Scripture for someone. Write it down and share it when you conclude your prayer time.

3. People of God

Your third priority in declaring God's kingdom is claiming it for the people of God in your church. You will pray for your pastor, leaders, faithfulness, and the harvest.

Your pastor. Did you know that when you pray for your pastor, you pray a prayer that could save *your* life? When Joshua and the people of Israel were battling the Amalekite enemy, Moses observed the battle from a nearby hillside. As long as his hands were lifted with the rod of God stretched over the conflict, Israel prevailed. When his hands grew weary, Israel began to lose the battle, so Aaron and Hur stood alongside Moses and supported his arms until the battle was won (Ex. 17:8–16). As long as God's leader, Moses, was strong, the people prevailed in battle and their lives were saved. When you are in the valleys of life fighting your battles, your success is affected by your spiritual leaders. That is why when you pray for them, you pray a prayer that could save your life.

You will adopt an attitude of accusation or intercession toward your leaders. Aaron and Hur were intercessors who held up Moses' hands. They didn't accuse him by asking, "What's the matter with that guy? He can't hold up his own hands. He is supposed to be our leader!" When Peter was imprisoned, the church prayed earnestly for him. They didn't raise accusations by questioning, "If he is a man of faith, why is he in jail?" Their consistent intercession activated the angel who delivered Peter from prison, enabling him to fulfill the call God had on his life to lead the early church.

Pray that God will preserve your pastor in spirit, soul, and body, that he will be able to finish his course and fulfill the purpose God has for him. Ask God to anoint him as a channel through which God's Word can flow, and pray that the spiritual fruit he brings forth will remain. Pray that the kingdom of God will reign in his life with righteousness, joy, and peace. Declare that he will have a shepherd's heart to care for the people and feed them with God's Word. Ask for direction for your pastor, so he will be able to guide the people into the ways of God. Ask for protection because he is on the front lines for God and subject to intense attack by the enemy.

Leadership. Pray for each leader of your church by name and for the area of his or her responsibility. (Perhaps you can obtain a church organizational chart to assist you in doing this.) Ask for anointing and guidance for your spiritual leaders. Pray that the kingdom of God will reign in their lives with righteousness, joy, and peace. Ask God that every program and each leader will be used to extend God's kingdom in your community. Pray for harmony between leaders, and between the pastor and the leaders. Ask for protection for your spiritual leaders because they are on the front lines for God and subject to intense attack by the enemy.

Members of your church fellowship. Pray that members of your church community will be faithful to God, their families, and your church. Pray that the kingdom of God will reign in their lives with righteousness, joy, and peace. Ask God to plant them in the fellowship as intercessors and soul winners and to make them faithful in tithes and offerings to enable the work of the ministry. Intercede for prayer requests that have been voiced by members of your church fellowship. Pray for revival!

Harvest. Prayer affects the spiritual harvest. Because the harvest is great, our prayers are to be directed to the Lord of the harvest, which indicates it is His harvest; Satan has no right to claim it (Luke 10:2). Pray for spiritual harvest in other churches in your community where the gospel is being proclaimed. Every church is responsible for its own harvest. In praying for the harvest in my church, God directed me to follow the pattern revealed in this passage:

> *Fear not, for I am with you;*
> *I will bring your descendants from the east,*
> *And gather you from the west;*
> *I will say to the north, "Give them up!"*
> *And to the south, "Do not keep them back!"*
> *Bring My sons from afar,*
> *And My daughters from the ends of the earth—*
> *Everyone who is called by My name,*
> *Whom I have created for My glory;*
> *I have formed him, yes, I have made him (Isa. 43:5–7).*

Although this text concerns the Jewish people being harvested from the nations of the world by God, as a spiritual type of Israel we can use its pattern to pray in the harvest. Direct your prayers to the northern part of your city, and command the north to release souls

64

to enter the kingdom of God. Do the same for the southern, eastern, and western portions of your community. When I began to follow this pattern in prayer in Rockwall, Texas, 3,659 new people were added to our church during the next year.

God's kingdom is a spiritual kingdom extended by spiritual means, but the evil forces of the enemy try to prevent the harvest from being reaped. Command these forces to release the souls of men and women, boys and girls for the kingdom (Matt. 16:19). When you do this, you are clearing the road between them and God. As you bind the spiritual darkness that is blinding their eyes, God releases the angels to minister in their behalf (Heb. 1:14). Your intercession clears the path to the lost, releases the ministry of angels in their behalf, and activates the Holy Spirit to draw them to salvation. After you pray the pattern of Isaiah 43:5–7, praise God for the harvest.

4. Political Entities

Now you are ready to enlarge the focus of your prayers to include the political entities of your community, your nation, and the world. Your prayers are not limited by your geographic location or restrictions imposed by governmental regimes. Intercession can take you anywhere in the world in the spirit.

Pray for the spiritual and political leaders of your community, state, and nation. Call them by name. (Your telephone directory should list the names of community, state, and national political leaders responsible for your area.) Obtain lists of the schools and churches in your community, and declare God's kingdom over each of them. (Lists are usually available in the telephone directory or at the chamber of commerce.) Ask God to help you identify strongholds or evil "ruling spirits" in your area and bind these wicked powers of Satan. Pray for the growth and development of the church in every nation and for unity between existing congregations, denominations, and organizations.

Pray for specific missionaries. Collect newsletters and magazines from mission agencies and pray about their needs. Pray for special outreaches throughout the world, such as television and radio ministries, gospel recordings, prison ministries, the work among immigrants and refugees, and more. Pray for the five major unreached people groups of the world: Chinese, Muslims, tribal peoples, Hindus, and Buddhists. Use the headlines of your newspaper to pray about major world issues influencing the spread of the gospel. Pray for the spiritual and political leaders of nations. Use a map to pray for your city, your nation, and the countries and regions of the world. The book *Operation World* by Patrick Johnstone provides a wealth of information and specific prayer requests for every nation in the world.[6]

Pray for the peace of Jerusalem. God commands us to do so (Ps. 122:6) because our prayers preserve the Jewish nation and are instrumental in opening the doors for the coming restoration that will precede the return of the Lord Jesus Christ. Pray for peace in all their houses and for social, civil, and spiritual peace (Ps. 122:7). Above all, pray that Israel comes to know the Prince of Peace. Psalm 122:6 indicates that we are blessed by God if we pray for Jerusalem. We will have complete confidence to receive the petitions articulated in the remainder of the model prayer when we obey this command to pray for God's chosen people.

When You Pray, Say . . .

As you declare your heavenly Father's kingdom to come, you can use the words Jesus used when He said, "When you pray, say these words." For example, to pray the entire model prayer for your wife, you might say something like this:

> *Let Your name be hallowed in my wife. (Declare the benefits of the blood and the names of God in her life.) Let Your kingdom come and Your will be done in her life here on earth, even as Your will is done in heaven. (Articulate the specific requests for her previously discussed in this chapter.) Make provision for my wife this day, forgive her sins, and help her to forgive those who have wronged her. Lead her not into temptation, but deliver her today from the evil one.*

You can use the model prayer in this way to intercede for yourself and others.

As you prioritize your personal prayer life and declare, "Your kingdom come," in the four areas we have discussed, you will be automatically catapulted into the perfect will of God. This happens because you have taken Christ's command "when you pray, say" and responded in obedience to it. The psalmist David noted that when the law of God is written upon your heart, you will delight to do His will (Ps. 40:8).

When you allow the kingdom of God to rule your inner life with righteousness, peace, and joy, the will of God will be done in your outer life. The Bible declares, "For we are His workmanship, created in Christ Jesus for good works, which God prepared beforehand that we should walk in them" (Eph. 2:10), which means it is preordained of God that we should walk in His will. When we declare, "Your kingdom come," all we are doing is clearing the rubbish of Satan off the path God has already made for us. The inner life is established by declaring, "Your kingdom come," and the outer life by proclaiming, "Your will be done."

When you make these faith declarations, you will witness a supernatural change as your will comes into harmony with the purposes and plans of your heavenly Father because you have declared that you will live this day in His kingdom on earth. That is why I am calling you to an anointing of prayer that will enable you to do the Father's will without groping and struggling to find it.

As we close this chapter, pray this prayer with me:

Heavenly Father, I declare Your kingdom to come and Your will to be done in my life, my relationships, my church, and my ministry. By making this declaration, I clear the rubbish off the spiritual paths of my life so I can walk in the prayer anointing that God foreordained for me. I believe it is done right now in the name of Jesus! Amen.

Having declared the kingdom to rule and reign in your life, you are now ready to make an easy transition to fulfilling your God-given destiny. I will explain how to do this in the next chapter.

10

—✠—

How to Know and Do Your Father's Will

W hat is God's will for me?" This question is perhaps the one most often asked by believers. It is also a question that frequently confronts Christian leaders as men and women turn to them for guidance in decision making. In the model prayer Jesus taught, we are instructed to pray for our heavenly Father's will to be done on earth as it is in heaven, but is it truly possible that this petition can be answered?

Phillip Keller asks, "How can the will of our Father really be done in earth as it is in heaven? How can His desires, His wishes, His intentions be realized on an earth dominated by evil; held under the tyranny of Satan; and populated by stubborn, self-willed men?"[1]

As sons and daughters of God on a quest to develop intimacy with our heavenly Father, we must know and do our Father's will. But what is the will of God, and how can we do it?

When we say we want God's will, we desire to know His general plan for our lives so we can make wise choices. We want guidance in the circumstances of life, and we want to be led by His Holy Spirit. Every day we constantly make choices that determine whether or not we will do the perfect will of God. It is essential to know His will and make right choices because each minor decision affects the discovery of God's will for a lifetime. The Bible commands, "Therefore do not be unwise, but understand what the will of the Lord is" (Eph. 5:17).

Two Greek words are used for the English word *will* in reference to God. One word is *boulema*. It refers to God's sovereign will, which is His predetermined plan for everything that happens in the universe. This type of God's will is fulfilled regardless of human decisions. It is His master plan for the world to bring to pass all things on the basis of His sovereign will (Eph.1:11). The *boulema* will of God does not require human cooperation because the outcome is predetermined. There is no need to seek this *boulema* will of God because it is revealed in the Bible.

The other word for God's will is *thelema*. It points to His individual plan or will for each man or woman. You have the power to choose whether you will walk in the *thelema* or individual will of God for your life. We refer to this *thelema* will, or God's will for you as an individual, when we speak of seeking God's will. God also has a "moral" will, which is revealed in the commandments in His written Word teaching how believers should live. The individual and sovereign wills of God for persons will never conflict with the moral will of God revealed in His Word.

God's sovereign will for each individual includes redemption (2 Peter 3:9), but His purpose for us goes beyond redemption. Just like an earthly dad, our heavenly Father has an individual plan for each of His children. The Bible confirms this by many accounts where God placed men and women in specific situations at exact times for special purposes. For example, God told the prophet Jeremiah,

> *Before I formed you in the womb I knew you;*
> *Before you were born I sanctified you;*
> *And I ordained you a prophet to the nations (Jer. 1:5).*

What greater witness is there to the personal plan of God?

The Father's Personal Plan

Everywhere we look in the universe intelligent planning is apparent—the arrangement of planets, the stars, and the individual design of each snowflake and flower. Given this evidence, we must conclude that the divine Creator also has a personal plan for us, the highest of His created beings.

Psalm 37:23 states, "The steps of a good man are ordered by the

LORD." The same word used here for "ordered" is translated "ordained" and used in Psalm 8:3 in relation to the moon and stars God created. The science of astronomy has recorded the amazing precision of the movement of heavenly bodies. The same precision that schedules the movement of the planets orders the steps of believers.

Our Father in heaven promises,

> *Your ears shall hear a word behind you, saying,*
> *"This is the way, walk in it,"*
> *Whenever you turn to the right hand*
> *Or whenever you turn to the left (Isa. 30:21).*

John Wesley once made the comment that he lived each day as a lifetime. He likened the morning to childhood, the afternoon to adolescence, the evening to old age, and sleep to death. For each day, as well as an entire lifetime, our heavenly Father provides direction, just as an earthly dad does for his children. But just like an earthly father, God has plans for us that are sometimes contrary to our own:

> *"For My thoughts are not your thoughts,*
> *Nor are your ways My ways," says the LORD.*
> *"For as the heavens are higher than the earth,*
> *So are My ways higher than your ways,*
> *And My thoughts than your thoughts" (Isa. 55:8–9).*

God's will is not always the path we would select, but that does not mean His will brings unhappiness. The Bible teaches that God's will is always good and that we will delight in the way ordered by the Lord (Ps. 37:23). Paul also confirmed that God's will is "good and acceptable and perfect" (Rom. 12:2).

God is constantly working in your life. Ephesians 2:10 indicates that "we are His workmanship." The word *are* reveals a continuing, progressive process of God's will being revealed. It is God's desire to "make you complete in every good work to do His will, working in you what is well pleasing in His sight, through Jesus Christ, to whom be glory forever and ever" (Heb. 13:21). *Working* is in the present tense. God is continually guiding, developing, and speaking to you regarding His plan.

The Importance of Our Father's Will

Doing God's will is important because it is the basis of your relationship with your heavenly Father. Jesus said, "Whoever does the will of God is My brother and My sister and mother" (Mark 3:35). If doing God's will relates us as "brothers and sisters" to Christ, it also intimately links us with God as His children. We should be motivated to obey our heavenly Father's will because we love Him: "He who has My commandments and keeps them, it is he who loves Me. And he who loves Me will be loved by My Father, and I will love him and manifest Myself to him" (John 14:21).

Your heavenly Father's will is important because

• it determines your eternal destiny:

> *Not everyone who says to Me, "Lord, Lord," shall enter the kingdom of heaven, but he who does the will of My Father in heaven (Matt. 7:21).*

> *And the world is passing away, and the lust of it; but he who does the will of God abides forever (1 John 2:17).*

• you are incapable of directing your own way:

> *O LORD, I know the way of man is not in himself;*
> *It is not in man who walks to direct his own steps (Jer. 10:23).*

• you are commanded by God's Word to know His will:

> *Therefore do not be unwise, but understand what the will of the Lord is (Eph. 5:17).*

• it results in success because a man who walks in God's way:

> *shall be like a tree*
> *Planted by the rivers of water,*
> *That brings forth its fruit in its season, . . .*
> *And whatever he does shall prosper (Ps. 1:3).*

71

- it frees you from the curse:

  If you [the nation of Israel] do not obey the voice of the LORD your God, to observe carefully all His commandments and His statutes which I command you today, that all these curses will come upon you and overtake you (Deut. 28:15).

- it is the key to receiving God's promises:

  For you have need of endurance, so that after you have done the will of God, you may receive the promise (Heb. 10:36).

- it results in answered prayer:

  And whatever we ask we receive from Him, because we keep His commandments and do those things that are pleasing in His sight (1 John 3:22).

Your Will Be Done

In the model prayer that Jesus taught, He told us to declare to the Father, "Your will be done on earth as it is in heaven." Some people hesitate to make this declaration. They consider the will of God remote, and they are fearful to declare it because they do not understand it. Others resign themselves that God will do what He wants anyway, so why worry? Some people have reservations, afraid of what God's will might entail, while others accept it with bitter resentment. William Barclay comments, "The root reason why we find it so difficult to accept the will of God is that we so often in our heart of hearts think that we know better than God. We really believe that, if we could only get our way, we would be happy, that, if we could only arrange life and the events of life to suit our ideas, everything would be all right."[2]

"Your will be done" is not a prayer to be made with a sigh of resignation, with fearful reservation, or with teeth clenched in bitterness. It is a cry of triumph for God's children. "Your will be done" is the same type of faith declaration that we make when we pray, "Your kingdom come." It is like a person putting a foot down and stating emphatically, "Be done, Your will." You can boldly make this declaration because you already prayed, "Your kingdom come," in the prioritized areas of your personal life and primary relationships, and in behalf of your church, community, nation, and world.

These two dimensions of "kingdom" and "will" are intricately entwined because the declaration of your faith plus the will of God equals the kingdom of God every time! Because you have declared, "Your kingdom come," over every area of your life, you can be assured that He will guide you in each decision you make that day. "Your kingdom come" linked with "Your will be done" means you are claiming your Father's reign over every circumstance and problem because God's kingdom is governed sovereignly and absolutely by His Word. You are praying a *petition,* "Your will be done on earth," in conformity to a divine *pattern,* "as it is in heaven." Heaven provides the pattern for earth in that His will is done joyfully, completely, and obediently: "In heaven it is no hardship to do God's will, but a joy. Likewise in my heart, if God's Kingdom on earth is there, doing the will of God should be a delight and not a drudgery."[3]

You control a bit of your heavenly Father's kingdom by doing His will. At every moment throughout the day, you can fulfill the prayer for the kingdom of God to come by controlling your individual realm of the kingdom and doing your Father's will. You can be assured you *will* do it because you have declared His kingdom to reign supreme.

The kingdom comes within you with righteousness, peace, and joy. The will of God is done through you and effected in your life, your family, and your church. What goes on internally (the kingdom within) lays the foundation for what occurs externally (the will of God being done).

God has a preordained plan for you, and when you pray, "Your kingdom come. Your will be done," you embrace the eternal destiny planned for you before your birth. David declared,

Your eyes saw my substance, being yet unformed.
And in Your book they all were written,

The days fashioned for me,
When as yet there were none of them (Ps. 139:16).

The accuser says, "No way." Self says, "My way." Intercession says, "His way . . . Your will be done!"

11

—✣—

How to Access Your Spiritual Inheritance

Let me ask you a question. What would you do for God if you were unlimited by material resources, that is, finances, equipment, personnel, and so on? Dream big. Just what goals and visions would you accomplish? What changes would you make in your life and ministry? What desperate needs around you would you be able to meet? Did you know that you don't have to be limited by your present means? You can learn how to access limitless spiritual resources to fulfill your God-given goals and visions.

We earthly fathers are interested in our children's every need, from necessities like food and shelter to wishes for bicycles and toys. If we are interested in all that concerns our kids and long to provide for them, surely our heavenly Father is not indifferent to anything that concerns His children: "If you then, being evil, know how to give good gifts to your children, how much more will your Father who is in heaven give good things to those who ask Him!" (Matt. 7:11).

Jesus articulated the strategy for having all our needs met: "Therefore do not worry, saying, 'What shall we eat?' or 'What shall we drink?' or 'What shall we wear?' For after all these things the Gentiles seek. For your heavenly Father knows that you need all these things. But seek first the kingdom of God and His righteousness, and all these things shall be added to you" (Matt. 6:31–33).

In the model prayer, we seek first the kingdom when we declare,

"Your kingdom come," over every circumstance in our lives. We submit in righteousness to our heavenly Father's will, declaring, "Your will be done." Now we can pray with assurance, "Give us this day our daily bread."

What Is Our Daily Bread?

"Give us this day our daily bread" is the first of three personal petitions in this model prayer. Curtis Mitchell notes, "All the phrases of this prayer are stated in the form of commands in a verb tense known as the imperative mode in the Greek text that indicates an attitude of intense urgency. In fact, these petitions are given with the most intense urgency and earnestness that it is possible to convey with Greek grammar."[1] If this request is urgent and we are going to pray with assurance that we will receive this "bread," we need to understand the exact meaning of the petition.

First, we must recognize that our heavenly Father is the source of our daily bread. Our source is not the company from which we draw a paycheck, a bank account, stocks, bonds, or a family inheritance. Some people question, "If God is our source, He already knows our needs, so why pray?" That is a negative attitude. The positive approach is that *because* the Lord knows our needs, we can pray with complete confidence.

The second thing we note in this petition is that we are appealing for *our* daily bread to be given to *us*. The use of these words precludes any selfishness in our petition. We are asking not only for ourselves but also for others in our spiritual family.

Third, the prayer is for *daily* bread. As William Barclay writes, "It does not look fearfully into the distant future; it is content to take the present and to leave it in the hands of God."[2] The Greek word translated "daily" in this model prayer occurs nowhere else in the Bible. It means "necessary or essential bread, sufficient for our sustenance and support."[3] Its use in this context confirms that the model prayer Jesus taught is to be prayed each day.

Fourth, the prayer is for *bread*. But just what is this bread? One meaning of this bread obviously refers to spiritual bread. Jeremiah said of God's Word, "Your words were found, and I ate them, and Your word was to me the joy and rejoicing of my heart" (Jer. 15:16).

Jesus is described as the "bread of life" (John 6:35). But I believe that the word *bread* includes material as well as spiritual sustenance, for the Scriptures reveal a close relation between physical and spiritual food just as there is between material and spiritual prosperity (3 John 2). While the petition "Give us this day our daily bread" echoes the cry of the soul for the spiritual bread by which it grows, it also references the practical need of material sustenance.

This daily bread is a spiritual parallel of the Old Testament manna because, like manna, it is something collected daily and of which God is the source. While manna met the physical needs of Israel, Moses emphasized that provision for spiritual needs was also necessary (Deut. 8:3). William Barclay states, "In praying this petition we in trust ask God to supply all the physical and the spiritual needs of this life."[4] This dual nature does not in any way rob the daily bread of its spiritual connotations but adds to it the practical dimension of earthly realities.

How to Pray for Daily Bread

There are four basic requirements for successfully petitioning for daily bread. Each starts with a *B*. First, you must be in the will of God. Second, you must believe it is God's will to prosper you. Third, you must be specific when you pray daily for what you need. Fourth, you must be tenacious.

1. Be in God's Will

To pray in what you need, you must be in God's will. This implies several things.

It implies that Jesus is Lord of your life. You declare your Father's kingdom to come and His will to be done in every area of your life. The order of the model prayer establishes the proper sequence of priorities for having your needs met.

Being in God's will implies being attached to a community of believers. Hebrews 10:25 commands us to not forsake the assembling of ourselves together. God often meets our material needs by using others in the body of Christ (Rom. 15:26).

Being in God's will implies balanced, diligent work habits. Paul indicated that we are to earn our living with our own hands and not be a burden to others (1 Thess. 4:11–12). He said we should not be idle or too busy with other people's affairs to attend to our own (1 Tim. 5:13), and he declared, "If anyone will not work, neither shall he eat" (2 Thess. 3:10).

Paul also gave specific instructions regarding sound work ethics, encouraging employees to be submissive to their employers, to please them in every way, and not to talk back, contradict, or steal things (Titus 2:9–10). Peter directed employees to work honorably even in the face of persecution (1 Peter 2:18–23). Diligence is a virtue promoted in Scripture: If you will be faithful and diligent, God, who is in charge of promotions, will advance you (Ps. 75:6–7).

Being in God's will implies proper stewardship, that is, managing your money wisely, budgeting, living within your means, and consistently giving to the work of the Lord. Scriptural ways to give to God include the following: alms, which are gifts to the poor (Ps. 41:1; Matt. 6:1, 3, 4); tithes, which are a minimum of 10 percent of your income; and offerings, which are special gifts given in addition to your tithes (Mal. 3:8). Malachi indicated that God's people robbed Him in tithes and offerings. He challenged them to bring their gifts and prove the veracity of God's Word (Mal. 3:8–11).

You can give your way out of your financial dilemma, as evidenced in the Old Testament parable of the woman who used her last flour and oil to feed the prophet of God. Her limited resources were supernaturally multiplied through her generosity (1 Kings 17:10–16). Certain laws for people in the will of God are immutable. For example, Isaac sowed his seed during the time of famine, and he received a one hundredfold harvest (Gen. 26). If we obey the Word of God, we can claim its promises and boldly petition, "Give us this day our daily bread." God promised that if we obey His Word and are in His will, multitudes of blessings will overtake us (Deut. 28:1–4).

2. Believe It Is God's Will to Prosper You

Because my father made a fortune in oil and gas in Texas, I grew up surrounded by luxury, but because my material possessions did not satisfy, I concluded that anyone who had money could not be right with God. Also, some in that era seemed to equate poverty with spirituality.

But the more I studied the Bible, the more it defied this philosophy. I read about wealthy Abraham (Gen. 24:35) and how his son sowed and reaped a hundredfold during a time of famine (Gen. 26:1, 12–14). I learned how God blessed Jacob, despite his manipulative personality. I read about Job who, although he lost everything in a severe trial of faith, received twice as much as he had before.

I analyzed the words that Moses spoke to the nation of Israel: "And you shall remember the LORD your God, for it is He who gives you power to get wealth, that He may establish His covenant which He swore to your fathers, as it is this day" (Deut. 8:18).

Then I read the promise of Jesus: "Give, and it will be given to you: good measure, pressed down, shaken together, and running over will be put into your bosom. For with the same measure that you use, it will be measured back to you" (Luke 6:38). The command is "give," but the emphasis of this verse is on what we will receive.

I went on to discover what Jesus promised to those who had sacrificed for the sake of the gospel: "Assuredly, I say to you, there is no one who has left house or brothers or sisters or father or mother or wife or children or lands, for My sake and the gospel's, who shall not receive a hundredfold now in this time—houses and brothers and sisters and mothers and children and lands" (Mark 10:29–30).

I read that Paul said I was an heir with Christ (Rom. 8:17) and that God would supply all of my needs in Christ Jesus based on His resources in heaven (Phil. 4:19). From these and a multitude of other Scriptures that reiterated the message of blessing, I reached the conclusion that it is God's will that I prosper materially.

God does not bless us just so we can tear down our old barns and build bigger ones, get the latest gadgets, and accumulate more stuff. God's blessings are sometimes withheld when we consume our resources by indulging our own pleasures (James 4:3). His purposes for increasing wealth are clear:

> And God is able to make all grace (every favor and earthly blessing) come to you in abundance, so that you may always and under all circumstances and whatever the need, be self-sufficient—possessing enough to require no aid or support and furnished in abundance for every good work and charitable donation. . . . And [God] Who provides seed for the sower and bread for eating will also provide and multiply

your [resources for] sowing, and increase the fruits of your righteous-
ness [which manifests itself in active goodness, kindness, and charity].
Thus you will be enriched in all things and in every way, so that you
can be generous (2 Cor. 9:8, 10–11 AMPLIFIED).

God meets your needs so you can meet the needs of others. He
puts wealth into your hands so you can be a channel of His blessing
through which He can implement His covenant in the nations of the
world (Deut. 8:18–20). The pattern established by the New Testament church was the redistribution of wealth to help needy people
and advance the spread of the gospel.

3. Be Specific

James indicated that one reason we have not is because we ask
not (James 4:2). Be specific in your prayers. When Dr. Yonggi Cho
of Korea first started his ministry, he prayed specifically for a bicycle,
a desk, and a chair, and he received exactly what he asked for. It gave
him faith to ask for bigger things, and now he has raised up one of
the greatest churches in the world, built on the foundation of prayer.
Analyze any prominent prayer of the Bible and you will find it is
specific. Your prayers should be specifically targeted because, as the
old saying goes, "Aim at nothing and you hit it every time."

4. Be Tenacious

In Luke 18:1–8, Jesus told a parable about an unjust judge and
a widow who repeatedly begged, "Get justice for me from my
adversary." Finally, because of the woman's tenacity, the un-
righteous judge granted her request. Jesus used the story to illustrate
that if an earthly judge responds to persistence, how much more does
a righteous judge, our heavenly Father, respond to His children who
cry day and night to Him.

The Amplified Bible translates Matthew 7:7, "Keep on asking
and it will be given you; keep on seeking and you will find; keep on
knocking [reverently] and the door will be opened to you." The Bible
indicates that we should always pray and not faint and that we will
reap if we do not grow weary. Do not allow yourself to give up! You
must believe that our heavenly Father is a rewarder of His children

who diligently seek Him, for without faith it is impossible to receive from God (Heb. 11:6).

When you get these four things in your spirit and begin to declare, "Give us this day our daily bread," you will be able to pray in what is needed in your life. Remember that one of the compound names of your heavenly Father is Jehovah-jireh, meaning "the Lord will provide." Unlimited resources are already provided. The prayer anointing is prepared for you. All you must do is lay claim to these fatherly provisions.

12

— ✠ —

Forgiving Father's Way

Which part of the model prayer do you consider to be the most important? If your emphasis is on praise and worship, you probably consider "hallowed be Your name" of greatest significance. Those enmeshed in kingdom theology focus on "Your kingdom come" as preeminent. Believers who advocate the prosperity doctrine claim "give us this day our daily bread" of primary importance while those with deliverance ministries might advocate "deliver us from the evil one."

Would you like to know which part of the model prayer really is the most important? It is the part Jesus emphasizes. In Matthew 6 where Jesus teaches the model prayer, He reiterates only one portion in an addendum to His teaching. It is the phrase, "And forgive us our debts, as we forgive our debtors." At the conclusion of the teaching Jesus adds, "For if you forgive men their trespasses, your heavenly Father will also forgive you. But if you do not forgive men their trespasses, neither will your Father forgive your trespasses" (Matt. 6:14–15).

Jesus could speak with authority on this matter of forgiveness because He had multiple opportunities to be offended. His cousin John doubted who He was, religious leaders declared He was using witchcraft and teaching heresies, He was not accepted in His own hometown, and the multitudes who followed Him were more interested in physical food than spiritual truths. His disciples forsook and denied Him, and He suffered the humiliation and pain of death by crucifixion. What was Christ's secret for dealing with all these offenses? It is revealed in this phrase of the model prayer, "Forgive us our debts, as we forgive our debtors."

Forgiveness must be exercised in two major arenas of life: "In any serious sense there is no such thing as a debt towards our fellow men which is not also a debt towards God. And there is no debt towards God which does not also involve our fellow men."[1] We must learn to both receive and give forgiveness for personal offenses and injustices caused by others.

Personal Offenses

Personal offenses occur when you offend yourself and God through your sin. You deal with the offense by asking Him to forgive you when you say, "Forgive us our debts." The Bible declares, "If we say that we have no sin, we deceive ourselves, and the truth is not in us. If we confess our sins, He is faithful and just to forgive us our sins and to cleanse us from all unrighteousness" (1 John 1:8–9). When you confess your known sin, God forgives your unknown sin as well as what you have confessed, cleansing you from all unrighteousness.

The word *confess* in this Scripture means "to speak the same thing." Have you noticed how in recent years we have veiled evil with "educated" terminology such as *having an affair, a woman's right to choose,* and *alternative lifestyle?* Adultery isn't an affair; it is sin. Abortion isn't a woman's right to choose; it is murder. Homosexuality isn't an alternative lifestyle; it is a transgression of God's law. To be forgiven, we must confess or come into agreement with what God says about sin. His Word says that all have sinned and that we must confess sin and accept the sacrifice of Jesus Christ as God's provision for our forgiveness.

Several words in the Bible describe what sin is, but all of them emphasize the fact that sin is an offense against God. In the model prayer, Jesus described human sin as a debt. The word *debt* means "dues, duties, what is owed, what is legally due."

When you confess your sins, you are assured by God's Word that they are forgiven. You may not *feel* forgiven. But forgiveness is not a feeling; it is a fact based on faith. It is a fatherly function in your behalf, which is assured by your position as a child of God.

John MacArthur comments regarding this:

> *Every petition in the prayer promises us something that God already guarantees. So when we bring those petitions to God, we aren't begging God for what is reluctantly dispensed on our behalf; rather, we are simply claiming what is already promised to us. . . . It's as if we have a policy with God and when we want to lay a claim, we have the right to do so.*[2]

As a child of your heavenly Father, you have a right to claim His forgiveness. You must confess or agree with God not only about what He says about your sin but also about what He has done about it. God views your sin as forgiven from the foundation of the world and declares, "Their sin I will remember no more" (Jer. 31:34).

Offenses of Others

The second area in which forgiveness must be manifested is in forgiving others of direct and indirect offenses. A *direct offense* occurs when you are offended by someone. An *indirect offense* occurs when someone hurts a friend or relative and you take up your loved one's offense. Jesus taught that we were to deal with such misdeeds by praying, "Forgive us our debts, as we forgive our debtors."

One day Peter came to Jesus with a question about forgiveness: "Lord, how often shall my brother sin against me, and I forgive him? Up to seven times?" (Matt. 18:21). You see, the rabbis of Peter's era taught that you should forgive an offender three times. By suggesting he would forgive seven times, Peter felt he was being quite spiritual and going beyond the call of duty. Jesus responded, "I do not say to you, up to seven times, but up to seventy times seven" (Matt. 18:22). Jesus indicated that we should forgive our brothers and sisters as many times as we are offended because that is how many times our heavenly Father is willing to forgive us.

Then Jesus taught a powerful parable to illustrate His response to Peter's inquiry. Take time to read Matthew 18:23–35, which is the story of a servant who owed his king 10,000 talents (an amount of approximately $10 million). The king knew the servant was struggling beneath a load of debt so enormous that he would never be able to repay it, so he pardoned the debt. Someone else owed this same servant a debt of a hundred denarii (about $20). Instead of forgiving as he had been pardoned, the servant had the debtor thrown in prison. When the king discovered the servant's lack of compassion, he asked him a question that God asks each of us: "Should you not also have had compassion on your fellow servant, just as I had pity on you?" (Matt. 18:33).

Note that the unjust servant "would not" forgive (Matt. 18:30). He *should* have forgiven, and he *could* have forgiven because he had been pardoned, but he *would* not.

This parable makes three crucial points: (1) God's forgiveness precedes human forgiveness; (2) human forgiveness is a reflection of God's forgiveness; and (3) God's forgiveness becomes real for us only when we are willing to forgive one another.[3] Jesus summarized these truths when He declared, "If you have anything against anyone, forgive him, that your Father in heaven may also forgive you your trespasses. But if you do not forgive, neither will your Father in heaven forgive your trespasses" (Mark 11:25–26).

We are to forgive at the same level we are forgiven by God. Because we have been forgiven, we can freely forgive others. The final picture in this parable is of the unforgiving servant being delivered to tormentors. Being unforgiving of others attracts bitterness and anger, which torment your spirit.

Be forewarned: Satan causes offenses in your family, between friends, in your business relationships, and in your church. The Bible states, "Offenses must come" (Matt. 18:7). How will you deal with these issues when they arise?

Here are four keys to help you give and receive forgiveness:

1. Don't Curse It

When you sin or you are offended by someone, don't curse it. Don't dwell on the issues of "if only I had" or "why me?" or get angry. Romans 8:28–29 indicates that all things work for good to conform you to the image of Jesus Christ. Ask yourself, How is God going to take what was intended for evil and work it out for my benefit? As Joseph did, boldly declare in the face of your offense, "But as for you, you meant evil against me; but God meant it for good" (Gen. 50:20).

Remember that "where sin abounded, grace abounded much more" (Rom. 5:20). God's grace is manifested in its greatest measure in the midst of your sin, your weaknesses, and the offenses you suffer.

2. Don't Nurse It

You nurse offenses through self-pity. When you think, *Poor me; I don't deserve this kind of treatment,* you nurse your offense. Refuse to let self-pity crawl into your heart because it is self-destructive.

3. Don't Rehearse It

What constantly consumes your thought life? Is your mind focused on your heavenly Father or on someone who has hurt and offended you? Rehearsing the wrongs done to you creates inner turmoil and torment. Isaiah 26:3 promises perfect peace if you keep your mind on your heavenly Father.

Whether it is a sin you have committed or an offense committed against you, stop talking about it! Once God forgives, He forgets, so why should you remember what God has forgotten? By an act of your own will, you must do as the apostle Paul did and forget the things that are behind (Phil. 3:13). Rehearsing offenses results in mentally and emotionally dwelling in yesterday, and you will never have a future as long as you are living in the past.

4. Disperse It

Covenant in your heart each day that you choose to forgive as an act of your will. Remember the unjust servant who *could* have forgiven and *should* have forgiven his debtor but *would* not. When you choose to forgive as an act of your will, you disperse the offense that was committed against you, which means you disarm it of its power over you.

In the Greek, forgiveness and remission are represented by the same word, which means "to send off" or "send away." In Old Testament times on the Day of Atonement, the sins of the people were confessed over the head of a scapegoat. The animal was then led away to the wilderness, never to return. That is exactly what happens when you are forgiven and what should happen when you forgive others. The offenses are carried away, never again to return.

Does a dark cloud of emotion rise up within you when you think of certain people? Then you need to forgive these individuals. Do specific memories still cause pain when you think about them? Do you hold prejudices you have not been able to release? Such feelings indicate that you need to forgive.

Since the Bible declares that offenses will come in this life, it is a matter not of *whether* they will come but of how you will deal with them *when* they come. Forgiveness is not justifying someone else's wrongs with an excuse: "She was under a lot of pressure." It is not denying you were hurt in the first place or accepting with resignation what was done to you. Neither does forgiveness come by waiting for time to heal the hurt because it usually doesn't.

True forgiveness comes by recognizing the wrong done to you, confessing the hurt to God, and releasing the negative emotions associated with the offense and the offender. The process is like peeling back the outer layers of an onion, and when you do this, you position yourself for God to work supernaturally in your life and the life of your offender. It clears the refuse of bitterness from your spirit and prepares the way for the prayer anointing to flow into your life.

Forgiving Father's Way

I have had to live the message I've shared in this chapter. After my dad divorced my mother, remarried, and was diagnosed with terminal cancer, I traveled to Mexico to see him. I told him, "I have come as three persons. I have come as your pastor to say that you are wrong in what you have done. I have come as your son, asking you to come back home with me. I have come as your friend, for a friend loves at all times." I had to stop cursing, nursing, and rehearsing the wrong and by an act of my will choose to forgive my father.

Before my dad's death, he confessed his sin and made things right with God. He couldn't come back home because he was so sick, so he died on foreign soil. If you need to forgive someone, don't postpone it. Don't wait until it is too late. Do it right now as you pray this prayer:

Heavenly Father, I bring to You the wounds that have come to me through the offenses of others. I forgive _____ right now and release them, forgiving even as You have forgiven me. I will no longer curse the wrong done to me. I will not nurse it or rehearse it. I disperse it right now, in Jesus' name. Amen.[4]

13

Delivered from
the Evil One

Dawn was breaking over the six-lane expressway that links the
northern region of England with the sprawling metropolis of London. My son John and I were en route to the city from the Manchester
area, accompanied by a local pastor and a bishop. We had been
ministering for several days throughout the nation and experiencing
powerful confrontations with the controlling spirits of witchcraft
and homosexuality.

The calm of the early morning was shattered when two motor-
cycle policemen and several assault vehicles screeched into position
surrounding our car. Laser weapons were targeted on us as the
officers screamed, "Exit the vehicle with your hands up and get on
the ground!" One burly officer put his foot on me as I lay face down,
and John's clothing was ripped by a police dog loosed on him while
he was being handcuffed.

"Do you arrest people in England without telling them the reason
why?" I asked the officer who had me in custody. Hearing my Texas
drawl, the policeman looked surprised and said, "Who are you
anyhow?"

"I am a minister of the gospel returning from a meeting in Leigh,
and tonight I will preach in London," I answered. The officer stared
at me intently with a perplexed look, and then he said, "If you are
who you say you are, we may owe you an apology."

We were transported to police headquarters, and it took some time to sort out the facts. It turned out that two days previously, a police officer was killed by a terrorist, and someone called in the license and make of the vehicle in which I was riding, telling the police, "Your shooter is in that car."

This terrifying experience illustrates the importance of the passage we will consider in this and the succeeding chapter, "Do not lead us into temptation, but deliver us from the evil one." William Barclay comments regarding this final petition in the model prayer: "This concluding petition of the Lord's Prayer does three things. First, it frankly faces the danger of the human situation. Second, it freely confesses the inadequacy of human sources to deal with it. Thirdly, it takes both the danger and the weakness to the protecting power of God."[1]

This is a petition you need to lift every day, for it is a prayer that could save your life, as it did mine in the satanically motivated attempt to destroy me in England. You must be able to identify the enemy, know how to arm yourself against his attacks, and learn how to live within God's hedge of protection. In this chapter, we will discuss the tempter, temptation, and our spiritual armor. In chapter 14, we will learn how to surround our lives with God's hedge of protection.

In the previous chapter, we learned to forgive as our heavenly Father forgives. Forgiveness always precedes deliverance, for if you cut the root of evil (bitterness and unforgiveness), you kill its fruit (temptation and evil).

The Tempter

Jesus taught us to pray, "Do not lead us into temptation," but James indicates God does not tempt man. Our loving heavenly Father is *not* the tempter: "Let no one say when he is tempted, 'I am tempted by God'; for God cannot be tempted by evil, nor does He Himself tempt anyone" (James 1:13).

So who is the tempter to whom Jesus is referring? The Bible reveals that this is our enemy, Satan (Matt. 4:3; 1 Thess. 3:5). The Scriptures repeatedly warn of temptations that come from the devil (Matt. 4:1; 1 Cor. 7:5).

The Bible explains that "each one is tempted when he is drawn away by his own desires and enticed. Then, when desire has conceived, it gives birth to sin; and sin, when it is full-grown, brings forth death" (James 1:14–15). Satan is the tempter, but we are drawn into his snare when we allow our fleshly desires to entice us. Such desires birth sin, and sin results in death.

When it comes to temptation, Satan is no respecter of persons. He tempted King David, Peter, and Jesus. He deceived Achan right in the midst of the camp of God's people and snatched Judas from the ranks of the disciples. We see that even in a holy environment like the Garden of Eden, the subtle voice of the tempter was heard.

Some of Satan's attacks arise from uncontrolled evil passions from within, while other temptations come from without through our senses of hearing, seeing, feeling, touching, and tasting. Whatever their source, the apostle Paul assures us, "No temptation has overtaken you except such as is common to man; but God is faithful, who will not allow you to be tempted beyond what you are able, but with the temptation will also make the way of escape, that you may be able to bear it" (1 Cor. 10:13).

We need to know what is meant by this word *temptation* that is "common" to all. No single English word does justice to the word *temptation,* as William Barclay explains:

> It has three ideas. It has in it the simple idea of proving or testing the quality of a person or a thing. It has in it the idea of putting a person in a situation which is in reality a test by which involves the possibility of failure. And it has in it the idea of the deliberate invitation and seduction to sin. . . . The English word which comes nearest to containing both ideas is the word trial.[2]

Three Arenas of Temptation

There are basically three arenas of temptation. They were illustrated in the story of Adam and Eve's fall into sin and in the account of Jesus overcoming it during His wilderness temptation. They are the lust (uncontrolled desire) of the flesh, the lust of the eyes, and the pride of life. The lust of the flesh is an unholy desire for what will satisfy sinful passions. The lust of the eyes is evil that is triggered visually. The pride of life is an insidious attitude that often comes disguised as self-esteem.

Satan's ultimate target in all temptation is to destroy our relationship with our heavenly Father. In the Garden of Eden, Adam and Eve had intimate fellowship with God until the serpent led them to doubt Him ("Has God indeed said?" [Gen. 3:1]), which resulted in disobedience ("[they] took of its fruit and ate" [Gen. 3:6]). In the next scene we see this couple who once shared an intimate relationship with their Father hiding from His presence.

Satan always attacks in our area of weakness. It is much like the story of the famous Greek, Achilles. According to legend, this hero of the Trojan War was dipped as a child into the sacred waters of the Styx by his mother. The result of this plunge was that every part of his body was invulnerable to the enemy and "wound proof" with the exception of one heel, which was not submerged. One day in the midst of a fierce battle, a poisoned arrow of the enemy found its mark at this weak spot and inflicted a death wound. In a similar manner, sin and temptation attack where we are weakest.[3]

When we pray, "Do not lead us into temptation," we ask God to preserve us from the enticement to sin: "It is apparent therefore that this is not a prayer in which we ask God to exempt us from trials. This is a prayer to be kept from enticement to sin. It is a prayer to be delivered out of all sin and evil."[4]

Hebrews 11 is a tremendous record of godly men and women who experienced temptation and trials. They were not exempt because of their faith, but they were preserved by it. Even Jesus was not delivered from temptation but was preserved in it (Heb. 4:15). The apostle John assures us,

> We know [absolutely] that any one born of God does not [deliberately and knowingly] practice committing sin, but the One Who was begotten of God carefully watches over and protects him—Christ's divine presence within him preserves him against the evil—and the wicked one does not lay hold (get a grip) on him or touch [him] (1 John 5:18 AMPLIFIED).

It is possible to successfully overcome temptation, and to those who do so, God promises, "Blessed is the man who endures temptation; for when he has been approved, he will receive the crown of life which the Lord has promised to those who love Him" (James 1:12).

Delivered from the Evil One

Jesus taught us to pray, "Deliver us from the evil one." The Scriptures identify our enemy, Satan, as the evil one, and our deliverance from his wicked clutches is assured if we daily appropriate our spiritual armor and learn to live within God's hedge of protection. In Ephesians 6:10–18, the apostle Paul provides detailed information about the evil one and the spiritual armor God provides for our defense. First, Paul identifies the enemies that confront us: "For we do not wrestle against flesh and blood, but against principalities, against powers, against the rulers of the darkness of this age, against spiritual hosts of wickedness in the heavenly places" (Eph. 6:12).

Paul emphatically declares we should be strong in the Lord and in the power of His might and stand boldly in the face of these evil forces (Eph. 6:10–11, 13). He decrees that it is possible to stand against every wile (deceit, cunning, craftiness) of the devil. Paul admonishes that we should wage good warfare (1 Tim. 1:18), fight an effective fight of faith (1 Tim. 6:12), and battle intelligently with purpose (1 Cor. 9:26–27).

Paul emphasizes that the battle is not a natural one and natural weapons are ineffective. Spiritual battles must be fought with spiritual weapons. Let us examine in detail each piece of our spiritual armor described in Ephesians 6:13–18.

The Belt

The belt held the other pieces of armor in place, so the first piece of our spiritual armor to be buckled on is the girdle or belt of truth. The truth of God's Word is the spiritual belt to which all other pieces of armor are attached. Satan's first attack on people in the Garden of Eden was upon the truth when he whispered, "Has God indeed said?" The truth of God's Word will protect you from lies and doctrinal errors of the enemy. Truth is the undergirding of your spiritual armor.

You are to have your loins (your spiritual vital organs) covered with truth (Eph. 6:14), which means you are to appropriate Jesus who is declared to be truth (John 14:6) and the power of the Holy Spirit who is the "Spirit of truth" (John 14:17). God is truth (Rom. 3:4), His Word is truth (Ps. 119:151), and the gospel is declared to be true (Col. 1:5). All these are woven into the fabric of our belt of truth.

The digestive, reproductive, and bowel systems are located in the loins. The spiritual analogy is that when our belt of truth is in place, the Word of God will be properly digested, we will be able to reproduce by guiding others to the way of truth, and our spiritual impurities will be eliminated.

The Breastplate

The breastplate covered the upper body of a warrior to protect his vital organs, such as his heart and lungs. The spiritual breastplate of righteousness refers not to your righteousness but to the covering of the righteousness of Christ (Phil. 3:9), which must be buckled onto the belt of truth.

You cannot face the enemy without the protection of the righteousness of Christ, which is described as surrounding the Christian warrior on "the right hand and on the left" (2 Cor. 6:7). The righteousness of Christ protects your spiritual vital organs from the attacks of Satan and from unrighteousness. If you should fail in spiritual battle, you do not have to try to justify yourself, excuse your defeat, or agonize from guilt. Simply declare, "I do not stand in my own righteousness. I stand clothed in the breastplate of the righteousness of Jesus Christ!"

The Shoes

A soldier's shoes are designed specifically for warfare because a warrior who cannot advance on the battlefield is disabled in battle. In Roman armies the soldiers' shoes had spikes or hobnails in their soles to prevent slipping. Feet shod "with the preparation of the gospel of peace" indicate a readiness to advance in the spiritual realm. These spiritual shoes protect you from the temptation of the enemy who would lead you in wrong paths. These spiritual shoes enable you to grind your spiritual hobnails into the ground and take a firm stand against the enemy (Eph. 6:15).

The Shield

The shield provided protection to the warrior's entire body. Your spiritual shield is called the "shield of faith." Several types of faith are mentioned in the Bible: saving faith, the gift of faith, and the spiritual fruit of faith. But the word *faith* when used in relation to the shield of faith speaks of *defensive* faith. This faith is a firm trust in God, which protects your whole being. It protects you from flaming missiles of doubt and unbelief sent by the enemy. It is a calm and confident trust in God, which deflects all the fiery arrows of the enemy from their target.

The shield of faith is the constant application of God's Word to the issues of life. It is a faith that enables you to overcome the evil forces of the world because "this is the victory that has overcome the world—our faith" (1 John 5:4). Without faith, you have no grasp of truth nor can you claim the helmet of salvation. Without faith, you cannot go forth with the gospel of peace, claim the righteousness of Christ, or effectively use the sword of the Spirit. Faith is not an assumption or a presumption; rather, it is a fact based upon God's Word, and you increase it by hearing His Word (Rom. 10:17), acting upon your present faith (Rom. 1:17), and seeking God (Heb. 12:2).

The Helmet

The helmet of salvation is not something you put on when you get saved because we are dealing here with spiritual armor. The helmet of salvation represents a regenerated mind, a transformed and renewed thought life. Satan desperately fights for control of your mind. An undisciplined mind makes you an easy target for the sinful deceptions of the enemy.

Paul speaks of the helmet as the "hope of salvation" (1 Thess. 5:8). This helmet of hope declares you have been saved from the guilt and penalty of *past* sins, you are being saved from the power of sin in the *present,* and in the future you will be saved from the *presence* of sin when Jesus returns. The hope of such comprehensive salvation strengthens your mind against the attacks of Satan.

The Sword of the Spirit

The "sword of the Spirit" is the Word of God, which can be used to defend against the attacks of Satan by quoting specific verses that apply to an immediate temptation. Jesus used specific sayings of God when He was tempted by Satan. The term for "word" in Matthew 4 means the *rhema* word of God. Peter encourages us to "resist him, steadfast in the faith" (1 Peter 5:8–9). To resist in the faith means to resist on the authority of God's Word. It is a powerful spiritual weapon: "For the word of God is living and powerful, and sharper than any two-edged sword, piercing even to the division of soul and spirit, and of joints and marrow, and is a discerner of the thoughts and intents of the heart" (Heb. 4:12).

Prayer

After describing the Christian soldier's armor, Paul comments, "Praying always with all prayer and supplication in the Spirit, being watchful to this end with all perseverance and supplication for all the saints" (Eph. 6:18).

When you do warfare praying, you do not just pray for your personal wants, needs, and problems. You intercede for people, leaders, and nations, pulling down strongholds of Satan and his demonic forces and waging battle in the unseen realm. You will learn more about this type of praying later on in this book.

Appropriating Your Father's Armor

The purpose of the armor is to be able to stand against the wiles of the enemy, Satan. Paul commands you to "put on" this spiritual armor, which means it is your responsibility to appropriate what God has provided. To put on means to take hold of something and apply it to yourself.

Putting on the armor of God is the application of Jesus in your daily life. Paul instructs us to put on the armor of light and further clarifies, "Put on the Lord Jesus Christ" (Rom. 13:12, 14). Just as an earthly father buys clothing for his children, our heavenly Father provides a spiritual covering for us in this armor of God.

Paul advises us to put on the "whole" armor of God (Eph. 6:11). Some of us are preoccupied with one piece of God's armor to the extent that others are neglected. You must have on the whole armor, or you may find yourself being an expert in the use of the sword of the Spirit and still defeated because you have forgotten the shield of faith.

This account of the armor of God is not just a beautiful metaphor. It is something for us to appropriate as we go daily into the spiritual trenches of life's battles. I have also learned it is important to bind the opposite spirit as I appropriate the armor. Here is a summary of your spiritual armor, the declaration you should make each day in prayer to appropriate it, and the opposite spirit to bind:[5]

Armor	Declaration to Make	Promise to Claim	Opposite Spirit to Bind
Loins girded with truth	Jesus, You are my truth.	John 14:6	Deception
Breastplate of righteousness	Jesus, You are my righteousness.	2 Corinthians 5:21	Unrighteousness
Feet shod with the preparation of the gospel of peace	Jesus, You are my readiness.	Philippians 4:13	Lethargy
Shield of faith	Jesus, You are my faith.	Galatians 2:20	Unbelief, doubt
Helmet of salvation	Jesus, You are my salvation.	Hebrews 5:9	Vain imaginations, evil thoughts
Sword of the Spirit (Word of God)	Jesus, You are my living Word.	John 1:14	Lies of the false father
Praying always in the Spirit	Jesus, You are my baptizer in the Spirit.	Romans 8:27	Prayerlessness

As we close this chapter, I want to pray a special prayer for you:

Heavenly Father, as each piece of this spiritual armor is appropriated, I claim deliverance from the evil one and release angelic forces to war in behalf of each person who now holds this book. As he or she marches forward in the name of the Lord, may liberation from the forces of darkness be effected in every area of his or her life and ministry in the name of Jesus. Amen.

When you appropriate your spiritual armor and cry out to the Father, "Deliver us from evil," God releases angels to battle in your behalf in the spiritual realm. You position yourself to begin construction on a hedge of protection that inhibits access by the evil one. In the next chapter, I will share exactly how to erect this protective barrier in your life.

14

Your Father's
Hedge of Protection

One of the chief functions of a good earthly father is the protection of his children. Our heavenly Father has provided a hedge of protection that can guard our families, businesses, churches, and all that pertains to us. Even the evil one, Satan, recognizes the power of this spiritual hedge. In Job 1:10, we find Satan complaining to God about a man named Job: "You have made a hedge around him so that I cannot touch him!"

This hedge provided by your heavenly Father very well may save your life, as I believe it did mine in the fearful encounter with the English police force. When you claim this hedge of protection, you also declare its associated benefits of prosperity, happiness, and increase. The tremendous benefits of this hedge are listed in Psalm 91:

- You will "abide under the shadow of the Almighty" (v. 1). The word *abide* here means being "seated" or "settled" in God, to "possess a place and live therein."
- You will be delivered from "the fowler" (v. 3). *Fowler* means "hunter," a credible description of Satan who creeps throughout the earth seeking his victims.
- You will be delivered "from the perilous pestilence" (v. 3).

Perilous pestilence means "annoying evil" or "rushing calamity, the nature of which sweeps everything before it."

- Your Father will cover you with His wings and feathers (v. 4). Wings and feathers speak of the gentle, comforting nature of your Father's protection.

- His truth will be "your shield and buckler" (v. 4). The shield and buckler on a soldier's uniform protected the vital organs from the attacks of the enemy. These terms reflect the powerful nature of your Father's protection.

- You will not be afraid of the terror by night or the pestilence in darkness (vv. 5–6). People huddle behind closed doors as terror reigns at night in many communities of our nation, but there are no locks and bars strong enough to shut out evil. Your heavenly Father's hedge of protection not only keeps you safe, but it also delivers you from the fear associated with these terrors.

- You will not be afraid of the arrow that flies by day or the destruction at noonday (vv. 5–6). Even in the daytime of your life with friends about you, there is danger. It does not say that arrows will not fly or destruction will not be evident; it says that you need not fear them.

- Thousands may fall around you, but "it shall not come near you" (v. 7). You will be untouched by the destroyer. No matter who around you might fall prey to Satan's destruction, you can be preserved in God's hedge of protection.

- Only with your eyes will you witness the reward of the wicked (v. 8). You will witness the destruction of the wicked, but you will not be part of it.

- No evil will befall you, and no plague will come near your dwelling (v. 10). This verse speaks of household preservation within the hedge of God's protection. You, your family, and your dwelling are safeguarded from plagues and evil!

- God will give His angels charge over you in all your ways (v. 11). Angels will be dispatched to keep you in all your ways, even when there is no apparent danger. They will bear you up in their hands and keep you from spiritual injury. It is their responsibility to minister to you because you are an heir of your Father's salvation (Heb. 1:14).

- You will tread upon the lion, adder, young lion, and dragon (v. 13 KJV). The lion, adder, young lion, and dragon are all symbols of Satan. You can tread upon your enemy because Jesus crushed the enemy's head (Gen. 3:15; Col. 2:15). "Treading" is a symbol of complete and powerful victory over the enemy.
- God will deliver you and set you on high (v. 14). You will function above the negative circumstances of life.
- When you call, He will answer and be with you in trouble (v. 15). God will pour out the prayer anointing on you and will respond to your petitions.
- He will honor you, satisfy you with long life, and show you His salvation (vv. 15–16). You will be a reflection of God's glory as you complete the work you were destined to do, and you will not die prematurely. You will experience the eternal benefits of your Father's salvation including forgiveness from the penalty for past sins, power to overcome sin in the present, and deliverance from the presence of sin in the future.

The Hedge of Protection

Every known need is covered in this psalm. Wouldn't you like to live with such reliable security? You can! The psalmist identifies three reasons you can claim your heavenly Father's protection and live in this tremendous supernatural realm. Each of these begins with the word *because*.

1. Because You Have Made the Lord Your Habitation (Ps. 91:9 KJV)

The word *habitation* refers to being at home with God, communing with Him, delighting in and depending upon Him as a child does his earthly father. We make our heavenly Father a habitation by praising Him (Ps. 22:3). As we praise Him, God dwells among us enthroned in our praises. That is why the apostle Paul encourages us to be filled with the Spirit and constantly lift psalms, hymns, and spiritual songs to the Lord in our hearts (Eph. 5:18–20).

David obviously made God his spiritual habitation, as evidenced by the tremendous collection of his psalms preserved in God's Word. He also declared God to be his refuge, fortress, and sheltering protection. David said God would hide him in His pavilion in times of trouble (Ps. 27:4–6). The word *pavilion* means both "a temporary, movable tent" and "a more permanent building." In Old Testament times, during war the royal pavilion, or king's tent, was erected in the center of the army and surrounded by a constant guard of mighty men. David, who had occupied one of these royal tents in battle, is saying, "In the time of trouble, God hides me in His royal tent in the very center of His army and surrounds me by a constant guard of His mighty angels." You can occupy this same secret place of protection by making God your spiritual habitation through praise and worship.

2. Because You Have Set Your Love Upon Him (Ps. 91:14)

"You still lack one thing," Jesus told the rich young ruler in an encounter recorded in Luke 18:18–27. "Martha, . . . one thing is needed," Jesus stated during a visit in Bethany (Luke 10:41–42). "One thing I do," declared the apostle Paul (Phil. 3:13). In each of these incidents, the priority of the claims of our heavenly Father on a true believer's life is emphasized. One thing is of supreme importance: God must come first!

In Psalm 91, God declares that a hedge of safety surrounds His people when we give Him first priority in our lives. Set your affections on God until your spirit can truthfully echo these words of David:

> *Though an army may encamp against me,*
> *My heart shall not fear;*
> *Though war may rise against me,*
> *In this I will be confident.*
> *One thing I have desired of the LORD,*
> *That will I seek:*
> *That I may dwell in the house of the LORD*
> *All the days of my life,*

To behold the beauty of the LORD,
And to inquire in His temple.
For in the time of trouble
He shall hide me in His pavilion;
In the secret place of His tabernacle
He shall hide me;
He shall set me high upon a rock.
And now my head shall be lifted up above my enemies all around me;
Therefore I will offer sacrifices of joy in His tabernacle;
I will sing, yes, I will sing praises to the LORD (Ps. 27:3–6).

3. Because You Have Known His Name (Ps. 91:14)

The third reason you can claim the hedge of God's protection is that you have known His name. The name of the Lord is described as a strong tower into which the righteous can run for safe haven (Prov. 18:10). It is obvious that the psalmist knew his heavenly Father's name and appropriated its benefits and relationships because he refers to God as "Most High," "Almighty," "Lord," and "God."

You learned the meanings of your Father's names in chapter 8. As you appropriate these names in prayer and begin to live in their inherent benefits, you will develop an even more intimate knowledge of His name because it will become a reality in your everyday life.

Living Within the Hedge of Protection

Just as an earthly father protects his children, your heavenly Father provides protection as one of His fatherly functions. It is an inherent benefit of His name Jehovah-nissi. Your Father's name is the banner of security that unfurls in victory above you proclaiming your deliverance from the evil one.

Each day when you pray, "Deliver us from the evil one," claim this hedge of protection around you, your loved ones, your business, your home, and all that pertains to you. Use Psalm 91 to make a verbal declaration, saying,

I choose to dwell in the secret place of the Most High this day, and I will abide under the shadow of Your wings. You are my refuge, my

fortress, my God, and I trust in You. I have confidence that You will deliver me from every snare and pestilence because I have made Your truth my shield and buckler. I am not afraid of any terrors, dangers, or destruction. I have confidence that the plagues slaying those around me will not come near me or my household. Father, I have made You my habitation, and I have set my love upon You. Your name is my refuge this day, and I can boldly declare that You are my fortress and You will deliver me from evil. I will be kept in all my ways, and when I call upon You in any situation I face today, You will answer me.

Three Personal Petitions

In the last few chapters we have analyzed three personal petitions in the model prayer: (1) "give us this day our daily bread"; (2) "forgive us our debts, as we forgive our debtors"; and (3) "do not lead us into temptation, but deliver us from the evil one."

Now that we are assured of daily provision, we have received and given forgiveness, and we are confident that our deliverance from the evil one is effected, we move forward to raise a final crescendo of praise in this model prayer. A simple phrase of thirteen words has the profound capacity to literally change your world, drawing you deeper into the supernatural realm of the prayer anointing.

15

Thirteen Words That Can
Change Your World

As we placed this model prayer under the intense analysis of the microscope of the Holy Spirit, we observed the beauty of its structure that, like the delicate pattern of a snowflake, is not readily apparent to the casual observer. We have now come to what is called the doxology of the model prayer, "For Yours is the kingdom and the power and the glory forever. Amen" (Matt. 6:13). This doxology is a powerful climax paralleling that of a final, moving crescendo of a symphony concert.

To fully comprehend the tremendous meaning of these concluding words, let us once again use our spiritual microscope for a closer look. We will examine each individual word in proper sequence and discover that these thirteen words have the capacity to change our world.

"For"

The word *for* indicates the authority by which the model prayer has been prayed. It means because the kingdom, power, and glory belong to our Father, we can claim the provisions, promises, and protection of this prayer. Because we are His children, we have the right to these benefits as part of our family inheritance.

"Yours Is the Kingdom"

In chapter 9 we discussed the kingdom of God in detail as we examined the segment of the model prayer that declares, "Your kingdom come." We learned that the kingdom is a demonstration of God's nature in action. We also learned of the past, present, and future dimensions of this kingdom and how it is currently manifested in the inward qualities of righteousness, peace, and joy.

When we arrive at this final portion of the model prayer and declare, "Yours is the kingdom," we come into agreement with everything God says about His kingdom. Like David, we proclaim, "The kingdom is the LORD's" (Ps. 22:28). But if we really understand what we are saying, our confession is even more powerful than it appears on the surface because Jesus said, "Do not fear, little flock, for it is your Father's good pleasure to give you the kingdom" (Luke 12:32).

When we proclaim, "Yours is the kingdom," our Father declares to us, "I have given My kingdom to you!" It is a powerful Father-child partnership, a relationship that links us intimately with our heavenly Father. It is His kingdom, but because we are heirs, it is our kingdom, also. It is a legacy conferred by our Father, and it pleases Him to give it to us.

"Yours Is the Power"

The Greek word for power is *dunamis* from which the English words *dynamic* and *dynamite* come. When we end our prayer with, "Yours is the power," we acknowledge the dynamic power of God with its dynamitelike potential for fulfilling our petitions.

But once again, just as when we proclaimed, "Yours is the kingdom," confessing, "Yours is the power," has an even greater depth of meaning. When we declare, "Yours is the power," God echoes to us the words of Jesus: "I give you power over all the power of the enemy." This delegated power is stronger than demons and disease (Luke 9:1) and it gives us the ability to put all the power of the enemy under our spiritual feet (Luke 10:19).

This inherent power provides the authority to claim every promise, provision, and protection for which we have prayed. This power gives strength (Ps. 68:35) and revives the faint (Isa. 40:29). It is the power to get wealth (Deut. 8:18) and to abide in covenant relationship with the Father (2 Peter 1:4).

You may think this tremendous power can be attained only by spiritual giants, but the Word of God is filled with examples of ordinary men and women who tapped into this power supply: Abraham, who lied about Sarah being his wife, yet God designated him to be the father of the nation of Israel; Moses, who killed an Egyptian in anger, yet God used him to lead a multitude to the Promised Land; Peter, who denied Jesus before a young servant girl but later gave a powerful witness before thousands on the day of Pentecost; and Gideon, who was a young man hiding in fear as he threshed the harvest grain, yet God used him to deliver an entire nation from oppressive captors.

Change was effected in these individuals when they learned to tap into the tremendous power provided by their heavenly Father. When you say, "Yours is the power," God echoes, "All power is given *you*." If you will receive this gift of power from your heavenly Father, you will encounter a dynamic life force and experience a new prayer anointing that you have never before known.

"Yours Is the Glory"

Glory is one of the richest words of the English language. No single word is an appropriate synonym, but here are some words that describe it: *honor, praise, splendor, radiance, power, exaltation, worthiness, likeness, beauty, renown,* and *rank.* The glory of God is the displayed excellence, beauty, majesty, power, and perfection of His total being, an expression of His divine essence. The Bible indicates that God is marked by glory, represented by glory, and surrounded by glory. Glory is a sign of His nature, so to relate intimately to our heavenly Father, we must know Him in the revelation of His glory. That is why Moses cried out, "Show me Your glory" (Ex. 33:18).

God originally revealed His glory in the Old Testament tabernacle and temple. He also revealed His glory in creation (Job 38–41), in heaven and earth (Pss. 57:11; 72:19), and in the plan of salvation (Ps. 21:5). The greatest revelation of God's glory, however, is in Jesus

(John 17:5). Jesus did not seek His own glory; He reflected that of His Father (Heb. 5:5; John 13:31–32).

In Old Testament times, God revealed His glory in Israel, but when they entered into idolatry, He declared they had "changed their Glory for what does not profit" (Jer. 2:11). Now God reveals His glory through the church. The new group of people are described as "Israelites" by adoption and are heirs of the glory originally promised to Israel (Rom. 9:4).

The church is composed of individual believers, so for the glory of God to be revealed in the church corporately, it must be revealed in each believer individually. Haggai 2:3–9 notes that in this "latter temple" (the body as temple), the greatest glory of the Lord will be revealed.

The glory of God is contained in the "earthen vessels" of our lives (2 Cor. 4:7). If our lives were flawless (like gold vessels), people would be attracted to the vessels instead of the content. We are created for God's glory (Isa. 43:7). We are admonished to walk worthy of our Father who has called us unto His kingdom and glory (1 Thess. 2:12), and God wants us to know the riches of glory (Col. 1:27).

You probably have caught on that we are to be partakers of our heavenly Father's glory, but you may ask, "How do I get this glory?" This wonderful glory of God, with its inherent wealth of meaning, has been reserved as a gift for you. It is freely given, just like the kingdom and the power. Jesus said, "The glory which You gave Me I have given them, that they may be one just as We are one" (John 17:22). The same glory with which Jesus was glorified by the Father is a gift to you. All you have to do is claim it, for Psalm 84:11 declares, "The LORD will give grace and glory."

As you are changed by the Word of God, prayer, and the experiences of life, you are in the process of receiving this glory: "But we all, with unveiled face, beholding as in a mirror the glory of the Lord, are being transformed into the same image from glory to glory, just as by the Spirit of the Lord" (2 Cor. 3:18).

The glory of our Father is reflected from the mirror (the Word) to our lives. God wants to take people like us who are utterly void of His glory and change us into instruments that will reveal it. Just as the reflection of an earthly father is seen in his child, we should reflect the image of our heavenly Father. Observing the divine nature of this glory, William Barclay comments, "We end the prayer by reminding ourselves that we are in the presence of the divine glory; and that means that we must live life in the reverence which never forgets that it is living within the splendor of the glory of God."[1]

"Forever"

Forever means exactly what it says, that is, "eternal, having no end." As you conclude your prayer, you ascribe the kingdom, power, and glory to your Father *forever*. You link yourself in an eternal bond with your Father because you acknowledge that you share in His kingdom, power, and glory. It is a Father-child partnership that can never be severed.

"Amen"

Consider the power of a single word. For example, the word *D day* and what it meant to the troops involved in World War II. Such is the power of this final word in the model prayer, *amen,* which literally means "so be it."

The word *amen* dates as far back as the time of Moses. When the solemn duties were performed by the priest, the response of the person who was adjured consisted simply of the word *amen.* In like manner the people of Israel responded, "Amen," when the blessings and curses of God's law were pronounced from the heights of Ebal and Gerizim.

Using the word *amen* seals our prayer with powerful authority because "Amen" is one of the names of Christ (Rev. 3:14). Christ is called the "Amen of God," for all of God's promises are fulfilled in Him. When we say, "Amen," we pray all our petitions in the name of Jesus.

Jesus gave us authority to use His name, and it is one of the keys to effective prayer. We often fail in prayer because we depend on our own ability or authority. We must realize it is not our name, position, or authority that assures an answer from our Father; rather, it is the name of Jesus.

The power in the name of Jesus is not in the chanting of it but in your having faith in it. The disciples emphasized this after the healing of a man who could not walk. Peter said that "through faith in His name," the man was healed (Acts 3:16). When you say, "Amen," you say, "In the name of Jesus." Exercising faith in that name wields tremendous spiritual authority.

Jesus said that whatever we ask the Father in His name, He will give it to us (John 16:23). What a powerful promise! But this promise must be received in harmony with the other principles of prayer taught in the Bible. We can never isolate one verse on a subject; we must consider all that is taught on that topic in the Word of God.

The Bible teaches you cannot ask selfishly: "You ask and do not receive, because you ask amiss, that you may spend it on your pleasures" (James 4:3).

You must also live righteously before God. If you have sinned, you are to confess and pray for forgiveness: "Confess your trespasses to one another, and pray for one another, that you may be healed. The effective, fervent prayer of a righteous man avails much" (James 5:16). You cannot continue to live in sin and think just because you ask in the name of Jesus you will be granted your requests. The prayers of *righteous* men and women avail with God because Jesus said, "If you abide in Me, and My words abide in you, you will ask what you desire, and it shall be done for you" (John 15:7).

Praying in the name of Jesus is also subject to the will of God. Jesus prayed that "if" it was the will of God, the "cup" of His suffering would be removed (Luke 22:42). In the weakness of human flesh, Jesus wanted His cup of suffering removed, but when He prayed, He submitted His will to God's will.

In some matters clearly defined in Scripture, we know the will of God and exactly how to pray. In other matters, we can express our will as Jesus did, but then we must submit our wills to God's will—all in the name of Jesus. We do this because we often pray according to human reasoning and cannot always discern God's higher purposes (Isa. 55:8–9).

Some may disagree with this biblical teaching and claim you can ask anything in the name of Jesus and it will be done. When you pray in arrogance without submitting your requests to God's will, He may answer your prayer, but it may not be in your best interests (Ps. 106:15).

We must also realize that when we ask for something on behalf of another person, that person's will enters into the situation. Nobody, even by prayer in the name of Jesus, can push something onto someone else that the person does not want. That would be spiritual witchcraft. God does not take away the free will of a person.

For example, Jesus prayed a great prayer concerning the men God gave Him as disciples (John 17). All these men received the same training, witnessed the same miracles, and received the same instruction from the Word of God, yet one of them was lost. Judas had a will of his own, and despite all he had heard and seen, he rejected God's Word in unbelief.

The word *amen* does not mean "over and out I'm finished praying!" The actual meaning of this word is, "Even so, as I have prayed it, even so shall it be done." When you say, "Amen," you make a declaration of faith. It reflects the picture of a man driving a boundary stake into the ground and declaring his rightful claim to a piece of property.

When we repeat this final segment, "For Yours is the kingdom and the power and the glory forever. Amen," we worship God for who He is and what He has shared with us as heirs, and we praise Him for responding to the petitions raised as we prayed our way through the model prayer.

The End That Is Really a Beginning

What do you think would be the greatest ministry you could ever fulfill? Perhaps your mind goes immediately to evangelism on the scale of that done by Billy Graham or you dream of the tremendous impact of a ministry of healing and deliverance. Maybe you think no particular ministry is greater than another, but God's Word identifies the greatest ministry in which any of us could ever engage. The model prayer we are studying opens and closes with this ministry. It is the ministry of praise and worship.

Why do I make this claim? Because praise and worship restore you to the spiritual state God intended and provide the supernatural energy force vital for victory. When you begin your prayer with praise, you enter into the courts of the Lord where His presence dwells. When you end with praise, you send the power of praise ahead of you to do battle in every circumstance of your day. You put on the "garment of praise" in your prayer time, and as you leave the place of prayer you determine to leave it on all day. You set your mind that all day long what will come out of your mouth is praise to God: "Therefore by Him let us continually offer the sacrifice of praise to God, that is, the fruit of our lips, giving thanks to His name" (Heb. 13:15).

The climax of the model prayer builds to a rising crescendo of praise as we declare, "Yours is the kingdom, Yours is the power, and Yours is the glory forever. Amen!" Praise is the language of faith that God inhabits. When we conclude with these words, we focus our attention on our heavenly Father's provisions rather than our problems. We thank Him for an inheritance that assures a position in His kingdom where we can claim His power and reflect His glory.

Just as an earthly father relishes the praise of his children, so our heavenly Father desires sincere, uninhibited adoration based on the truth of His Word and lifted from the depths of the spirit. You can praise Him by being silent before Him (Zech. 2:13); speaking, shouting, and singing (Ps. 146:2); playing instruments (Ps. 150:3–6); standing in His presence (2 Chron. 20:19); lifting up your hands (Ps. 63:3–4); clapping (Ps. 47:1); bowing and kneeling (Ps. 95:6); walking and leaping (Acts 3:8); and dancing (Ex. 15:20).

With these thirteen powerful words we come to the conclusion of the model prayer that Jesus taught His followers. But this is an end that is really a new beginning. When Solomon ended the dedicatory prayer for the temple at Jerusalem, it is recorded, "When Solomon had finished praying, fire came down from heaven and consumed the burnt offering and the sacrifices; and the glory of the LORD filled the temple. And the priests could not enter the house of the LORD, because the glory of the LORD had filled the LORD's house (2 Chron. 7:1–2).

When Solomon concluded his prayer, there was a mighty revelation of the power and anointing of God. Like Solomon, you have completed the first level of prayer. You have learned to pray the way Jesus taught, and you have developed an intimate relationship with God as your heavenly Father. But this is not an end, for by receiving the anointing of personal prayer, you are positioned to receive a new revelation of your Father as His presence fills your spiritual temple with power.

You have enrolled in the school of prayer, a spiritual institution from which there is no graduation. Do not naively assume that your commitment to personal prayer and your developing relationship with the Father will go unchallenged, however. Lurking in the spiritual shadows is the false father who would target for destruction all you have received because "he was a murderer from the beginning, and does not stand in the truth, because there is no truth in him. When he speaks a lie, he speaks from his own resources, for he is a liar and the father of it" (John 8:44). The insidious strategies of this false father will be exposed as we advance to the second level of the prayer anointing, that of power prayer.

PART 2

Releasing the Anointing of Power Prayer

16

The False Father

In Part 1, you learned to release the anointing for personal prayer using the model Jesus taught. You learned how Jesus cleansed the temple, it became a house of prayer, and a mighty demonstration of God's power resulted as blind eyes were opened, deaf ears heard, and paralyzed limbs were healed.

When the temple became a house of prayer, in the midst of the joyful celebration of praise and power, opposition began. The voice of accusation was raised, emanating from the chief priests and scribes. This account is an example of where you are now spiritually, having cleansed your spiritual temple and become a house of prayer by receiving the anointing for personal prayer. You are poised at the threshold of a new dimension of power in prayer, but as Israel at the borders of Canaan, you will not enter without opposition.

You must experience the anointing of personal prayer before you can move into the new dimension of prayer we are now ready to address, that of power prayer. Personal prayer is objective by nature. You can use the outline of the model prayer; you know when you start and when you finish. Power prayer, however, is subjective rather than objective, meaning it is something grasped by your spirit instead of your intellect. Because it is subjective, there is no defined starting or stopping place, and it cannot be reduced to a simple outline.

The anointing of power prayer takes you into a new realm of intercession where you battle for the hearts and minds of men and women, boys and girls. You pray with the same powerful results that Jesus experienced, releasing people from the clutches of sin, sickness, oppression, and possession. Your prayers affect the destiny of entire nations.

Power prayer is actually warfare praying, for you battle in the spirit realm with unseen wicked forces operative in the world. To be successful, however, you must know the enemy you are confronting, recognize his strategies, and use the tremendous spiritual resources God provides for this type of prayer.

The Enemy Is a Father

Jesus called Satan a "father" when He warned the Pharisees: "You are of your father the devil, and the desires of your father you want to do. He was a murderer from the beginning, and does not stand in the truth, because there is no truth in him. When he speaks a lie, he speaks from his own resources, for he is a liar and the father of it" (John 8:44). This Scripture reveals that deception is Satan's primary method of operation because he is the father of lies. It also reveals that just like our heavenly Father, Satan has a will. His will, however, is destructive because "the thief does not come except to steal, and to kill, and to destroy" (John 10:10).

The Heritage of the False Father

This deceptive father was originally created by God as an angel with a free will to choose good or evil (Ezek. 28:12–17). He was one of the cherubim class of angels, holy, wise, beautiful, and perfect. He was the leader among the cherubs and was called a "guardian" or "covering" cherub. His name was originally Lucifer, which means "light bearer" (Isa. 14:12). He was bedecked with precious stones set in gold (Ezek. 28:13; see also Ex. 28:15–21). He was given a position on God's holy mountain and apparently led in worship (Ezek. 28:14).

But Satan did not retain the intimate relationship with God. The Bible describes his tragic rebellion in Isaiah 14:12–14. Satan's fall occurred because of pride demonstrated by his attempt to occupy

God's position, with equal recognition, rule, and worship. Satan said he wanted to be like the "Most High," selecting this title because it reflects God as possessor of heaven and earth. Satan wanted to be God, the Father.

Because of his sin, Satan was banished from the presence of God, his character was corrupted, and his power perverted to oppose all that God is and does (Ezek. 28:16–17). Part of the heavenly force of angels joined Satan in his defection, and they are now demonic spirits that do his bidding. Satan formed his own kingdom, an evil family of which he is the father.

In Job 1, Satan is pictured trying to infiltrate the ranks of the "sons of God" appearing before the Father (Job 1:6). From this passage we learn Satan is present in spirit form in the world today: "And the LORD said to Satan, 'From where do you come?' So Satan answered the LORD and said, 'From going to and fro on the earth, and from walking back and forth on it'" (Job 1:7).

The Strategy of the False Father

Some people believe spiritual warfare to be a battle between God and Satan, but the devil is no match for God's power. Spiritual warfare is a family feud, a spiritual parallel that makes the legendary battle between the Hatfield and the McCoy clans pale in comparison. When God created the first man and woman, the battle began between the "children of God" belonging to the heavenly Father and the "children of disobedience" belonging to the false father. This familial division between the children of God and the children of Satan engulfs the whole of society in spiritual conflict.

What is the target of Satan's deceptive, destructive strategies? It is the Father-child relationship of intimacy between you and your heavenly Father. That is evident from the very first temptation when Satan, disguised in the form of a serpent, came to Eve in the Garden of Eden. He tempted her to eat from the forbidden tree of knowledge, claiming, "God knows that in the day you eat of it your eyes will be opened, and you will be like God" (Gen. 3:5).

Eve was created in the image of her heavenly Father, and she shared intimate fellowship with Him daily as He came to walk and talk with her and Adam in the Garden. When Satan challenged Eve's relationship with God, her answer should have been, "I am already like God!"

This identical strategy is evident in the satanic attacks on Christ. At the baptism of Jesus, there was a powerful witness of His sonship when God declared, "This is My beloved Son, in whom I am well pleased" (Matt. 3:17). Immediately after that tremendous spiritual encounter, Satan attacked the Son of God relationship during the wilderness temptation. The devil whispered, "*If* You are the Son of God, command that these stones become bread. . . . *If* You are the Son of God, throw Yourself down [from the pinnacle of the temple]" (Matt. 4:3, 6, emphasis added). At first, Philip viewed Jesus only as the "son of Joseph" (John 1:45).When Jesus did miracles of healing and deliverance, the people also asked, "Is this not Joseph's son?" (Luke 4:22).

Satan's attacks on the intimate union between Jesus and His Father continued right up to the time of Christ's death. As Jesus was being led to the council of the Sanhedrin, the chief priests and scribes questioned, "Are You then the Son of God?" (Luke 22:70). Some of the Jews declared, "We have a law, and according to our law He ought to die, because He made Himself the Son of God" (John 19:7).

When Jesus hung on the cross, the religious leaders mocked, "If He is the King of Israel, let Him now come down from the cross, and we will believe Him. He trusted in God; let Him deliver Him now if He will have Him; for He said, 'I am the Son of God'" (Matt. 27:42–43). All of these attacks on the sonship of Jesus proved futile, however, for on the cross Christ addressed His last words to His Father.

The Strategy Has Not Changed

Some two thousand years later, Satan's strategy has not changed, for he still targets the intimacy of the Father-child relationship. Satan contradicts everything declared by the Father in the model prayer taught by Jesus. When you say, "Our Father," the enemy whispers, "God is not your Father, and you cannot come into His presence because you are unworthy." When you declare God's will to be done in your life, the enemy taunts, "What makes you think you can ever do His will? Look at what you have done, the shame and guilt of your past. You will never be used by God, and you will never finish the plan God has for you." Satan relentlessly and subtly instills his lies into your spirit, questioning, "If God is really your Father, why are you so poor? Why are there no miracles in your ministry? Why did He let this tragedy happen in your life? Why doesn't God help you?"

To receive the anointing of power prayer and war effectively against the false father, we must expose his deception and learn how to address these lies. Jesus told His disciples that when they stood before the accusation of the enemy, they should allow the Spirit of the Father to speak through them (Matt. 10:20).

In the next few chapters we will analyze the model prayer again, this time focusing on how Satan attacks every benefit of sonship assured us by our heavenly Father. We will use the biblical example of King David to illustrate these attacks and ways to overcome them, for he is the only person in Scripture referred to as "a man after God's own heart." If we seek a similar level of intimacy with our heavenly Father in prayer, we must learn how to let the Spirit of the Father rise up within us to address every lie of the false father as we experience the deeper anointing of power prayer.

17

—✛—

He Is Not Your Father

The young woman's arms were tattooed with hideous designs and evil phrases. Her hardened countenance reflected the harsh effects of drug addiction and belied the fact that she was only in her early twenties. She was a repeat offender serving time in a state prison for women. Tara's disillusionment was evident as she declared, "I believe the whole world is divided into good and evil people. I asked God to forgive me, but I know He won't do it because of what I have done. I am one of the bad ones, and I am destined to be evil, so why fight it?"

Tara was a victim of the deception of the false father who says, "You are not worthy to enter God's presence. He is not your Father, and you cannot appropriate the benefits of His name. Who do you think you are anyhow? Look at the bad things you did and the mess you made of your life."

Our study of the personal prayer anointing revealed that by the blood of Jesus, you have authority to enter God's presence when you pray to "our Father in heaven." As soon as you utter these opening words of the model prayer, however, the false father begins his relentless attack. The enemy wants you to believe, like Tara, that there is no way you can develop intimacy with the heavenly Father. Satan wants to alienate you from the family of God and deceive you into believing you are unacceptable and unworthy to enter God's presence. But you can come to know, as Tara eventually did, that his claims are invalid. Today, Tara is a child of God.

A Man After God's Own Heart

David was the only man in Scripture who was called "a man after God's own heart," meaning he had a kindred spirit and was someone in whom God found a special affinity. David models the intimacy we seek to develop with our heavenly Father, and for this reason we will analyze his life to see how he successfully dealt with the attacks of the enemy.

David was the greatest king in Israel's history, whose descendants would always reign, and from whose lineage the Messiah would come. But David didn't spend all his life in a palace surrounded by luxury. His life began in the fields around Bethlehem as a shepherd boy. He was devalued by his family and was someone who did not always feel worthy and accepted.

David was just a youth when Israel rejected God's rule over them and demanded of the prophet Samuel, "Give us a king to judge us" (1 Sam. 8:6). Saul was selected as the first king of Israel, but when he lost his position through disobedience, God commanded Samuel to go to the house of Jesse to anoint a new king.

When Samuel arrived in Bethlehem, he invited Jesse and his sons to participate in a sacrifice where he would anoint God's chosen man, after which they would share a special dinner together. It was a unique privilege for a family to host the prophet of God and to participate in a sacrifice and fellowship with him.

Jesse made appropriate preparations for the occasion and summoned his sons. When the young men had assembled, the first to catch Samuel's eye was Jesse's oldest son, Eliab:

> So it was, when they came, that he looked at Eliab and said, "Surely the LORD's anointed is before Him!" But the LORD said to Samuel, "Do not look at his appearance or at his physical stature, because I have refused him. For the LORD does not see as man sees; for man looks at the outward appearance, but the LORD looks at the heart" (1 Sam. 16:6–7).

123

Eliab had the outward appearance of a king, but God saw what was in his heart. In 1 Samuel 17, we, too, are permitted a glimpse of Eliab's true nature when he angrily accused David of pride and insolence. God's anointing will rest not on the accuser but on the one who, like David, is an intercessor and praiser.

Next, Jesse's sons Abinadab and Shammah were called, but they were both rejected. One by one, seven of Jesse's sons passed before Samuel, but each time God said, "Neither has the LORD chosen this one."

Finally, Samuel asked, "Are all the young men here?" Jesse answered, "There remains yet the youngest, and there he is, keeping the sheep." Apparently, David was not highly esteemed by his father and his brothers, for although the prophet of God was hosting a sacrifice and feast, David was not summoned to participate. He was just an insignificant boy in the fields tending the sheep.

Samuel told Jesse to send for David, and when the young boy arrived, God said to Samuel, "'Arise, anoint him; for this is the one!' . . . And the Spirit of the LORD came upon David from that day forward" (1 Sam. 16:12–13). He was a young man whose family didn't even think enough of him to call him to the dinner table, but God said, "He is the one . . . I have chosen him."

When God anoints you, it is not on the basis of education, physical appearance, financial status, intelligence, or popularity. Your acceptance does not depend on such outward achievements, for God evaluates from the inside out. Robbie Castleman notes, "Our appointment as kings and priests to God does not depend on external qualifications, but on who we are in relationship to God Himself."[1]

It was said of Saul that from his shoulders up, he was taller than anyone in Israel (1 Sam. 9:2). But Ivor Powell writes that Saul was measured from his shoulders, and David was measured from his heart.[2]

Come Up to the Father's House

Have you sometimes felt like David, rejected by your family, the least in your father's house, abandoned in the fields of this world? Do you feel insignificant and unworthy to enter the Father's house to receive this precious anointing of intimate relationship?

When Jesus said to pray, "Our Father in heaven," He extended a spiritual summons to you that parallels Samuel's call for David to come up to the father's house. Like David, you may be forgotten, rejected, or abused by your earthly father or others around you, but God sees the cry of your heart and has prepared an anointing for you.

When the prodigal son was sitting in the pigpen, he thought to himself, *I will go to my father and say, "I have no right to be called your son."* Satan will try to make you believe that, but when he whispers his lies, remember that you have been summoned by the Prophet (Jesus) into the Father's house to receive His anointing. Like the father of the prodigal son, the heavenly Father will receive you with great joy. It is there, right in the presence of the enemy's false claims, that you will receive your anointing and the table of provision will be spread for you (Ps. 23:5–6).

New Destiny and Purpose

From the time of his anointing, David's life was never again the same, for it was marked with a new sense of destiny and purpose. It didn't matter what his father thought of him or how his brothers treated him. It didn't matter that he didn't look like a king and that he still kept sheep in the field and hid in a cave. He knew he was destined to be a king! You will experience this same sense of purpose and destiny when you are linked with your heavenly Father in the intimate union of sonship and come under the prayer anointing.

When you begin your prayer by saying, "Our Father in heaven," you affirm your anointing as a child of God and heir of His kingdom. Whenever Satan attacks your right to this inheritance, make this declaration: "I am chosen in my Father before the foundation of the world, predestined to be adopted as His child (Eph. 1:3–5). *Now* I am the child of God (1 John 3:2). I am anointed to serve as a priest and a king before God. He *is* my Father!"

After David was anointed he returned to the solitude, obscurity, and monotony of the fields. Charles Swindoll comments that "David didn't run out to try on crowns or shine up his chariot and ride through Bethlehem announcing his new position of royalty! He immediately went back to the fields with the sheep."[3] But from that day when "the Spirit of the LORD" came upon him, David's life was never again the same.

Like David, you may still be in the field, laboring through the dull monotony of the routine duties of another day, but everything is different now. You are experiencing the anointing of power prayer, which enables you to release the Spirit of the Father and declare from the depths of your spirit, "You are my Father!"

18

—✢—

Unhallowed Is His Name

Adolf Hitler—a name that strikes terror in our hearts. It represents intense suffering, a worldwide holocaust, and the deaths of at least six million people. It is a name that is forever etched in our minds as a grotesque memorial to evil.

In personal prayer we learned of the tremendous importance attached to the meaning of names and how God's names reflect His attributes and provisions. We learned the meanings of the eight compound names of God and how to appropriate their inherent benefits when we pray, "Hallowed be Your name."

The false father also has titles reflecting his personality and provisions, but these names are more evil in their connotations than even Hitler's name. Whenever we declare the benefits of one of God's names, the false father immediately counters with an antithetical name of his own. For each name of our heavenly Father, the false father has an opposing title.

The Heritage of His Name

By examining the meanings of Satan's unhallowed names, we will be more cognizant of the deception he peddles to estrange us from the Father.

127

Accusation

When we analyzed our heavenly Father's names, we learned that we are assured forgiveness and *salvation from sin* through appropriating the names Jehovah-tsidkenu (Jehovah our righteousness) and Jehovah-m'kaddesh (Jehovah who sanctifies).

The false father is called the "accuser of our brethren," which reflects his purpose to counter these claims of forgiveness and deliverance from the dominion of sin (Rev. 12:10). As you appropriate forgiveness through the blood of Jesus, Satan will counter with accusations of guilt and shame. When this happens, let the Spirit of the Father within you rise up to declare that you are righteous and sanctified through the blood of Jesus. Praise God because you can enter His presence through the righteousness imputed by the blood of Jesus Christ. Declare, "I am delivered from the penalty for sins of the past, the power of sin in the present, and the presence of sin in the future. I stand before God because of the blood, clothed in the righteousness of Jesus Christ."

An Unholy Spirit

The *fullness of the Holy Spirit* is reflected when we appropriate our Father's names Jehovah-shalom (Jehovah is peace) and Jehovah-shammah (Jehovah is there). Satan also has a spirit, but it works in the "sons of disobedience" (Eph. 2:2). It is not a spirit of peace, for he is described as a roaring lion (1 Peter 5:8), a serpent (Rev. 12:9), and an adversary (1 Peter 5:8). It is not a holy spirit, for Satan is called the "enemy" (Matt. 13:39) and the "wicked one" (1 John 5:19).

When we claim peace, the false father whispers fear and stirs up agitation. Satan is called Abaddon and Apollyon, which mean "destruction" and "destroyer" and reflect his objective to obliterate the peace of God in our lives (Rev. 9:11). When we claim the presence of the God who is there, the father of lies murmurs words of alienation and abandonment: "God doesn't love you. If He really cared about you, your circumstances would be different."

When Satan disturbs your peace and tries to alienate you from God, let the Spirit of the Father rise up within you and declare on the basis of God's Word, "You are my peace, You are the God who is there. You are Jehovah-shalom and Jehovah-shammah to me!"

Unsoundness

We have the right to *soundness* as we appropriate our heavenly Father's name Jehovah-rapha (Jehovah heals), but the false father's name of murderer reflects his antithetical evil intents (John 8:44). He plants the fear of sickness and death and sows seeds of doubt concerning our healing. "It might work for others," he says, "but not for you." He also argues, "The day of miracles and healing is past," or "You are not good enough to get healed. You deserve this. Look at what you did!" Counteract the false father's claims by declaring your heavenly Father's name Jehovah-rapha. Confess with your mouth, "Father, You are the God who heals me. I am healed by the stripes of Jesus!"

Failure

Our *success* is guaranteed by the name Jehovah-jireh (Jehovah my Provider). Our heavenly Father is a provider, but Satan is a thief who comes to steal (John 10:10). The false father says, "You aren't going to make it. How are you going to pay these bills? If God was really your Father, He would provide better for you." When this happens, allow the Spirit of the Father to rise up within you and declare, "Jehovah-jireh *is* my Provider!" Continue to say it until it comes from your innermost being. If necessary, shout it in the face of the devil until its message rings true in your spirit.

Insecurity

Our *security* and freedom from the fear of death and hell are guaranteed by our Father's names Jehovah-raah (Jehovah my Shepherd) and Jehovah-nissi (Jehovah my Banner). Satan wants to set up a banner over your life, too, but instead of one of a caring shepherd, it is the banner of a self-made prince. Satan is called "the ruler of the demons" (Matt. 9:34), "the ruler of this world" (John 12:31), and a prince of the evil powers of the air (Eph. 2:2). Satan comes disguised as "an angel of light" (2 Cor. 11:14) and as "the god of this age" (2 Cor. 4:4), and his noisy claims to power would all but drown out the tender voice of our Shepherd.

Let the Spirit of the Father rise up to counter Satan's claims to power over your life by declaring, "Father, You are my Shepherd.

You are the Banner over every circumstance of my life. Your power is greater than that of the god of this world and the prince of evil."

David Knew His Name

The young man David, whose steps we are tracing through these chapters, was not idle in the fields around Bethlehem while he waited in obscurity following his anointing to be king. His compositions in the book of Psalms reveal that he was learning to appropriate his heavenly Father's names and, in so doing, becoming a man after God's own heart.

David learned how to counter every claim of the false father through appropriating God's name. After questioning, "Who may ascend into the hill of the LORD? Or who may stand in His holy place?" David boldly declared, "[He who receives] blessing from the LORD, and righteousness from the God of his salvation" (Ps. 24:3–5). David realized that *salvation from sin* through God's name enabled him to come boldly into the Father's presence.

David acknowledged the fullness of the *Spirit* and his right to the peace and presence of his Father. He declared, "The upright shall dwell in Your presence" (Ps. 140:13), and noted that there was no place he could go that was void of God's presence (Ps. 139:7). When David sinned, he pleaded with God not to remove His Spirit from him, which reveals he fully understood its necessity and value (Ps. 51:11).

David claimed the benefit of *soundness* through appropriating God's name, crying out, "O LORD, heal me" (Ps. 6:2), and expressed his trust in God for healing from both physical and spiritual afflictions (Ps. 25:18).

David knew his *success* came through the name of God. When the enemy threatened him with failure, David declared that whatever he did would prosper (Ps. 1:3). He boldly declared God was his Provider, saying, "The LORD is my shepherd; I shall not want" (Ps. 23:1).

David claimed the *security* afforded by his Father's name. He knew God as his Shepherd (Ps. 23:1), his Banner (Ps. 20:5), and his defense (Ps. 20:1). While others trusted in chariots and horses, David trusted in the name of the Lord (Ps. 20:7). He conquered the fear of death, confidently proclaiming that he would dwell in his Father's house forever (Ps. 23:6).

When you read through the book of Psalms, it is obvious by the many references to God's name that David recognized its tremendous significance and continually appropriated its benefits. We find him declaring God's name in the midst of the congregation of the righteous (Ps. 22:22) as well as before the heathen (Gentiles; Ps. 18:49). He extolled God's name as excellent, above all others in the earth (Ps. 8:1), and admonished everything that breathes to give God the glory due to His name (Ps. 29:2). David recognized the tremendous inheritance in his Father's name, and that is why he cried out from the depths of his being, "Bless the LORD, O my soul; and all that is within me, bless His holy name!" (Ps. 103:1).

Proclaiming the Name

David was destined to reign as a king, but the enemy tried to prevent him from fulfilling his destiny. David had to conquer Goliath, enemy nations, King Saul, the shame of his transgression with Bathsheba, and the subsequent family problems that troubled his life. But because David knew the benefits inherent in his Father's name, he could boldly declare in the face of every enemy, "I come to you in the name of the LORD of hosts. . . . This day the LORD will deliver you into my hand" (1 Sam. 17:45–46).

As believers, we are kings and queens spiritually who are destined to reign in our Father's kingdom, but we will be able to do so only as we claim the inheritance of our family name. David declared, "In the name of our God we will set up our banners," meaning he had declared the name of God to reign over every circumstance of his life (Ps. 20:5). We must do likewise if we are to fulfill our destiny and serve the purpose of God in our generation as David did in his. It is under this banner of the Father's name that this anointing of power prayer functions. David wrote in Psalm 20,

> *May the LORD answer you in the day of trouble;*
> *May the name of the God of Jacob defend you;*
> *May He send you help from the sanctuary, . . .*
> *May He grant you according to your heart's desire,*

And fulfill all your purpose. . . .
May the LORD fulfill all your petitions.
Now I know that the LORD saves His anointed;
He will answer him from His holy heaven
With the saving strength of His right hand (vv. 1–6).

This is truly power praying, is it not?

Do you want God to answer you in the day of trouble and defend you? Do you want assistance from the sanctuary of God with the saving strength of His right hand? Do you want to accomplish God's purpose for your life and have your petitions and desires fulfilled? Do you want to remain standing when everything around you crumbles in the dust? When the false father whispers his lies, do you want to counter his attacks with an answer straight from heaven? If so, then like David, proclaim the name. Say to the enemy, "You come to me with a sword, with a spear, and with a javelin. But I come to you in the name of the Lord of hosts. . . . This day the Lord will deliver you into my hand." Then set up your banners in the name of the Lord!

19

—✟—

Kingdom in a Cave

This anointing of prayer of which we are learning is obtained when we begin to pray as Jesus taught, but it is more difficult to maintain the anointing than to receive it. While the anointing oil is fresh upon your spirit, Satan begins his relentless attacks. When you declare, "Your kingdom come, Your will be done," over the priorities of your life, the false father immediately counters by whispering, "You will never fulfill God's plan for your life. You won't be able to do His will."

As a young man, David was anointed king by the prophet Samuel, and he immediately began to move into his calling by conquering the giant Goliath and subsequently becoming a great warrior in Israel. Eventually, David became so successful that King Saul was jealous and tried to kill him, so David fled his wrath and went into exile. Four hundred men who were experiencing distress, debt, and discontent joined him hiding in a cave called Adullam, a rocky mountain fortress southwest of Jerusalem.

Many of us burrow down in a spiritual cave of Adullam, lingering somewhere between enemy territory and our spiritual destiny. Was the cave of Adullam to be the final destiny of this man who was anointed of God as a king? Was his monarchy to be over a bunch of "cavemen" and his kingdom in a cave?

Caught in a Cavern

How did David, so full of faith and promise, end up in a dark, lonely cavern? If we retrace his footsteps, perhaps we can discover reasons for the spiritual "caves" we encounter as we seek to do our Father's will.

David was just starting to move into his anointing when his mentor, the prophet Samuel, died. David's wife, Michal, betrayed him, and he was separated from his dearest friend, Jonathan. David also lost his military position and became a target for the jealous wrath of King Saul.

When faced with similar devastations in life, our tendency is to try to escape the circumstances, and that is exactly what David did. He said to himself, "Now I shall perish someday by the hand of Saul. There is nothing better for me than that I should speedily escape to the land of the Philistines" (1 Sam. 27:1). Charles Swindoll notes, "When we listen to ourselves, it's important that we're saying the right things. David wasn't. . . . There is nothing ethically, morally, or spiritually wrong with those feelings of despair that chill us like an unexpected downpour. It's when we run for cover in an enemy camp that disobedience begins."[1] Instead of confessing his anointing as king, David confessed negative words of defeat: "I will perish someday by Saul's hand. I will never fulfill my God-given destiny."

Believing he had lost everything, David fled to Gath, Goliath's hometown, but found himself in even greater peril there because the people recognized him as the giant's killer. To save himself, David feigned insanity and in doing so experienced the loss of self-respect. Ivor Powell asserts, "He who was destined to become the king of Israel had become a disgusting sight, clawing at doors and dribbling spittle over his chin, beard, and clothing. . . . To compare this man with the simple, trusting, dignified lad who fearlessly went to meet Goliath, confounds the mind."[2]

The Diary of a Cave Dweller

Living as a fugitive, David dwelt for sometime in the cave of Adullam, most likely convinced he had reached the end of his usefulness in God's kingdom. As David sat in the cave, tormenting memories paraded through his mind. He remembered the day when the sweet anointing oil of the prophet flowed over his head, and he recalled the battle with Goliath when he triumphed victoriously in the name of the Lord. The voices of the women of Israel singing his praises echoed down the corridors of his mind.

Then David looked around him. Some kingdom! He sat in the darkness of a rocky hideout, with a ragtag army of men guarding his fortress. He longed for the intimate fellowship of his heavenly Father with the intensity of a thirsty deer seeking water, but instead he heard the tormenting voice of the enemy whisper, "If you really are a king, what are you doing here? God doesn't care about you, or you wouldn't be hiding in a cave. You will never be able to fulfill God's will for your life."

In deep despair, David recorded his emotions. He described himself as being hunted like a partridge (1 Sam. 26:20) and said he felt like a pelican of the wilderness and an owl of the desert (Ps. 102:6). He pictured his soul as being among lions (Ps. 57:4) and acknowledged that the enemy had prepared a net for his steps (Ps. 57:6).

Can you identify with David's emotions? Have you desired intimacy with your heavenly Father, to fulfill your anointing, and to do great things for the kingdom, only to find yourself seemingly deserted and abandoned in some cave of circumstances?

A Coming Out Party for Cavemen

David had a choice to make. He could remain in the cave of Adullam forever, listening to the sinister taunts of the false father, or he could rise up and seize the destiny for which he was created. David penned the words of Psalm 142:

> *I cry out to the LORD with my voice;*
> *With my voice to the LORD I make my supplication.*
> *I pour out my complaint before Him;*
> *I declare before Him my trouble.*
> *When my spirit was overwhelmed within me,*
> *Then You knew my path.*
> *In the way in which I walk*
> *They have secretly set a snare for me.*
> *Look on my right hand and see,*

For there is no one who acknowledges me;
Refuge has failed me;
No one cares for my soul.
I cried out to You, O LORD:
I said, "You are my refuge,
My portion in the land of the living. . . .
Bring my soul out of prison,
That I may praise Your name;
The righteous shall surround me,
For You shall deal bountifully with me."

Although his circumstances had not changed, David changed the direction of the rudder of his life, his tongue. He rose up spiritually and began to declare his destiny. He confessed to his heavenly Father, "You are my refuge. You shall deal bountifully with me! You will bring my soul out of prison. I will fulfill my destiny."

David remained in the strongholds of the wilderness for a time after composing this psalm, and he was still a target of the enemy. His adversity was not altered, but his attitude changed. David had learned the secret of declaring his heavenly Father's will to reign over all the negative circumstances of his life while living in a cave.

The Kingdom Come

David did not realize it, but during the difficult time in the cave of Adullam, God was at work laying the foundation of his kingdom. God gave David a ministry in the cave, that of helping the warriors who joined him there. Charles Swindoll writes: "In our lives, too, God often uses cave experiences to give us purpose and direction. So next time you find yourself in the cave, be aware of how God may be wanting to use you. Prepare yourself to be brought out of that cavern and into a new ministry."[3]

Could God establish David's kingdom on such an unreliable foundation as that disillusioned group of men? Indeed He did. When David assumed his position as king, the men became mighty men of valor, warriors who won great victories for his kingdom. Ivor Powell observes,

Centuries later, another group of people sought the aid of David's far-greater son. Lepers, fishermen, impoverished folk from all walks of life, and people who were frightened and depressed were willing to leave their possessions to answer the call of the Savior. Could God build a church with such poor material? He evidently made the attempt, and today after two thousand years that church stands supreme—against it, even the gates of hell cannot prevail![4]

Not long after David wrote Psalm 142, his destiny was affirmed by the mouth of his enemy when King Saul declared, "And now I know indeed that you shall surely be king, and that the kingdom of Israel shall be established in your hand" (1 Sam. 24:20). Acts 13:36 confirms that David achieved God's purpose for his life, serving his generation by the will of God.

Are You Living in a Cave?

As God's child, you have enemies all around you that threaten your relationship with your heavenly Father. The world, the flesh, and the devil are your sworn spiritual enemies, and they wage relentless attacks. If you are hiding in some spiritual cave right now, remember that "being a person after God's heart doesn't mean never experiencing . . . the despair of the cave. It means being able to sing in the silent darkness like David did, confident that one day God will deal bountifully with you again."[5]

The false father whispers that God's will cannot be done in your life because you are too far off the track, but the Word declares that God's will is already done: "For we are His workmanship, created in Christ Jesus for good works, which God prepared beforehand that we should walk in them" (Eph. 2:10). You do not have to struggle along making your own way in life, trying to do God's will.

David did not have to fight his way to the throne, for Samuel had already prophesied it would come to pass. God has declared the same thing over your life. All you need to do is come into agreement with that declaration by the confession of your mouth. His kingdom will come in your life and His will will be done!

Right now, in the cave of your confining circumstances with the accusations of the false father reverberating in your ears, rise up to declare your destiny by praying this prayer:

> *Dear God, like the spirit of Your servant David, my spirit is overwhelmed within me because of the snare of the enemy. There is no one to help, and all other refuge has failed me. But You know exactly where I am. You are my refuge and my hedge of protection from the enemy. I declare by faith that You will bring my soul out of the cave of my circumstances and that I will rise up to fulfill my destiny. In Jesus' name, Amen.*

20

---✛---

Deadbeat Dad

The children were teenagers, and their mother had struggled for years to provide for them after their father deserted them as infants. Finally, Mom was forced to apply for public assistance, and the family survived on welfare, living in abject poverty. Their father was coming into a large inheritance, but he refused to pay the child support that rightfully belonged to his children. The man was what social services departments label a deadbeat dad.

Jesus said to pray, "Give us this day our daily bread," claiming the provision inherent in the name of Jehovah-jireh, our Provider. But the false father intends to steal, kill, and destroy. Like a deadbeat dad, Satan wants to rob you of your possessions, finances, physical health, mental stability, and the spiritual inheritance that is rightfully yours as a child of God.

A vital element of power prayer is learning how to take back what the enemy has stolen from you because as long as you are burdened by financial losses, failing health, and emotional problems, you cannot be concerned with your heavenly Father's kingdom priorities. When you discover the strategies for retaliating against the enemy, the phrase "give us this day our daily bread" becomes pregnant with powerful spiritual authority that enables you to claim your Father's inheritance.

The strategies to effect such reprisals are revealed in an account recorded in 1 Samuel 30:1–25, which occurred just before Saul died and David assumed his position as king. Satan always attacks just before you are to move into your God-given anointing, and adversity will become either a tombstone or a stepping-stone to your destiny.

David lived like a fugitive after his anointing by Samuel. Fearing for his life because of King Saul's jealousy, David left Judah and sought refuge in Philistine territory where he befriended a leader named Achish and asked him for a city named Ziklag (1 Sam. 27:5–6). After settling their wives and families there, David and his men invaded the Geshurites and the Gezrites for the Philistines. Fearful that David would someday turn against them in battle, the Philistine warriors convinced Achish to send David and his men back home to Ziklag. (Actually, that was the intervention of God to prevent David from being involved in a situation where he would be forced to attack his own people, Israel.)

In 1 Samuel 30, we find David and his men returning home from the battlefield tired and weary only to find Ziklag invaded, burned, and their wives and children taken captive by the Amalekites. When David and his men viewed the scene at Ziklag, they wept until they had no strength left to cry. David was distressed not only because of his losses but also because his men were so angry that they were talking about stoning him to death (1 Sam. 30:4–6). Ivor Powell explains, "David's men rebelled because they felt they had been involved in an expedition which was none of their business. They could have been at home defending their families against the attack of the Amalekites. They angrily questioned his decision to participate in an unnecessary crusade."[1] The voice of the accuser is one that says, "We have lost everything and it's your fault," and it always leads to taking up stones of retribution.

What a predicament! David was in a foreign land living as an exiled fugitive, he had lost his family and possessions, and his own men were turning against him. Matthew Henry comments,

This was a sore trial to the man after God's own heart. . . . Saul had driven him from his country, the Philistines had driven him from their camp, the Amalekites had plundered his city, his wives were taken prisoners, and now, to complete his woes, his own familiar friends . . .

140

instead of sympathizing with him and offering him relief . . . threatened to stone him.[2]

When we get into a situation of similar desperation, many of us either remain in the midst of the ashes mourning our losses or, like David's men, rise up in accusation looking for someone to blame.

It was a pivotal moment of decision for David. His resolution of the situation would make the difference between ascending into his anointing or remaining in the ashes of his losses with the voices of accusation echoing in his ears.

Rising from the Ashes

Four factors are evident in David's response, actions you can take when faced with similar attacks by the enemy. They are (1) praise, (2) pray, (3) pursue, and (4) provide.

1. Praise

In David's predicament, the Bible records that he "strengthened himself in the LORD his God." He didn't conduct an emotional pep rally; he rose up spiritually to embrace his God-given destiny.

David knew that he was anointed by God to be a king and that from his lineage the Messiah would be birthed, but to make this promise a reality, he had to rise up spiritually to claim his rightful inheritance. If you will rise from the ashes of your losses to claim provision in God, you, too, will fulfill your destiny and give birth to God-given dreams and visions.

When everything went awry in David's life—the circumstances were terrible, the city was destroyed, and everyone was pointing the finger of blame and saying, "It's your fault"—David turned a deaf ear to it all and encouraged himself in the Lord. David didn't have someone to lead him in worship or to counsel him about what to do. He didn't even have a family to turn to for loving support, for they had been taken by the enemy. But David began to encourage *himself* in the Lord! The fact of the matter is that no one can do it for you. You may be stirred in your emotions when you get around some charismatic person who prays for you and encourages you, but true strengthening comes from God alone and from the inside out, not the outside in.

David learned how to encourage himself in the Lord prior to this enemy attack through an intimacy with God developed in the solitude of the fields of Bethlehem and in the isolation of exile. David didn't get the psalms he wrote while attending seminary, praying in a monastery, or relaxing in the palace in Jerusalem. He got them on the battlefields of the everyday circumstances of life while wandering the hills and hiding in caves with the enemy in hot pursuit.

David did not deny his circumstances at Ziklag, for the Bible records that he wept until he could weep no more, but he did deny circumstances the power to dictate his future. He rose up, dried his eyes, and encouraged himself in God.

2. Pray

After David encouraged himself in the Lord, he called for Abiathar the priest to bring the ephod. J. Vernon McGee explains, "The ephod was a portion of the high priest's garments which speaks of prayer. This garment went over the garment that the regular priest wore. The ephod set the high priest apart. It was the garment he wore when he went to the golden altar of prayer."[3]

David and Abiathar took the ephod, the garment of prayer, and prayed together for God to reveal what action to take (1 Sam. 30:8). The New Testament calls this agreeing in prayer. The Greek word translated "agreement" does not mean two people saying a prayer together. It is a covenantal word that means, "I'm going to pray a prayer with you and agree on it until we get the answer." Most of us spend our whole lives reacting to circumstances like spiritual Ping-Pong balls. We need to enter into the prayer of agreement until we hear God speak and we can act instead of react against the enemy.

David did not want to just react to his circumstances; rather, he wanted to act against them. Ivor Powell notes, "All his instincts suggested an immediate pursuit of the enemy; it seemed essential that he should hurry to the rescue of his wives. Yet, he paused to ask God for guidance. . . . The grief-stricken captain realized that without the _____ of God, even his best plans would be useless."[4]

_____ responded to the covenant prayer of David and Abiathar, directing them to "pursue, for you shall surely overtake them and without fail recover all" (1 Sam. 30:8).

3. Pursue

In the midst of your need, you must first praise God to encourage yourself in the Lord and then enter into covenantal agreement in prayer to determine the action you should take. Next, you must get up from the ashes of your circumstances and move out on the word He gives you to pursue the enemy. You don't wait to recover to move out for God. You rise up and move from a position of defense to offense, and *then* you recover it all.

When my children were young and I was traveling extensively in ministry, the enemy often attacked them with sickness. Despite our prayers, they were not always healed right away. My wife, Melva Jo, finally got tired of it and declared, "When my kids are sick, I am going to pray for every sick person who crosses my path. I will continue to retaliate against the enemy until the health of my children is restored!" Do you know what happened? It worked!

We began to practice this principle of pursuing the enemy to retaliate in every area of our lives. When our finances were devastated and there seemed to be no way out, we retaliated by sacrificial giving. When depression attacked me to the extent that I didn't want to preach anymore, I increased my ministry schedule and crisscrossed the United States and traveled to the nations of the world.

David pursued the enemy to retaliate, and the Scriptures record that he recovered all that the Amalekites had carried away (1 Sam. 30:18–19). David not only recovered what was rightfully his but also brought back more than he had lost, for he took the flocks and herds of the Amalekites as spoil.

4. Provide

When David recovered his possessions from the enemy, he immediately began to provide for others. He divided the wealth among the men who went to battle and those who were weak and remained behind. Portions were also sent to Bethel (which means "the house of God"). "Here is a present for you from the spoil of the enemies of the LORD," said David (1 Sam. 30:26).

When you recapture all that Satan has taken from you, don't hoard it. Give to the work of the Lord and to those in need. David declared, "Whatever I get, I am going to give." As a result, the man who had lost everything became the wealthiest man in the world.

Recovering It All

God had a plan for David, just as He has an eternal destiny for each of His children, but David could not fulfill that destiny as long as he was poverty-stricken and worrying about his stuff. David learned how to claim the daily bread of provision that was rightfully his and, in so doing, established four vital principles of recovery. Are you ready to apply them to your circumstances?

1. *Praise.* Lift up your hands right now and declare, "I will bless the Lord at all times. Circumstances, you be quiet! I will not let you dictate my future, but I will fulfill my God-given destiny." Give praise to God and encourage yourself in the Lord.

2. *Pray.* Come under the covenant mantle of agreement in prayer. Ask God to provide direction about how you are to act instead of react against the enemy. I agree with you in covenant relationship right now, as I write these words, that when you pray, God will reveal the appropriate action you should take.

3. *Pursue.* What are you doing to retaliate against the enemy? Have you just resigned yourself to sit in the ashes of your losses? Do not settle down amidst the ashes of your circumstances hoping things will change. When you receive your answer in prayer, by faith step out and pursue the enemy.

Hope is confident assurance that God is able to do it, but faith is an action. Hebrews 11 indicates that by faith Noah built an ark, Abraham departed for the Promised Land, and Moses led Israel out of Egypt. These are all acts. Faith is the "evidence of things not seen," which means it is a fact, but it is also an act.

4. *Provide.* Claim the promise of Isaiah 61:7 that you will take back from the enemy double your losses. When you have recovered all from the enemy (and you will), give to those in need and to "the house of God." When you become productive instead of just con-

suming your resources, out of the ashes of your life will come reparation:

> *The Spirit of the Lord GOD is upon Me,*
> *Because the LORD has anointed Me . . .*
> *To proclaim liberty to the captives . . .*
> *To comfort all who mourn . . .*
> *To give them beauty for ashes,*
> *The oil of joy for mourning (Isa. 61:1–3).*

When you become involved in producing for the kingdom, God says your flocks will be fed, you will eat of the riches of the nations, and you will have a double portion and everlasting joy (Isa. 61:4–7).

When you employ these principles—praise, pray, pursue, and provide—then from the ashes of your circumstances, you will rise to rebuild the ruins of your life, repair every desolation, and recover all from the deadbeat dad. Your tombstone of defeat will become a stepping-stone to your destiny. David's destiny was a palace. Yours is a place—the place of the prayer anointing.

21

—✠—

Breaking the Shame Barrier

Forgive us our debts, as we forgive our debtors"—an elementary phrase Jesus taught us to pray. It is a simple request, but perhaps the most difficult facet of the model prayer in terms of countering the claims of the false father. We may say these words and give intellectual assent to the cleansing power of the blood of Jesus until the false father launches his shameful assaults.

Shame is a painful emotion generated by guilt and condemnation. It arises from the consciousness of something dishonorable, improper, ridiculous, or sinful, done by oneself or another. Very often when you pray, "Forgive us our debts," you will hear the shaming voice of the false father saying, "Look what you did. God can't forgive you, and even if He does, you can't be used by Him. You're finished!"

Satan brings shaming accusations into your mind and spirit, such as,

- "You are divorced; therefore, you cannot be a minister."
- "You committed adultery, and you can never rise above this."
- "You aborted your baby. How can God ever forgive you?"

These are examples of the voice of shame, which is one of the most powerful forces you must defeat in order to come under the anointing of power prayer. Shame erects a spiritual barrier that must be removed before you can boldly enter God's presence. The power of shame must also be shattered to experience perpetual prayer, the persevering type about which we will study later in this book, because that kind of prayer is "shameless asking."

For years I carried the shame of being the son of an alcoholic. I battled the shame of my sins and shame imposed by negative words spoken over me by my dad. My shame made me feel unworthy to enter God's presence, and it erected an insurmountable barrier in relating to Him as a loving heavenly Father.

Have you experienced similar feelings? If so, you are not alone in your frustration, for shame is common to all people. Even Jesus had to deal with it during His life and ministry, for many people considered Him to be an illegitimate child. His hometown was not highly respected, and people questioned, "Can anything good come out of Nazareth?" His earthly father's profession apparently was not esteemed either, for people cynically commented, "Isn't this the carpenter's son?" Jesus bore the shame of people accusing Him of false claims to deity, and on the cross He bore the shame of public humiliation and degradation.

The Power of Shame

The power of shame is manifested in these areas in our lives: inherited, imposed, institutional, individual, and incessant shame.

Inherited Shame

Inherited shame results from the basic sin nature that we all received at birth due to the original transgression in the Garden of Eden. Immediately after Adam and Eve sinned, they suffered the shame of their act, covering their nakedness with fig leaves and hiding from the presence of the Lord. The Bible reveals that because of this original sin, a sinful nature was transmitted to succeeding generations, resulting in the sad reality that "all have sinned and fall short of the glory of God" (Rom. 3:23). All of us must deal with the inherited shame of our basic sin nature.

Imposed Shame

Imposed shame is inflicted upon you by others who put you down or say you are not good enough. Abandonment by parents or a spouse always results in imposed shame because you think it is your fault that the relationship terminated. Imposed shame is expressed by constantly trying to prove yourself and measure up to someone else's standards.

Institutional Shame

Institutional shame is put on you by the institutions of society. You may be shamed because of the color of your skin or your personal background. You may be ostracized because you bear the institutional label of felon or ex-convict. You may even bear institutional shame because of the city or nation in which you were born. For example, many Germans still bear the institutional shame of the Jewish holocaust of World War II.

Individual Shame

Individual shame comes from sins you commit personally, which result in guilt and condemnation. This is the most difficult type of shame to deal with, for it is hard to forgive yourself for mistakes and unwise decisions.

Incessant Shame

If you do not deal with shame successfully, you will pass it on to your children, and they will duplicate it by passing it on to the next generation. Thus, the cycle of shame continues incessantly from generation to generation.

David Confronts the Shame Barrier

Shame erects a barrier that inhibits you from fulfilling your spiritual calling. In our continuing analysis of David, this issue of shame represents his greatest crisis in conquering the enemy who sought to prevent him from fulfilling his purpose. David's season of shame began when he was well on his way to fulfilling his God-appointed destiny. He had survived the trying years of exile and reigned as king of Israel. Charles Swindoll observes, "David's career was at an all-time high. Fresh from a series of victories in battle, he had reached the peak of public admiration. He enjoyed an endless supply of money, power, and fame. Never are we more vulnerable than when we have it all, and David was no exception."[1]

One afternoon, David arose from his afternoon nap to take a walk on the roof of the palace where the cool breezes offered relief from the heat of the day. David should not have been relaxing in the luxury and ease of the palace, for Israel was at war and it was the duty of kings to lead the battle. Matthew Henry notes, "Had he been now at his post at the head of his forces, he would have been out of the way of this temptation. When we are out of the way of our duty we are in the way of temptation."[2]

From the palace roof, David saw a beautiful young woman bathing. The pause in the way of temptation, like that of Eve on the path winding by the tree of knowledge, catapulted David into the devastating cycle of sin and its associated shame.

Despite the fact that Bathsheba was another man's wife, David brought her to the palace and had intimate relations with her. A short time later, Bathsheba sent word to David that she had conceived a child from their adulterous union. The news that Bathsheba was pregnant panicked David. Her husband, Uriah, was one of David's mighty men and a national hero (2 Sam. 23:39). As Matthew Henry points out, "Uriah . . . was a person of honor and virtue, one that was now abroad in [David's] service, hazarding his life in the high places of the field for the honor and safety of [David] and his kingdom, where [David] himself should have been."[3]

David also knew that according to the law, both he and Bathsheba deserved death by stoning. To conceal his sin, David sent for Uriah to come back to Jerusalem and bring news of the battle. David wined and dined Uriah and encouraged him to spend the night with Bathsheba, but Uriah refused that pleasure (2 Sam. 11:11). Manipulation having failed, David conceived an even more diabolical plan. He sent orders to the commander of the army to set Uriah in the front of the hottest battle and then abandon him to the enemy. One sin led to another in David's life. First there was transgression, then manipulation, and next murder. Charles Swindoll warns, "Playing with sin is playing with fire. If you don't snuff out temptation when it first sparks in your mind, the fire may burn out of control. What started as a lustful thought in David's mind spread to adultery, which spread to deception, which culminated in murder. . . . Take temptation seriously. Stop sin before it ever starts."[4]

After Uriah was killed in battle and Bathsheba had properly mourned his death, David sent for her, she became his wife, and she bore him a son.

The Shame of Sin

It looked for a while as if David got away with his double sin of adultery and murder, but the Bible records, "the thing that David had done displeased the LORD" (2 Sam. 11:27). You may think you get away with sin, but you really don't. And as long as you do not deal with your sin, you will never eliminate its associated shame.

It was several months before Nathan the prophet came knocking at the palace door to confront David with his sin. In the meantime, David suffered shame's reprisals. Psalm 32 describes his condition in the unrepentant state:

> *When I kept silent, my bones grew old*
> *Through my groaning all the day long.*
> *For day and night Your hand was heavy upon me;*
> *My vitality was turned into the drought of summer (vv. 3–4).*

This passage does not sound like the reflections of a man after God's own heart, does it? It seems our image of intimacy is shattered by sin and broken in the ruins of shame. But lest our voices are raised with those of the accusers, J. Vernon McGee writes, "The sin of David stands out like a tar-baby in a field of snow, like blackberry in a bowl of cream. It may cause us to miss the greatness of the man. Remember that sin was the exception in David's life, not the pattern of it."[5]

Breaking the Shame Barrier

The story of David's sin with Bathsheba does not end here. What happens next reveals the liberating truth that the power of sin and shame can be broken. The strategy for doing this is revealed in three vital steps David took to deal with his transgressions and their related shame.

Step 1: Act Against Your Shame

Several months after David's sin, the Lord sent Nathan to David: "Notice that God didn't send Nathan to confront David immediately after he committed adultery—or even after the murder. He doesn't always settle up with us in the springtime of our sin. Often, He waits until we've experienced a barren winter in our souls."[6]

Nathan used a parable to expose David's unconfessed sin. It was a moving story of a poor man who had one lamb raised as a beloved pet and a rich man with many flocks and herds. When a traveler visited the rich man, he refused to kill his animals to prepare dinner but instead slaughtered the lamb that was dearly loved by the poor man.

The parable aroused David's anger, and he said to Nathan, "As the LORD lives, the man who has done this shall surely die!" A poignant hush fell over the throne room as Nathan said to the king, "You are the man!" Then he rehearsed a detailed account of David's transgressions (2 Sam. 12:7–9). When Nathan finished speaking, David did not try to justify or deny his sin, but he immediately acted against it. David said to Nathan, "I have sinned against the LORD" (2 Sam. 12:13). Psalm 51 reflects his response as he pleaded,

> *Have mercy upon me, O God,*
> *According to Your lovingkindness;*
> *According to the multitude of Your tender mercies,*
> *Blot out my transgressions.*
> *Wash me thoroughly from my iniquity,*
> *And cleanse me from my sin.*
> *For I acknowledge my transgressions,*
> *And my sin is always before me.*
> *Against You, You only, have I sinned,*
> *And done this evil in Your sight (vv. 1–4).*

When David repented, Nathan immediately responded, "The LORD also has put away your sin; you shall not die" (2 Sam. 12:13).

Jesus dealt with shame at the cross, for the Bible says that He endured the Cross and the hostility of sinners, "despising the shame" (Heb. 12:2). Because Jesus took your shame to the cross, you no longer have to live under the guilt of inherited, imposed, institutional, individual, or incessant shame. God wants the shame barrier broken in your life so you will never again be condemned in this world or the world to come, but for this to happen, you must, like David, act against your shame.

If the result of what you are doing or have done is shame, it is from Satan, and he is using it to destroy you. You must repent of everything that produces shame. True repentance is an inward decision that results in the outward action of turning away from sin. David said, "I will declare my iniquity; I will be in anguish over my sin" (Ps. 38:18). He asked God to search his heart, know his thoughts and ways, and cleanse him from even secret sins (Ps. 139:23–24).

Shame is a signal that something is wrong. One psychologist describes it as "the red light on our internal dashboard," cautioning,

> When you see the light's feverish glare, you have a choice to make. You can either pull over, get out of the car, open the hood and see what's wrong; or you can smash the light with a hammer and keep driving. The first option leads to fixing the problem. . . . The second only relieves the symptoms. You may be able to keep the light from glaring, but after a few more miles, the whole engine might burn up. How do you treat guilt's red light? Do you take it seriously, stopping to analyze why it's flashing?[7]

When you act against shame by repenting of the sin that propagates it, you have taken the first step in shattering the shame barrier.

Step 2: Address Your Shame

After acting against his shame by repenting, David addressed his shame. He spoke positive words to counteract the lingering accusations of shame resulting from his transgression:

> I acknowledged my sin to You,
> And my iniquity I have not hidden.
> I said, "I will confess my transgressions to the LORD."
> And You forgave the iniquity of my sin (Ps. 32:5).

Jesus bore your shame on the cross so that you do not have to bear it, but even after you repent of the shame-producing conduct, the voice of the accuser will continue to echo in your soul. You may be caught in the very act of adultery, as the woman in New Testament times, but you must make a decision that you will not listen to the voice of shame. The voice of accusation says, "She is guilty. Stone her!" The voice of intercession says, "Neither do I condemn you. Go, and sin no more." Judas listened to the voice of shame, and it led to suicide and death. Ask yourself, Is the result of the voice I am listening to death or life? This question will help you distinguish between the voice of shame and that of mercy.

The Bible teaches that confession is instrumental to experiencing salvation, for if you "confess with your mouth" and believe in your heart that Jesus is Lord, you are saved. You gain other spiritual victories as well by the confession of your mouth.

When you hear the voice of shame speak to you, you must address it instead of ignoring it. You must reprogram your inner computer. When the voice of accusation says, "Shame on you," respond by declaring, "No, shame was upon Him. Righteousness is on me. Jesus, who knew no sin, bore my sin and shame so I stand righteous before God through Him. So, shame, shut up!" Speak to shame in prayer just as you would address a man standing there with stones ready to kill you. If you surrender to shame, it will do to you what it did to Judas. You do not have to die in your shame because Jesus already died on the cross bearing your shame.

Step 3: Ask for a New Passionate Relationship with God

After you act on your shame and address it, ask God for a new passionate relationship with God, for that is the only way you will get out from under shame's dominion. After Peter denied Jesus, the Lord confronted him three times with the question, "Do you love Me?"—each time with increasing levels of intensity of relationship reflected in the Greek forms of the word *love*. Peter responded each time, "You know I love You, Lord!" Jesus then commissioned him, "Feed My sheep." In essence, Jesus was saying to Peter, "You failed Me, but you repented and you are forgiven. Now all you need to qualify to feed My sheep is a passionate relationship with Me."

After David acted against his shame and addressed it, he sought this passionate relationship with God. He prayed,

Do not cast me away from Your presence,
And do not take Your Holy Spirit from me.
Restore to me the joy of Your salvation. . . .
Open my lips,
And my mouth shall show forth Your praise (Ps. 51:11–15).

Many people let the shame of their failures prevent them from fulfilling their God-given destiny. After David was forgiven and his passionate relationship with God restored, he declared, "Then I will teach transgressors Your ways, and sinners shall be converted to You" (Ps. 51:13). His work wasn't over. He broke loose from the shackles of shame to fulfill his destiny.

The Shadows of Sin

When David confessed and repented of his sin, the prophet Nathan immediately responded, "God has forgiven you," but he also warned David that there would be consequences of his transgression. The child born to David and Bathsheba would die. Charles Swindoll comments,

> *If you have taken lightly the grace of God . . . if you have childishly skipped through the corridors of the kingdom, picking and choosing sin or righteousness at will . . . the storm is just brewing on the horizon. Though God's forgiveness is sure, so are sin's consequences . . . Don't be deceived. God's grace doesn't necessarily chase away the dark clouds of sin's consequences.*[8]

Even though you repent from sin and address its associated shame, there may be consequences as you live in the shadows of your former transgression. For example, if you are incarcerated and you ask God's forgiveness and conquer your shame, you may still be required to complete serving your sentence. But even if you dwell for a time in the shadow of sin, you no longer must live in the shame of it. Charles Swindoll observes, "Soon after David's loss, he held a new baby son in his arms. Likewise, neither will God punish you forever; He is not through blessing your life."[9]

In a few years, David and Bathsheba had another son and

named him *Solomon,* which means "peaceful," for his birth was a token of God's being at peace with them. The prophet Nathan said Solomon would be called *Jedidiah,* which means "beloved of God," "signifying that those who were by nature children of wrath and disobedience should, by the covenant of grace, not only be reconciled, but made favorites."[10] Even if you are experiencing lingering consequences of sin, do not let its shame prevent you from fulfilling your destiny.

1. Act against your shame. If the result of what you are doing or have done is shame, it is from Satan, and he is using it to destroy you. Repent of everything that produces shame.

2. Address your shame. When the voice of accusation says, "Shame on you," respond by declaring, "No, shame was upon Him. Righteousness is on me. Jesus, who knew no sin, bore my sin and shame, so I stand righteous before God through Him. So, shame, shut up!"

3. Ask for a new passionate relationship with God.

When you take these three steps, the power of shame will be broken over your life, and as happened with David and Bathsheba, you will soon give birth to new dreams and visions.

22

—✠—

The Spirit of Accusation

Among the grisly memorials of Nazi Germany, none is more horrible than the concentration camp in southwestern Poland known under German occupation as Auschwitz. Historians estimate that more than one million people from across Europe were put to death there, most of them exterminated in gas chambers disguised as showers. Others were starved, tortured, executed, or worked to death. There Josef Mengele conducted his infamous medical experiments on children, and mounds of corpses were burned in the open air because the crematories could not keep pace with the number of deaths.

Can such atrocities ever be forgiven? Can we pray, as Jesus taught, for our forgiveness and link it to our willingness to forgive others—even the "others" who commit atrocities like those recorded at Auschwitz?

Corrie Ten Boom proved it is possible. Her beloved sister and parents died in the concentration camp, and Corrie suffered inhumanities at the hands of the Nazis. But Corrie learned how to forgive, and she traveled the world with the message that there is no place so dark that the light of God's love cannot penetrate.

David, our model of intimacy with God the Father, also chose to forgive. Despite the evil perpetuated against him by King Saul, David refused to retaliate, and he saved Saul's life on one occasion. When

David sinned, he knew how to readily access God's forgiveness because he knew how to forgive. In contrast, King Saul never learned how to forgive, so he did not know how to seek and receive forgiveness.

The model prayer teaches us to pray, "Forgive us our debts, as we forgive our debtors," and this phrase precedes the appeal for deliverance from the evil one. Forgiveness for sins and deliverance are explicitly linked to our willingness to forgive others. Morris Cerullo tells us, "Time and again, Jesus linked human forgiveness to God's forgiveness. . . . He said that forgiving others was important . . . evidence of being forgiven by God."[1]

The Power of Unity

Satan seeks to divide believers and church fellowships because he knows the power of unity. Where two or three are gathered together in agreement, Jesus is there. When the early believers were in one accord in the Upper Room in Jerusalem, a tremendous move of the Holy Spirit resulted in thousands of conversions. The Bible indicates one can put one hundred to flight, but two cause ten thousand to flee.

The Bible declares that the world will know we are related to God the Father not by our faith, miracles, tongues, or evangelistic campaigns but by our love for one another. The Scriptures explain,

> *He who says he is in the light, and hates his brother, is in darkness until now. He who loves his brother abides in the light, and there is no cause for stumbling in him. But he who hates his brother is in darkness and walks in darkness, and does not know where he is going, because the darkness has blinded his eyes (1 John 2:9–11).*

This passage indicates the deciding factor between a child of darkness and a child of light is whether you love or hate. You cannot penetrate the darkness of Satan's kingdom in power prayer if you are walking in darkness, for only light can dispel the darkness. Unresolved anger, bitterness, and unforgiveness result in giving place to, or room for, the devil to operate in your life (Eph. 4:25–27).

Accuser or Intercessor . . . Your Choice

The Bible teaches that there are two forces at work in heaven and in the world today. One is that of the false father, the "accuser of our brethren," who according to Revelation 12:10 constantly slanders and accuses God's people. The other spirit, that of the Intercessor, Jesus Christ, intercedes in our behalf. These two forces are constantly operative in the universe, and you will conform to the spirit of one or the other in your personal relationships, in your attitude toward others, and in the words of your mouth.

Jesus silenced the voice of the accuser when He died on the cross, and the only way that spirit operates now is when you allow Satan to malign others through your unforgiving words, feelings, and actions. The spirit of accusation says, "You have a right to be mad. Look what your enemy did to you!"

The spirit of intercession, however, responds as Jesus did when He hung on the cross. Jesus had every right to accuse those around Him, for He knew their sins and He was suffering agony at their hands. But Jesus chose to intercede in their behalf, praying, "Father, forgive them."

The force of accusation works to fashion you into the image of the false father. The spirit of intercession seeks to conform you to the image of God. You put a death nail in the coffin of the accuser when you choose to follow the example of Jesus, forgiving those who wrong you and interceding for them.

How to Turn Your Enemies into Your Friends

The Hebrew word for *enemy* means "observer." Your enemy observes you, seeking grounds for accusation and offense, watching intently for your failures and faults.

Proverbs 16:7 states, "When a man's ways please the LORD, he makes even his enemies to be at peace with him." One day when I read this verse, I wondered, What must I do to have my ways please God so much that my enemies will be at peace with me? In answer to my question the Lord led me to this passage: "I say to you, love your enemies, bless those who curse you, do good to those who hate you, and pray for those who spitefully use you and persecute you, that you may be sons of your Father in heaven" (Matt. 5:44–45).

This passage lists four steps to take to turn your enemies into friends. These steps mark your identity as a true child of God because when you take them, you exhibit the supernatural nature of your heavenly Father.

Step 1: Choose to Love

True love is a choice, an act of the will, not of the emotions. For example, when God "so loved the world" that He decided to send Jesus to die for our sins, He made the choice as an act of His will. God didn't do it because He felt great about having His only Son suffer humiliation and a painful death. He acted in love by choice, not by emotion, for every divine emotion in His being opposed sacrificing His only Son.

If you want to please God, you must emulate His ways and, by an act of your will, choose to love. When you act according to the natural instincts of the flesh and hate someone, you fashion yourself after the killing, stealing, destroying nature of the false father. If you choose to respond in a supernatural dimension with divine love, you pattern yourself after the nature of your heavenly Father. Forgiveness is a choice based on the Cross. You forgive on the basis of the blood of Jesus.

Step 2: Choose to Bless

To forgive the way Jesus did, you don't just ignore an offense and pretend it never happened. You bless the person who wronged you. Negative power is released by enemies who speak or act against you with words that curse, tear down, and destroy. When you speak a blessing over them, you reverse the curse of their words and actions.

Step 3: Do Something Good for Your Enemy

Positive and negative wires create the power of electricity. There is a spiritual parallel, for rejecting the negative emotions of hatred and bitterness and choosing to bless instead result in a special endowment of power by which you can do something good for your enemy. Jesus said, "Do good to those who hate you." Find something nice to do for your enemy, and do it in Jesus' name.

Step 4: Intercede for Your Enemy

When you decide to love instead of hate, bless instead of curse, and do something good for your enemy, you are able to pray for those who have wronged you. This is true power praying because there is no way you can do it without a supernatural endowment of God's power. It isn't a natural response. Your sincere intercession releases the power of the Holy Spirit to work in your enemy's life, and the result is that "you shall be perfect, just as your Father in heaven is perfect" (Matt. 5:48). When you are perfected, your ways please the Father, and He causes your enemies to be at peace with you.

When you choose to love and bless your enemy properly, you will come under the anointing of power prayer. As you intercede in behalf of your enemy, you will align yourself with the force of intercession and reject the force of accusation.

23

Emancipation from the False Father

It was June 6, 1944, a day that would later be labeled in history books as D day. The Allied troops stormed the beaches of Normandy, France, dealing a decisive blow to enemy forces and marking the turning point of World War II. It was a full year after the battle, however, that the Germans and Japanese finally signed the official documents of surrender. That intervening year was the bloodiest of the entire war, for the enemy forces knew their time was limited and they intensified their fierce attacks.

The church today stands in a similar position spiritually. It was the D day of victory when Jesus Christ died on the cross and defeated the enemy forces of Satan. Until Christ returns to establish His kingdom and force Satan's ultimate surrender, however, believers are engaged in an intensified spiritual battle. The enemy knows his time is limited, and he has unleashed every demonic force at his disposal to wage the final campaign.

Satan is not a passive aggressor, for the Bible describes him as a roaring lion seeking to devour, a liar, and a thief coming to steal, kill, and destroy. When you pray, "Deliver us from the evil one," the spirit of this aggressor rises up to intimidate and program you for defeat. "You tried to live for God before and failed," Satan declares. "Face it. You are weak and destined to remain that way. If God was really your Father, He would help you."

If you are to survive the relentless onslaughts of the enemy, you must learn to wage both defensive and offensive spiritual warfare. To do this, like David, you must know your spiritual weapons and how to use them. In this and the following two chapters, you will learn how to use a spiritual arsenal that will permit you to declare with authority, "Deliver us from the evil one," knowing assuredly your prayer will be answered!

In Part 1, we discussed the importance of putting on the armor of God, which is your uniform for spiritual battle. We also learned how to build a spiritual hedge of protection as detailed in Psalm 91. These are basic defensive weapons you should employ each day when you pray, "Deliver us from the evil one."

But now, as you receive this deeper anointing of power prayer, you must learn more about the enemy's strategies and how to employ offensive weapons as well as the defensive ones of which you already have knowledge. These offensive weapons are the blood of Jesus, the power of His name, the word of your testimony, and the weapon of praise. You will also learn how to bind the strongman, rendering his powers sterile.

Exposing the False Father

Military forces spend much time gathering intelligence information on the nature and strategies of their enemy. As believers, we must do likewise. Charles Swindoll elaborates on this point:

> *Before any opponent can be intelligently withstood, a knowledge of his ways must be known. Ignorance must be dispelled. No boxer in his right mind enters the ring without having first studied the other boxer's style. The same is true on . . . the battlefield. Days (some times months) are spent studying the tactics, the weaknesses, the strengths of the opponent. Ignorance is an enemy to victory.*[1]

The false father, Satan, is the spiritual enemy who pursues believers in a similar fashion as King Saul did David. He continuously prowls about, seeking to destroy God's anointed. We can summarize these destructive strategies of Satan by noting that they are always directed against God's purposes, His plans, and His people. The enemy is crafty (2 Cor. 11:3), and his deception targets your intimate relationship with your heavenly Father (2 Cor. 11:13–15). That is why Satan continuously programs lies into your spirit to contradict every provision of your heavenly Father reflected in the model prayer.

The False Father's Family

Spiritual warfare is a battle between the children of God and the forces of the false father consisting of his demonic hosts and the "children of the wicked one," who are ungodly men and women. The battle in which we are engaged is not a conflict against "flesh and blood" (Eph. 6:12).

Satan is not omnipresent (present everywhere at the same time), but he dispatches a host of demon spirits throughout the earth to accomplish his purposes. When Lucifer rebelled against God, the angels who joined the rebellion were cast out of heaven with him (Rev. 12:7–9). There appear to be two groups of these fallen angels. One group actively opposes God's children while another group is confined in chains (Jude 6). Satan, who is called the "prince" or "ruler" of demons (Matt. 12:24), leads the host of active demons. Demons constitute the powers of the air (Eph. 2:2) and the powers of darkness (Col. 1:13). They are described as spirits (Matt. 8:16) who can speak (Mark 5:9, 12) and do evil (Luke 8:29). They are intelligent (Mark 1:24) and are endued by Satan with supernatural strength and presence (Acts 19:16).

As the false father, Satan seeks to imitate God. Satan has organized his demonic forces in ranks similar to those of God's angelic host. God's organization is described by the apostle Paul as thrones, dominions, principalities, and powers (Col. 1:16).

Our battle against Satan's hierarchy is described as a battle against "principalities, against powers, against the rulers of the darkness of this age, against spiritual hosts of wickedness in the heavenly places" (Eph. 6:12). These evil forces of Satan function as unclean evil spirits and spirits of infirmity and deception that affect men and women through oppression and possession. The good news is that Satan is not omnipotent (all-powerful). The power of God within believers is greater than the power of Satan: "You are of God, little children, and have overcome them, because He who is in you is greater than he who is in the world" (1 John 4:4).

Satan is strong only over those who yield to his authority instead of to the rightful authority of their heavenly Father. If you are living a defeated Christian life, lulled into passivity by the enemy, stripped of your intimacy with your heavenly Father, it is time to do something about it: "That they may come to their senses and escape the snare of the devil, having been taken captive by him to do his will" (2 Tim. 2:26).

Are you ready for D day liberation in your spiritual life? Are you ready for your emancipation from the false father? In the natural world, your name and bloodline identify you as a member of your family. The same is true in the spiritual world. The blood and the name declare your new identity and your emancipation from the clan of the false father and his children of wrath.

The Blood of the Lamb

We learned in discussing personal prayer that through the redemptive quality of the blood of Jesus, we can boldly access the presence of our heavenly Father. But the blood of Jesus has other tremendous spiritual benefits beyond its redemptive power. The blood is like a two-part document. One part guarantees our right to intimacy with our Father: "But now in Christ Jesus you who once were far off have been brought near by the blood of Christ" (Eph. 2:13). The other part guarantees our release from the false father's authority: "And they overcame him by the blood of the Lamb" (Rev. 12:11).

Throughout the Old Testament record, the blood of lambs was shed sacrificially to secure salvation from sin. When Jesus died, the blood of "the Lamb slain from the foundation of the world" was shed once and for all (Rev. 13:8). Salvation, healing, and deliverance are all assured through the blood of Jesus, and this blood emancipates you from the false claims of the enemy. The blood breaks Satan's legal hold on your life, terminating the parental rights of the false father. Hebrews 9:15 speaks of the Mediator of the new covenant, Jesus, who by means of His death secured this inheritance for you. Hebrews 10:19 declares that the blood of Jesus gives you boldness to enter the "Holiest," which means it leads you to the "holiest" level of life where you are totally saved, healed, and delivered.

You do not have to stand outside your Father's presence burdened with guilt, shame, and defeat. The anointing for power praying comes when, by the blood, you break through these barriers erected by sin and come boldly into God's presence. If you have experienced forgiveness from the sin that separated you from the Father, the blood has been applied to your life. Satan has no legal hold over you because you are now righteous in Christ. You do not have to struggle to measure up to some illusive standard, for you have assumed the family identity of righteousness.

The mission of the false father is to accuse you and undermine your identity with the true Father. When the false father comes with condemning words about your faults, hold up the legal document of the blood and say, "Just look at that, Satan! That's my righteousness. The blood is evidence of my true identity, and I have been emancipated from your claims in my life!" Terry Law offers this encouragement: "Our declaration has to be, 'I am righteous.' If we stay with it, if we continue to confess with our lips, God will open our spiritual eyes to the revelation of the truth. We will begin to see ourselves being the righteousness of God in Christ. Then Satan will have lost his ground of accusation."[2]

Blood type is determined at the moment of conception, and it comes from both parents. Jesus Christ was not conceived naturally but was placed in Mary's womb by the Holy Spirit. She did not supply any of her Adamic blood, so the blood of Jesus was immaculate because it was the blood of God.

You received your blood type at conception, and spiritually it carried with it the stains of the Adamic nature. When you were born again, you received a spiritual transfusion at the cross from Jesus. The blood of your heavenly Father now flows through your spiritual arteries and you are emancipated from the bloodline of the false father.

The Name of Jesus

We learned in Part 1 on personal prayer about praying in the name of Jesus, but His name is also a powerful spiritual weapon.

Your spiritual blood transfusion makes you a child of God, your adoption papers were signed in the blood of Jesus, and you have the authority of His name just as you have rights associated with your earthly family's name.

When David confronted Goliath in the "name of the LORD of hosts" (1 Sam. 17:45), he invoked the name of God that was reserved for use in wartime situations. Jesus is described as the captain of the Lord's host (Josh. 5:15), so when we use the name of the Lord of hosts, we access the inherent power of the name of Jesus and all the hosts of heaven. When we deploy the powerful spiritual weapon of His name, our entire spiritual family rushes to our assistance.

Great people obtain their names in three ways. Some people inherit a great name through birth by being born into a family with a name known for its wealth or political power. Other individuals make a great name by their personal achievements, becoming noteworthy writers, inventors, politicians, or leaders. Others have a name conferred upon them by another person. For example, a poor woman may receive the name of a rich politician when she marries him, or a king or tribal leader may give an important title to someone in his domain.

Jesus received His name in all three ways that great people receive their names on earth. The name of Jesus, which means "Savior," was bestowed as an inheritance from His heavenly Father. Hebrews 1:4 indicates, "He has by inheritance obtained a more excellent name." Jesus received His name by achievement because He conquered all the power of the enemy (Col. 2:15). He also had His name conferred upon Him by the heavenly Father: "God also has highly exalted Him and given Him the name which is above every name" (Phil. 2:9–11).

The name of Jesus is the most powerful name in the universe, secured in the way all great people come by their names, and it is a name far above all principalities, powers, and might. The name of Jesus is not a magical phrase used to conclude a prayer in order to guarantee its answer; it signifies power through invested authority. It is much like a police officer who has rights of arrest conferred upon him by his government. He functions, as do we, on the basis of his delegated authority. God gave Jesus authority to delegate power to us over all the powers of the enemy (Matt. 28:18). We can "arrest" these powers of the enemy in the name of Jesus just as a police officer arrests offenders in the name of his government.

Simply repeating the name of Jesus becomes "vain repetition" similar to that practiced by the Pharisees and scribes in Bible times. The power of the name is inherent in the faith exercised in it (Acts 3:16). We have been strong in the ritual of chanting the name of Jesus, but our faith in the name has been weak. How can we correct this? How can we move beyond mere repetition of His name to the kind of faith in it that results in power?

The Bible says, "Faith comes by hearing, and hearing by the word of God" (Rom. 10:17). Your faith in the name of Jesus is increased by hearing, believing, and confessing what the Word of God says about it. There is power for healing in the name of Jesus (Acts 3:6) and for signs, wonders, and miracles: "And these signs shall follow them that believe; In my name shall they cast out devils; they shall speak with new tongues; they shall take up serpents; and if they drink any deadly thing, it shall not hurt them; they shall lay hands on the sick, and they shall recover" (Mark 16:17–18 KJV).

A. L. Gill comments regarding these verses: "When the translators were trying to clarify this passage, they added punctuation after 'them that believe.' This passage could, just as correctly, read 'them that believe in my name.' Many believers do not know the power of believing in the name of Jesus. When we believe in that name, we will use the name and signs will follow."[3]

Demons are cast out in the name of Jesus, and we are protected from every power of the enemy (Mark 16:17). Authority for preaching, teaching, and baptizing comes through that name (Matt. 28:18–20). There is power for salvation (Acts 4:12) and power to become a child of God (John 1:12). Sanctification, which brings the ability to overcome the temptation of the evil one, is instilled by the name of Jesus (1 Cor. 6:11). You are to reign in this life and the one to come through His name (Rom. 5:17), which means you can reign right now over every negative circumstance of your life in Jesus' name.

When you really begin to hear with your spiritual ears what the Bible declares about the name of Jesus, your faith is increased, and you can use that name to conquer the powerful forces of the enemy in prayer. Jesus said, "Most assuredly, I say to you, whatever you ask the Father in My name He will give you" (John 16:23).

Claiming Your True Identity

You bear the name and bloodline of your earthly father, and in some cases, that familial association may not be highly respected by others. You may be the child of a convicted criminal or a notorious swindler. But remember that your true identity is spiritual. You are a child of your heavenly Father, His blood flows through your spiritual arteries, and you have all the inherent powers of His family name. When you fully grasp your true identity as a child of your heavenly Father, any feelings of shame or inferiority stemming from your earthly heritage will be totally eliminated.

As you conclude this chapter, here are some power prayer declarations to make concerning the blood of Jesus that secures your emancipation: "According to Romans 5:9, I am justified by the blood of Jesus. On the basis of Ephesians 1:7, the blood of Jesus has redeemed me out of the hand of Satan, and my sins are completely forgiven. Satan has no authority over me! According to Hebrews 13:12, I am sanctified by the blood of Jesus. I can live a holy life, set apart unto God. According to Hebrews 10:19, I can enter boldly into my Father's presence. Look out, devil. Here I come!"

Legacy of a Liar

The false father propagates a legacy of lies, drawing each fabrication from the limitless reserve of his evil resources. Jesus told the Pharisees, "You are of your father the devil, and the desires of your father you want to do. He was a murderer from the beginning, and does not stand in the truth, because there is no truth in him. When he speaks a lie, he speaks from his own resources, for he is a liar and the father of it" (John 8:44).

In personal prayer when we pray as Jesus taught, this lying spirit of the false father constantly rises up against us. Satan challenges every fatherly function of our heavenly Father. That is why we are working our way through the model prayer exposing his lies, disarming them of their oppressive power, and clearing these blockades from the pathway leading to the anointing of power prayer.

We have observed that when we pray, "Deliver us from the evil one," the false father intimidates us with threats that we can never be free from his clutches. We learned in the last chapter that our emancipation is assured when we employ the spiritual weapons of the blood of the Lamb and the name of Jesus. In this chapter we return to our spiritual family's armory to learn how to activate another forceful weapon, the word of our testimony.

The Word of Your Testimony

The lies of the enemy come from his evil spiritual resources. To counteract his false claims, you must draw from your spiritual resources, speaking the truth through the word of your testimony. Revelation 12:11 declares, "And they overcame him [the enemy] . . . by the word of their testimony."

Your testimony acknowledges that your Father's authority is greater than the power of the enemy. It is like evidence used in a court case to convict a criminal. As you testify, or give evidence, you wage offensive battle against the enemy, much like a prosecuting attorney does. That is why Jesus commanded people who were healed to tell others what God had done for them.

The authority of *your* testimony emanates from the power of the Word of *His* testimony, meaning your words must be permeated with God's Word to be effective. The testimony by which you overcome the enemy is not a long rehearsal of how bad you were when you were a sinner or how difficult things are for you now. It is a dynamic witness to the truth of the Scriptures that have become real in your life, making the Word a powerful sword of the Spirit in your mouth that slashes the deceiving lies of the enemy.

It is difficult to picture a sword coming out of your mouth. Usually, you hold a sword in your hand. That is also its position in every sketch I have seen illustrating the Christian soldier clothed in God's armor. But the apostle John portrayed it differently in a passage describing Jesus leading the armies of heaven: "He was clothed with a robe dipped in blood, and His name is called The Word of God. . . . Now out of His mouth goes a sharp sword" (Rev. 19:13–15). The apostle John described the ultimate war that will occur on earth during which the evil forces of the false father will be eradicated. Jesus will defeat the enemy in this battle the same way we must defeat him in the everyday battles of life, by the sword of the Spirit, which is the Word of God. A. L. Gill notes, "Our battles must be won by the Word of God, and that Word has to come forth from our mouths, even as it will from the mouth of the victorious Lord Jesus as He returns to this earth."[1]

This is not aimless positive confession that attempts to manipulate God's Word for selfish, greedy purposes. It is God's Word in our mouths targeted against the enemy who comes to kill, steal, and destroy.

The *Logos* Becomes *Rhema*

There are two different words in Scripture for the Word of God. One is *Logos,* which refers to the entire written revelation of God in the Bible. The second word is *rhema,* which refers to specific sayings of God that apply to individual situations. *Rhema* is the word used to describe the "sword of the Spirit" in Ephesians 6:17. The word of your testimony is a *rhema* illustration of God's *Logos* made real in your life. You testify when you confess what the Word has done for you in the past and declare by faith what it will accomplish in the future.

The writer of Hebrews relates that the worlds were framed by the word of God, and when God spoke, the universe came into existence because His words have tremendous creative power. If you are to receive the anointing of power prayer, you must begin to use the dynamic, creative, *rhema* words of your heavenly Father.

When Satan robs you of finances, do not talk about how bad the economy is or how you can't pay your bills. Instead, testify of the times God provided for you in the past, and acknowledge that He will once again supply your present needs according to His riches in glory by Christ Jesus. When sickness strikes, testify of the times God healed you in the past, and confess that you are once again healed by the stripes of Jesus. When you sin and Satan brings guilt and shame, confess your sin, and declare the righteousness of Christ to reign over your life.

David, our example of intimacy with the Father, knew the power of positive testimony. When he faced Goliath on the battlefield, he did not talk about how tall the giant was, how much he weighed, or the threat posed by his deadly weapons. David focused on what God did for him in the past, recalling how he had been endued with supernatural strength to kill a lion and a bear. He then declared a *rhema* word about what God would do in the future, claiming, "The LORD, who delivered me from the paw of the lion and from the paw of the bear, He will deliver me from the hand of this Philistine" (1 Sam. 17:37).

The Bible indicates that life and death are in the power of your tongue (Prov. 18:21). What comes out of your mouth when you are under attack by the evil one is a matter of spiritual life or death. If you speak negative words, death is released. When you meditate on the Word of God, it penetrates your spirit, and then through the word of your testimony, you release its life-giving power.

Speak the Word

When Jesus faced temptation in the wilderness, He met each challenge of the enemy with the word of God. Throughout His earthly ministry, Jesus constantly reiterated that His words were those of the Father (John 3:34; 14:10, 24; 17:8, 14).

Too often we testify about the power of the problem and witness to the lies of the false father:

- "I know God can heal, but I just can't get my healing."
- "This is just the way I am. Bad tempers run in my family, so I came by it naturally."
- "I know God wants my marriage to work, but my mate argues all the time and I just can't take it anymore."

The Bible indicates you snare yourself with your words, which means you get yourself into difficulties by what you say (Prov. 6:2). Satan uses your negative testimony to cause a breach in your spirit. The Bible declares, "A wholesome tongue is a tree of life, but perverseness in it breaks the spirit" (Prov. 15:4). This breach, or opening in your spirit, permits Satan to enter and establish spiritual strongholds in your life.

A negative testimony brings trouble (Prov. 21:23), destruction (Prov. 13:3), and a snare to your soul (Prov. 18:7). Your words affect your entire being: "And the tongue is a fire, a world of iniquity. The tongue is so set among our members that it defiles the whole body, and sets on fire the course of nature; and it is set on fire by hell" (James 3:6). When Satan controls the testimony of your mouth, he controls you. If you really want to be delivered from evil, you must speak your heavenly Father's language of faith and declare His Word instead of the legacy of lies propagated by the false father.

Numbers 13 illustrates the importance of proper confession. Israel stood poised at the border of the Promised Land. God said that the land was theirs and that He would empower them to conquer it. Spies were dispatched to determine how best to take possession, but ten of them returned with a negative confession. The men reported that the land was filled with giants who made the Israelites look like mere grasshoppers. They said there was no way the enemy could be conquered. Their negative confession convinced the people not to enter the land, a decision that resulted in forty years of suffering. Any report that is contrary to what God says is a negative confession and generates detrimental effects.

Power in the Word

The devil knows there is tremendous power in the word of your testimony, and that is why he wants you to speak his words. Satan recognizes that the Word of God in your mouth becomes a quick, powerful, and sharp spiritual weapon (Heb. 4:12). God's Word is powerful because He promised that it would accomplish what He purposed (Isa. 55:11) and that He performs His word (Jer. 1:12).

Jesus understood the dynamic power of the spoken word. He spoke the words of His Father to a man whose withered hand was healed (Mark 3:1–5) and to a man with leprosy whose skin was cleansed (Matt. 8:2–3). Jesus said to "rise and walk" to a sick man lying by a pool (John 5:8); "see" to blind people (Luke 7:21); "come out" to demons (Matt. 9:32–33); "hear" to a deaf man (Mark 7:32–35); and "come forth" to a dead man (John 11:44). The early church continued this dynamic witness to God's Word, for they went everywhere sharing God's Word, and their testimony was confirmed with miraculous signs.

When we speak covetous, idle, or foolish words, we testify to the power of the false father. When we rise up in the spirit of accusation and speak evil words about others, murmur, and complain, we become victims of the legacy of his lies. Signs follow these words, too—depression, division, discouragement, and defeat.

Romans 10 indicates that faith speaks. What does it say?

"The word is near you, in your mouth and in your heart" (that is, the word of faith which we preach): that if you confess with your mouth the Lord Jesus and believe in your heart that God has raised Him from the dead, you will be saved. For with the heart one believes unto righteousness, and with the mouth confession is made unto salvation (vv. 8–10).

These verses reveal that what you believe in your heart, combined with the confession of your mouth, results in the reality of that belief being manifested in your life.

Testifying to the Enemy

When David faced Goliath, he boldly proclaimed,

Who is this uncircumcised Philistine, that he should defy the armies of the living God? . . . Let no man's heart fail because of him; your servant will go and fight with this Philistine. . . . Your servant has killed both lion and bear; and this uncircumcised Philistine will be like one of them, seeing he has defied the armies of the living God (1 Sam. 17:26, 32, 36).

Whenever Satan comes to bring the shame of my past on me and tell fearful lies about my future, I deny him the power to use my past or present circumstances to dictate my future. I tell him about his past: He is the one who rebelled against God and was cast out of heaven, was defeated by the blood at the cross, and is under my feet. Then I tell him about his future: He is doomed to hell to be bound in chains for a thousand years and eventually cast into the bottomless pit of everlasting darkness forevermore.

As you conclude this chapter, why don't you employ this strategy right now? When you testify in the face of the enemy, his threats are stripped of their power, and you are one victory nearer to fulfilling your destiny and releasing the prayer anointing in your life. The legacy of the enemy's lies are defeated by your words of faith that, like David's stones, find their mark and strike down the enemy every time.

25

Breaking the Family Ties

You are a product of your parents. You may have your dad's height or your mother's eyes, and input from both determined your blood type at the time of conception. Each of your physical traits was dictated by the genetic heritage received from your parents. Medical science also recognizes the genetic predisposition to certain physical conditions, such as cancer, heart problems, and diabetes. That is why your doctor questions you regarding relatives affected by various diseases.

The transmission of certain types of deviant behavior is also a subject of clinical studies, and researchers have noted that children of criminal, abusive, or alcoholic parents often develop similar problems. *Newsweek* devoted an entire section to "Breaking the Divorce Cycle." The observation was that during the 1970s and 1980s, a million children a year watched their parents divorce, and these children, who are now adults, are the first generation to experience widespread divorce. Divorce remains a central issue in their lives, no matter how well adjusted they seem to be: "Adult children of divorce are more likely to have troubled relationships and broken marriages. When adult children of divorce get divorced themselves, the painful legacy is passed to a second generation of children, the offspring of these adult survivors."[1]

Many secular physicians and psychologists do not realize that spiritual forces are behind such observable phenomena as inherited deviant behavior, illness, and social problems. The Bible describes such forces as "curses" or "strongholds" of Satan.

You dispel the lies of the false father as you receive the anointing of power prayer. When you ask your heavenly Father to "deliver us from the evil one," the false father retorts, "You are my captive, bound by addictions, hostage to negative emotions, physically weak, and captive to the evil desires of the flesh." He reminds you,

- "Your mother died of cancer, so you will probably die of it, too."
- "Your father never conquered his addiction, and you won't be able to, either."
- "You can't change. You are just like your parents."

If you let him, the false father continues to reiterate these lies even after you are adopted into your heavenly Father's family. If you do not deal with his claims, you will be victimized by generational curses and strongholds, and you will continue to perpetuate them by passing them on to the next generation. This chapter identifies these generational links, explains how to recognize if they are operating in your life, and details how to extricate yourself from this evil heritage.

Hazards of Heredity

Heredity concerns the presence or absence of certain characteristics including physical, emotional, and personality traits passed from one generation to another. Science has long recognized that physical traits result from chemical heredity through sexual reproduction. It has also noted the effects of environmental heredity, observing that people are affected by food, climate, upbringing, education, income, and other factors in their environment.

But science does not recognize how spiritual heredity affects such observable phenomena. God's Word teaches that a person is a spiritual being with a spiritual heredity that is influenced by invisible forces. The Bible addresses both the negative and the positive aspects of this invisible generational link. God said, "I, the LORD your God, am a jealous God, visiting the iniquity of the fathers upon the children to the third and fourth generations of those who hate Me" (Ex. 20:5).

This indicates that spiritual curses are passed down through generations. The Bible also reveals that spiritual blessings are propagated the same way, but that they are passed on to "thousands" of descendants (Ex. 20:6).

Many people readily accept the concept of inherited blessings but are skeptical about curses, thinking it conjures up images of the Dark Ages. But the Bible is clear on this matter: Blessing and cursing are vehicles of spiritual power that produce either positive or negative results, and they can be passed through generational links.

How Family Ties Are Developed

The Bible warns that we should not give "place to" or room for Satan to operate in our lives (Eph. 4:27). When you give such opportunity to the false father, whether in your thought life or in sinful actions, a breach (opening) is created in your spirit. This can result in either a curse or a spiritual stronghold in your life.

Strongholds and sinful actions that perpetuate curses begin as thoughts. Paul admonishes us to cast down "arguments and every high thing that exalts itself against the knowledge of God" and bring every thought into captivity (2 Cor. 10:4–5). Thoughts become actions and actions become established patterns of behavior, strongholds perpetuated by the affected individual as curses to the next generation.

Strongholds are negative forces that become so forceful in your life that they constantly drive and overwhelm you. They never let up. Desire so overpowering that you don't know what to do about it is caused by a stronghold.

The Bible reveals that lust, addictions, and numerous other negative behaviors and emotions are caused by spirits established in and operating through a person's life. When I say that spirits cause these problems, I mean these things are satanically generated. For example, did you know that fear is a spirit? "God has not given us a spirit of fear" (2 Tim. 1:7). If a spirit of fear is not of God, whose spirit is it? What spirit makes people fearful of disease, death, and insufficiency? Why do people cower in their homes at night with windows and doors barred and bolted?

Everyone feels afraid at times, but the spirit of fear is a paralyzing force that prevents you from fulfilling your ministry. Paul admonished Timothy in the same passage to "stir up the gift of God" lest the spirit of fear prevent him from accomplishing God's purpose in his life (2 Tim. 1:6). When fear prohibits you from fulfilling God's purposes, it is no longer just an emotion or a panic attack; it is a stronghold.

How Curses Are Generated

The Bible indicates that "a curse without cause shall not alight" (Prov. 26:2), meaning that behind every curse is a spiritual cause. Deuteronomy 27:15–26 lists moral and ethical sins that start as thoughts, are expressed in evil actions, and create spiritual breaches that open us up to curses or strongholds. A summary includes worship of false gods, disrespect for parents, all forms of oppression and injustice, all forms of illicit and unnatural sex, and rebellion against God's Word (the latter is rather inclusive and covers sins not specifically itemized).

Other biblical references contribute to this list. People preaching a gospel of apostasy will be cursed (Gal. 1:6–9), and the Lord declared that those who trust in "flesh" (works) instead of Him are cursed (Jer. 17:5). Robbing God of tithes and offerings brings a financial curse (Zech. 5:1–4; Mal. 3:8–9). Anti-Semitism is dangerous spiritually, for God declared to the Jewish nation, "I will curse him who curses you" (Gen. 12:3).

Examination of Deuteronomy 28 reveals eight indicators of the operation of a spiritual curse or stronghold: (1) mental or emotional breakdown; (2) chronic sickness; (3) barrenness or a tendency to miscarry; (4) alienation and breakdown of marriage and family relationships; (5) a history of unnatural or untimely deaths; (6) a cycle of poverty; (7) constant defeat by the enemy; and (8) continual failure.

When I first married Melva, she was under generational curses of sickness and depression. Her mother struggled with a grieved spirit, and certain illnesses, such as rheumatoid arthritis, plagued her family. Melva was sick frequently and depressed the rest of the time. Chronic heart problems and alcoholism were curses operating in my ancestral line. When we recognized and dealt with these strongholds, they were eliminated and have not passed to our children.

How to Break the Family Ties

You may be continuously attacked in your body, struggling with the spirit of infirmity. You may be caught in the cycle of poverty or under attack in your marriage. Perhaps you are wrestling with lust, alcohol, drugs, or other addictions. All of these things are ties linking you to the family of the false father, the heritage of children of wrath.

You do not have to live in bondage to these negative inherited tendencies. As a child of God, you do not have to put up with these things, no matter how long they have run in your family. You can break generational curses and tear down the strongholds of the enemy in your life. *You* can be the one to break the cycle!

Jesus taught that satanic spirits were strong but that they could be conquered: "When a strong man, fully armed, guards his own palace, his goods are in peace. But when a stronger than he comes upon him and overcomes him, he takes from him all his armor in which he trusted, and divides his spoils" (Luke 11:21–22).

The Bible affirms that God's power in you is greater than the power of the enemy. It is your right, as a child of God, to declare that the spiritual powers of darkness will not govern your behavior or capture your thoughts. You can bind the strongman and get him out of your life! Here are the steps to take:

Step 1: Revelation

Ask God to reveal the presence of generational curses or strongholds affecting your life. He may do this when you are in prayer or bring to your attention controlling behavior patterns evident in your family's history.

Step 2: Recognition

As a child of God, you do not have to live under the curse of generational iniquities or strongholds of the enemy. The curse is broken over your life, and Romans 6:14 emphatically states that sin no longer has dominion over you. Your family roots are no longer in the sinful line of Adam but are in the righteous line of Jesus Christ.

Step 3: Repentance

When God reveals a curse or stronghold and you recognize you do not have to live under its power, the next step is repentance. If you or your family have had any involvement with witchcraft or the occult, you should renounce it when you repent. Generational spirits and curses often gain access to families through these avenues. When you confess a stronghold as sin, 1 John 1:8–9 assures that your Father forgives you and cleanses you from "all unrighteousness." "All unrighteousness" means that even strongholds of the enemy you fail to recognize are eradicated.

Step 4: Rebuking

The New Testament reveals that Jesus addressed the enemy, rebuking his powers and telling him to go. You have the same authority to speak to the evil spiritual powers behind the strongholds in your life. Say something like this: "In the name of Jesus Christ and on the authority of His blood, I bind you and you must go!" Address the spirit by name. Bind lust, anger, fear, depression, or whatever has controlled you. When the blood of Jesus is applied, that spirit of lust, addiction, fear, poverty, or whatever has no more right to you. The power of Satan stops at the bloodline of the Cross.

Step 5: Resisting

Strongholds start in the mind, which is the major battlefield of spiritual warfare. Satan will come back and whisper to you, as he did to Eve, "Hath God said?" He will try to reestablish his stronghold, claiming,

- "This may work for others, but you are different. It won't work for you."
- "You really weren't delivered."
- "Just do it one more time. It won't hurt. You can do it once and stop."

You must learn to resist such attacks instead of succumbing to the insidious lies of the false father. The Bible says to "resist the devil and he will flee from you" (James 4:7) and admonishes you to resist

Satan steadfastly in the faith (1 Peter 5:9). Resisting means that when Satan attacks, you stop where you are and replace his lies with the truth. Say, "I resist you, Satan. You are a liar. This spirit has been broken off my life by the blood of Jesus and in His name."

Step 6: Replacing

Jesus indicated that when evil spirits were cast out, a spiritual void was left that must be filled to prevent their return. Replace controlling strongholds by enthroning the Father as the Lord of your life. Replace fear with faith, lust with love, alcohol with the new wine of the Holy Spirit.

Step 7: Relating

Get into covenant relationship with other believers who will love you, pray with you, and help you when you are tempted to succumb to temptation and revert to old behavior patterns. Find a fellowship of true believers and submit yourself to the leadership. The therapeutic environment of faith will help you remain free of the curse.

The Curse Stops Here!

You may say, "This sounds too easy. You don't know my terrible family background. You don't know how bad I've been. I've been in therapy for years and nothing is different. How can I ever change?"

Joshua 2 recounts the story of a prostitute named Rahab who lived on the wall in the city of Jericho, a strategic location where she engaged in her illicit activities. Rahab came from a sinful profession and an evil environment, a city so wicked that God destroyed it. Despite all that, Rahab broke the curse over her life and her entire family. One day, she had an encounter with two men of God. Rahab acknowledged that their God was greater than any power in heaven and earth (Josh. 2:9–11). The scarlet rope that she hung from the window of her home was a testimony to her faith in the blood applied for deliverance for her and her entire household.

Rahab broke the generational curse of her bloodline. She became an ancestor of David, our example of intimacy, who was a "man after God's own heart." Because she broke the strongholds in her life, Rahab passed on a godly heritage and, ultimately, from her genetic line came the Lord Jesus Christ. You can secure a similar deliverance spiritually as you apply the seven steps described in this chapter.

You will pass on either curses or blessings, spiritual death or life, to your descendants:

I have set before you life and death, blessing and cursing; therefore choose life, that both you and your descendants may live (Deut. 30:19).

26

Finishing Strong

In Part 1, we received the anointing of personal prayer as we learned how to use the model prayer Jesus taught His disciples. In Part 2, we have worked our way through the model prayer once again, this time learning to dispel the deceptions of the enemy as we come under the anointing of power prayer. We learned that for each fatherly benefit provided by our heavenly Father in the model prayer, the false father has an antithesis.

As we did this, we traced the footsteps of an anointed man after God's own heart to illustrate each principle of power prayer. With this chapter we arrive at the conclusion of King David's story and of the model prayer as we consider the final phrase, "For Yours is the kingdom and the power and the glory forever. Amen."

When we utter these final words, we must dispel one last accusation of the enemy. We learned in regard to personal prayer that God has given us the kingdom, delegated to us His power, and that He wants to reveal His glory in our lives to enable us to fulfill His purposes. But the spirit of the false father threatens, "You will never reach your full potential. You will not finish your course."

Acts 13:36 declares, "For David, after he had served his own generation by the will of God, fell asleep, was buried with his fathers." Despite a host of enemies and his sinful failures, David fulfilled God's purpose for his life and served his generation by the will of God. Contrast that with the fate of King Saul: "Few men have had beginnings as bright as Saul's. Physically, emotionally, spiritually, professionally—he had it all. Yet from that high and noble beginning, Saul sank to an infamous ending. His epitaph could have read, 'behold I have played the fool.'"[1]

What do you want on your tombstone? Saul said, "I have played the fool." Jacob said, "Few and evil have been my days." It was said of Samson only that "he began." But David's biographer emphatically declared, "He served his generation by the will of God."

What has God given *you* to do in your generation? Will you be a finisher like David, or will you be like King Saul, who died on a lonely hill near Beth Shan having never fulfilled his potential and purpose? Charles Swindoll comments,

> *The city of Beth Shan wasn't far from where the trumpet's blast had inaugurated Saul as king. During his forty year reign, Saul gained no ground for his kingdom. . . . Symbolically speaking, when you die, will you be far from where you began your life in God's kingdom? Will there be miles of growth to mark the path of your spiritual journey? Will the kingdom have benefited because of your life?*[2]

The Spirit of a Finisher

God is a finisher. He instituted His plan from the foundation of the world, is constantly at work bringing all things to pass on the basis of His will, and has declared in the book of Revelation that it will be completed.

Jesus had a passion to finish what God gave Him to do. That desire transcended even His natural desires, enabling Him to proclaim, "My food is to do the will of Him who sent Me, and to finish His work" (John 4:34). Finishing motivated Jesus and kept Him going in the difficult times. His final words on the cross were, "It is finished."

The apostle Paul also had this attitude of finishing, which enabled him to conquer every problem and circumstance. He declared, "But none of these things move me; nor do I count my life dear to myself, so that I may finish my race with joy, and the ministry which I received from the Lord Jesus, to testify to the gospel of the grace of

God" (Acts 20:24). Paul constantly pressed toward the goal for the prize of his calling in God (Phil. 3:14) and was able to declare at the conclusion of his life, "The time of my departure is at hand. I have fought the good fight, I have finished the race, I have kept the faith" (2 Tim. 4:6–7).

Victory over the enemy comes through finishing, not just trying. When they put the first nail in Christ's hand, He might have said, "That's it. I'm out of here!" and called for the angels to effect His deliverance. But Jesus knew if He did that, He would not fulfill God's purpose. It was when He finished the sacrifice on Calvary that the rewards of salvation, healing, and deliverance were effected.

Either you will be an overcomer, or you will be overcome by the lies of the false father. If you are to overcome, you must program into your spirit that on the basis of God's Word, you will be able to finish your course. Paul assures you can be confident that "He who has begun a good work in you will complete it until the day of Jesus Christ" (Phil. 1:6) and that you can be "preserved blameless at the coming of our Lord Jesus Christ" (1 Thess. 5:23).

God determined before you were born what He wants to accomplish in your life. You are God's workmanship "created in Christ Jesus for good works, which God prepared beforehand that [you] should walk in them" (Eph. 2:10). God already ordained the path you are to walk, but the enemy comes through circumstances, failures, age, and so on and says you will not be able to finish your course.

The accuser says, "You are too young to fulfill God's purpose," but many of the great revivals in the history of the church were birthed through young people. David was a mere youth when he was anointed by Samuel and when he rose up to defeat Goliath and revive the failing spirits of God's people.

The accuser says, "You are too old. You already missed God's plan." For years in a desert wilderness, Moses heard the accuser whisper, "You missed it. God spoke to you and prepared you, but you failed. You are not going to be able to do it." But God said to Moses, "Get up and go tell Pharaoh, 'Let My people go!'"

The false father says, "You are too great a sinner to fulfill your purpose," but the biblical record is stained with the sinful blotches of men and women who failed miserably but rose up again to seize their destiny in God.

Attributes of a Finisher

A finisher has five attributes that are described in 1 Peter 5:5–10. Open your Bible to this passage as you study these characteristics.

1. Acknowledge Jesus as Lord of Your Life

Total commitment to God as Lord of your life is the first attribute of a finisher. That is why an intimate relationship with your heavenly Father is so important. A sinful tax collector named Zacchaeus was willing to make what I call this great exchange of commitment to God (Luke 19:1–9). The rich young ruler was not (Mark 10:17–22). Paul compared the great exchange to crucifixion, explaining, "I have been crucified with Christ; it is no longer I who live, but Christ lives in me; and the life which I now live in the flesh I live by faith in the Son of God, who loved me and gave Himself for me" (Gal. 2:20).

The great exchange requires a total change of heart, perspective, and priorities. It requires exchanging life in this world for life in Jesus, the riches of this world for the treasures of heaven. The first mark of a person who has the spirit of a finisher is this quality of submission to God the Father and the lordship of Jesus Christ (1 Peter 5:5).

2. Associate with a Local Church

Your ability to finish is enhanced by submission to the covering of a local church. Peter exhorts you to "submit [yourself] to your elders," and the Amplified Bible further identifies elders as the ministers and spiritual leaders of the church (1 Peter 5:5). It is in the church, where two or more are gathered in His name, that Jesus is present to work signs and wonders and where you will find comfort and help in times of crisis.

3. Abandon Worry

Next, Peter admonishes you to cast "all your care upon Him, for He cares for you" (1 Peter 5:7). People who have the spirit of a finisher do not sit down in the rubble of negative circumstances and cry. They resolve their circumstances by listening to God's direction and then getting up and acting on that guidance.

The Amplified Bible reads, "Casting the whole of your care—all your anxieties, all your worries, all your concerns, once and for all—on Him" (1 Peter 5:7). Paul said, "Be anxious for nothing, but in everything by prayer and supplication, with thanksgiving, let your requests be made known to God" (Phil. 4:6). Instead of worrying, pray about your problems, and let your requests be made known to God with thanksgiving. Worry is a negative force, but praise has positive potency and is the language of faith (Matt. 6:25).

When you face challenging circumstances or devastating problems, instead of crying, "What will I do now?" raise your hands and declare, "Father, You said You would finish what You began in me. You said everything was working for good in my life to conform me to Your image. Now, here's my problem. . . ." Then lay it out before Him, praise Him for an answer, and leave it there. Doing this releases the peace of God to guard your heart and mind from worry.

In 2 Chronicles 20, we find a story that illustrates this principle. King Jehoshaphat was in quite a dilemma, for he was completely surrounded by the enemy nations of Ammon and Moab. In the midst of those fearful circumstances, Jehoshaphat set himself to seek the Lord. He didn't worry or fret; he made up his mind to seek God about his problem. He went to God in prayer and acknowledged that he did not know what to do, but he declared, "Our eyes are upon You." King Jehoshaphat then arose from prayer and called God's people together to wait on the Lord for an answer.

God's response came through a man named Jahaziel who declared, "Thus says the LORD . . . 'Do not be afraid nor dismayed because of this great multitude, for the battle is not yours, but God's. Tomorrow go down against them. . . . You will not need to fight in this battle'" (2 Chron. 20:15–17). The next day the people advanced on the enemy, not with man-made weapons of warfare, but with the supernatural spiritual weapon of praise. A cloud of confusion descended on the enemy, causing them to turn on each other and kill their own comrades.

Men and women who have the spirit of a finisher are like Jehoshaphat. They have their eyes on God instead of on the problem. They don't worry over past, present, or future circumstances; they pray over each situation in faith believing that God will resolve it. Then they act on God's Word using the weapon of praise to cut a path through their difficulties and defeat the enemy.

4. Adopt a Wartime Mentality

Never forget that you live in a war zone. You must get serious about the battle and adopt a wartime mentality (1 Peter 5:8–9). The days are past when you can take a casual attitude toward the enemy. The devil is prowling around like a roaring lion seeking to devour, so don't be surprised when he roars at you. Put on the whole armor of God every day, resist his temptations, put up your shield to divert his fiery darts, and let the sword of the spirit of God's Word be in your mouth.

As A. L. Gill assures us, "The devil walks around as a roaring lion seeking whom he may devour. However, when we know our spiritual authority, we do not have to be afraid. We are covered with the blood of Jesus. We know the power of speaking the Word of God, and we have the authority of the Name of Jesus. He is a defeated foe."[3]

Satan may roar like a lion, but the Bible declares there is coming a day when God will "roar from Zion" (Joel 3:16). "Zion" is the church, and God says there will be a day when we will no longer lift up feeble voices, saying, "Oh, Lord, help us." There will come instead a militant roar of God from the depths of our beings, an intensity in prayer resulting from our spirits uniting with the Spirit of the Father. We will stand united in boldness to declare, "Your kingdom come. Your will be done . . . Yours is the kingdom and the power and the glory!"

There is a time for quietness and meditation in prayer, but from that place of waiting on God, it is time for the roar of power prayer to erupt. I am talking not about emotionalism but about your spirit touching the Spirit of the living God. Joel prophesied that when the priests (that's us now) ministered to the Lord between the porch and the altar (which was directly in front of the Holy Place in the Old Testament tabernacle), no longer would the nations question, "Where is your God?" When that kind of intercession occurs in power prayer, the latter rain of God's Spirit will fall, the years lost to the "locust" of the enemy will be restored, and His power will be poured out upon all flesh (Joel 2).

This restoration will result in the greatest harvest the church has ever seen as we reap the multitudes in the valley of decision before Jesus returns. Instead of the whining and complaining that some people call prayer, adopt a wartime mentality and let the roar of power prayer erupt from the depths of your spirit to wage effective warfare and pull down the strongholds of Satan.

5. Assert Your Determination to Win

Peter concludes this passage on the attributes of a finisher by declaring that the God of all grace who has called you to His eternal glory will "perfect, establish, strengthen, and settle" you (1 Peter 5:10). In other words, Peter declares that you will win if you determine to do so.

On one occasion my dad and I were discussing his experiences in World War II as part of the famous C Company of the Eighty-second Airborne Division. It was a contingent that once fought for more than three hundred days continuously without a break despite numerous casualties, and my dad was one of a handful of men who survived the battle.

I asked Dad, "What kept you going during that long siege when you saw your comrades falling and the battle raging fierce around you?"

"The knowledge that we had to win is what kept me going," he answered.

"Why did you believe this so strongly?" I questioned.

"I thought about Hitler and his Third Reich," said Dad. "Then I thought about my mother and brothers living under his dominion for the rest of their lives. I decided there was no alternative—we had to win!"

Today we fight an enemy who is more evil than Hitler. What happens to you, your children, and their children should we not win? Resolve within you that the battle is worth winning. Use the skills you have gained in power prayer to war against the enemy with the spirit of a finisher. Expect to keep your marriage together and to see your children grow up as godly men and women. Expect to see new souls added to the kingdom through your ministry. Determine that you will have your needs abundantly met, be successful, and walk in a spirit of forgiveness. Expect to see God save, heal, deliver, and overcome all the powers of the evil one. In short, *determine to win!*

The Infallible Posture

We have learned that power prayer brings us into a tremendous anointing of intercession that permits the Spirit of the Father to rise up within us and address every threat of the enemy. F. J. Hugel notes, "It has often been said that prayer is the greatest force in the universe. This is no exaggeration. It will bear constant repetition. In this atomic age when forces are being released that stagger the thought and imagination of man, it is well to remember that prayer transcends all other forces."[4]

It is no longer necessary for us to walk in the futility of our minds, having our understanding darkened, being alienated from the life of God because of the lies of the false father (Eph. 4:17–18). We know how to release the anointing of power prayer. In so doing, we assume an infallible posture in the midst of battle: "So use every piece of God's armor to resist the enemy whenever he attacks, and when it is all over, you will still be standing up" (Eph. 6:13 TLB).

Prior to starting Part 3, take some time to pray about these qualities of a finisher. They are vital to receiving the next dimension of the prayer anointing, that of prevailing prayer.

190

PART 3

Releasing
the Anointing
of Prevailing
Prayer

27

Pray Without Ceasing

The man was knocking on the closed door expectantly, but there was no answer. His knocks echoed down the long hallway. Finally, he kicked the door in exasperation, shrugged his shoulders, and sadly walked away.

God gave me that vision, and when I saw it, I cried out of my spirit, "Lord, what am I seeing?" God told me it was a picture of how many of us struggle in our prayer lives. We want to pray effectively, but we repeatedly come up against barriers like that closed door. With increased determination, we continue knocking and even try to barge through in our own strength, but it doesn't work. In sad defeat, many of us give up.

I could readily identify with the man I saw in my vision because for years I had struggled with my prayer life. When God gave me that vision, I asked Him, "What must I do to get the people through the door?"

In Parts 1 and 2, you received the anointing for personal and power prayer. In this part, you will experience the third dimension of a successful prayer life, the anointing for prevailing prayer. I will teach you how to get through the door. You will learn how to dialogue with your heavenly Father, pray in the Spirit, set purpose in prayer, and use dynamic trigger points for perpetual prayer. In the final chapter, you will arrive at a turning point in your prayer life as you experience the impartation of a prayer anointing that will empower you to "ask, seek, and knock"—and the door will open to you!

The Call to Perpetual Prayer

The Bible is filled with appeals for perpetual prayer, or to "pray without ceasing" as 1 Thessalonians 5:17 expresses it. In Ephesians 6:18, we find the Christian soldier equipped for battle with a constant spirit of prayer, "Praying always with all prayer and supplication in the Spirit, being watchful to this end with all perseverance and supplication."

We are admonished to "continue earnestly in prayer, being vigilant in it with thanksgiving" (Col. 4:2). Romans 12:12 indicates we should be "continuing steadfastly in prayer," 1 Corinthians 7:5 instructs us to give ourselves to fasting and prayer, and Jesus told us to "pray always" (Luke 21:36). These Scriptures do not present a picture of the closed doors many of us seem to encounter in prayer. Rather, our heavenly Father promises, "Those who seek me diligently will find me" (Prov. 8:17), and "You will seek Me and find Me, when you search for Me with all your heart" (Jer. 29:13).

Concerning these scriptural directives, Charles Spurgeon wrote, "Prayer must not be our chance work, but our daily business—our habit and vocation. As artists give themselves to their models, and poets to their classical pursuits, so must we addict ourselves to prayer. We must be immersed in prayer as in our element, and so pray without ceasing."[1]

Examples of Prevailing Prayer

The Bible is filled with examples of men and women who persevered in prayer. Abraham prevailed in prayer for a son despite his age and the barrenness of Sarah's womb, and he also interceded repeatedly for the evil city of Sodom. Isaac prayed for Rebekah to conceive, and Jacob wrestled all night in prayer, and their lives were never again the same.

Moses persevered in prayer during a lengthy battle between Israel and the Amalekites, assuring the victory for God's people. When

Israel sinned, he stood between them and God's judgment, doggedly interceding in their behalf. A barren woman named Hannah continued in earnest prayer until God gave her a son. King David declared, "I give myself to prayer." Elijah prayed repeatedly until a drought ceased and it began to rain.

The disciples determined they would give themselves continually to prayer. Believers prayed without ceasing for Peter to be delivered from prison. Jesus often continued all night in prayer to God, and in the Garden of Gethsemane He prayed the same petition three times "saying the same words" (Matt. 26:44).

Three Issues to Settle

As a loving earthly dad longs for communication with his children, so your heavenly Father seeks those who will enter into the intimacy of continual, prevailing prayer. The Bible provides clear directives about how we can experience this relationship, but before we move on to study them in subsequent chapters, three basic issues must be settled. They are key issues that are fundamental to receiving the anointing of prevailing prayer. They were revealed to me after I saw the vision of the man knocking on the door. These three issues deal with your past, your present, and your future.

Past

The first basic issue that must be settled is your past. You cannot boldly access the throne of God with a spirit of shame because the definition of *persistent prayer* is actually "shameless asking." In chapter 21, we dealt with the forces of inherited, imposed, institutional, individual, and incessant shame. We saw how Jesus bore our shame so that we do not have to carry it, and we took three steps to break the shame barrier by acting against shame, addressing it, and asking for a new passionate relationship with God. If for some reason you have not yet settled this issue of the shame of your past, then review chapter 21 again. Only when the force of shame is broken can you come boldly into the throne room asking, seeking, and knocking in shameless persistence.

Present

The second basic issue essential to the anointing of prevailing prayer is to make a commitment to pray each day using the model prayer Jesus taught. When you use this seven-point pattern of prayer, it functions much like the seven major arteries in your body, bearing life and health to your spiritual being.

In 1989, I was in Israel conducting a prayer seminar, and I used this example comparing the model prayer to the seven major arteries of the human body. At midnight there was a knock on my hotel door, and when I opened it, there stood a rabbi. He was a secret believer in Jesus Christ who had been in my seminar that day, and he came immediately to the point of his visit.

"Where did you come up with the idea of there being seven arteries of the spirit that parallel the arteries of the human body?" he asked.

"I discovered it by studying the seven major parts of the model prayer taught by Jesus," I answered.

The rabbi was thoughtful for a moment, and then he said, "The reason I ask this is that we rabbis have taught for years that there were seven major areas of man's spirit. Until today, however, we did not know how to access them."

The parts of the model prayer taught by Jesus are the seven spiritual arteries that channel mobility and strength to your spiritual being. If these arteries are blocked, you are rendered ineffective in prevailing prayer. You keep them functioning by praying the Lord's Prayer each day.

In Part 2, we moved into the anointing of power prayer, and now we are purposing to receive the anointing of prevailing prayer, but neither replaces the model Jesus gave us for daily personal prayer. Samuel Chadwick notes, "As the scholar can never in all his after studies or learning dispense with his ABC's, and as the alphabet gives form, color, and expression to all after learning, impregnating all and grounding all, so the learner in Christ can never dispense with the Lord's Prayer. But he may make it form the basis of his higher praying."[2]

If you are to move into the anointing of prevailing prayer, you must make a commitment now—in the present—to pray the model prayer each day.

Future

The third issue that must be settled if you are to persevere in prayer concerns the future. You must obey in the future without fear.

I will help you develop a hearing ear, which will enable you to recognize and respond to God's voice.

The Fire of Passion

Fire is one of the emblems representing the Holy Spirit, and as such it devours the spirit of false religion that makes prayer a ritualistic act of legalism. Religion is the human attempt to reach God, it drives you to try in your own strength, and then when you fail, it induces shame. Religion says, "You can do it on your own," but when you fail, it says, "Look how bad you are." The people who crucified Jesus were as religious as those who came with rocks in hand to stone the woman caught in adultery.

When you take the three steps I have shared in this chapter—release the past, pray in the present, and obey in the future—the fire of the Holy Spirit will ignite a passion for prayer in your life. The rich young ruler who came to Jesus had religion, but he lacked passion. His possessions were greater than his passion for God. What are you most passionate about? Is it a hobby? A person? Your job? When you allow the fire of the Holy Spirit to burn these roots out of your life and ignite a passion for praying, you will succeed in prevailing prayer.

Moses received his commission when he drew near a burning bush where God spoke words that ignited his spiritual passion. The prophet Elijah persevered in prayer because he knew the God who answered by fire. Malachi caught a vision of the refining fire of God. John the Baptist spoke of One who would baptize with the Holy Spirit and fire. On the day of Pentecost, the Holy Spirit appeared as cloven tongues of fire, and during the mighty revelation given to the apostle John on the island of Patmos, he described the eyes of God as fire. We are counseled to buy "gold refined in the fire" (Rev. 3:18), and the Scriptures proclaim that our God is a "consuming fire" (Deut. 4:24).

Submission to the purifying fire of the Holy Spirit breaks the force of religion that says to just keep trying harder. It releases you from struggling in prayer, making it your passion and the motivating force of your daily existence.

E. M. Bounds comments regarding this passion ignited by the fire of the Holy Spirit: "The Holy Spirit comes as a fire, to dwell in us. . . .

If our religion does not set us on fire, it is because we have frozen hearts. . . . It takes heat and fervency and meteoric fire, to push through to the upper heavens where God dwells."[3]

Make These Declarations

As you conclude this chapter, say these declarations aloud right now:

- "I release the shame of my past."
- "I make a commitment in the present to pray through the model prayer each day."
- "I will not be afraid to obey God in the future."

When these three issues are settled, the door to your prayer capacity will be opened to you. You will also be ready to move on to the basic principles of prevailing prayer I share in the next chapter.

28

—✦—

Principles of Prevailing Prayer

$\mathbb{A}$t that time Jesus answered and said, 'I thank You, Father, Lord of heaven and earth, that You have hidden these things from the wise and prudent and have revealed them to babes'" (Matt. 11:25). If you examine the passage where this verse occurs, you will see that no one asked Jesus a question, yet it says He "answered." So who spoke to Him?

Although there is no record of it, the speaker was obviously the heavenly Father, for He is the One to whom Jesus addressed the answer. Charles Spurgeon comments regarding Jesus that "God spoke into His heart so often, so continually, that it was not a circumstance singular enough to be recorded. . . . May we likewise have silent fellowship with the Father, so that often we may answer Him, and though the world knows not to whom we speak, we may be responding to that secret voice unheard of any other ear."[1]

Such dialogue with the Father, the nightlong prayer sessions, and the record of intercession in the Garden of Gethsemane evidence that Jesus lived under the continual anointing of prayer. He shared the principles that govern such prevailing prayer in two parables preserved in the New Testament record.

The Needy Host

The first parable is an account of a needy host who called on a friend at midnight. Jesus related this story immediately after teaching the model prayer to His disciples (Luke 11:5–8). It was late at night when an unexpected guest arrived, and his host had nothing to feed him. The host went to a friend's house and knocked on the door with boldness and confidence. His request was specific—"lend me three loaves"—and he continued to knock relentlessly until he received what he needed, even though his friend grew a bit irritated with him. Matthew Henry declares, "If importunity could prevail thus with a man who was angry at it, much more with a God who is infinitely more kind and ready to do good to us than we are to one another, and is not angry at our importunity."[2]

This is the only place in the New Testament where the word *importunity* occurs. It comes from the Latin word *importunas,* which means "troublesome or impudence." In Greek, the word means "shamelessness" or a freedom that enables a person to ask repeatedly. This illustrates why I have stressed the importance of breaking through the shame barrier. Curtis Mitchell explains, "Thus importunate asking involves dogged, tenacious persistence reaching the point of shamelessness. This is the way Jesus taught us to bring our petitions to the Father."[3]

Jesus drew a direct correlation between this parable and persistent prayer, telling His disciples:

> *I say to you, ask, and it will be given to you; seek, and you will find; knock, and it will be opened to you. For everyone who asks receives, and he who seeks finds, and to him who knocks it will be opened. If a son asks for bread from any father among you, will he give him a stone? Or if he asks for a fish, will he give him a serpent instead of a fish? Or if he asks for an egg, will he offer him a scorpion? If you then, being evil, know how to give good gifts to your children, how much more will your heavenly Father give the Holy Spirit to those who ask Him! (Luke 11:9–13).*

The verbs *ask, seek,* and *knock* imply continuous action and can be translated "keep on asking, keep on seeking, keep on knocking." The word *knock* pictures a man beating on the door with vigorous blows. The difference between the man in the parable and the one I saw in my vision is that this individual has mastered the persistence that elicits a positive response. The door is opened to him.

Jesus then gave an illustration of a son asking his father for bread, a fish, and an egg. Each object is similar in appearance to the object suggested as a substitute—a stone, a serpent, a scorpion—reflecting the deception of the false father analyzed in Part 2 of this book. If an earthly father responds to his child's continued appeals, how much more our heavenly Father answers our requests. Curtis Mitchell comments, "If earthly dads, with all their faults, will give good things to their children, how much more can we depend upon our perfect heavenly Father to answer the fervent, persistent petitions of His children in the best possible manner."[4]

The Widow and the Unjust Judge

The second parable Jesus taught to illustrate prevailing prayer is recorded in Luke 18:2-8, and it was prefaced by the admonition that "men always ought to pray and not lose heart" (Luke 18:1). The word *ought* reflects necessity; *always* means "continually"; and *not lose heart* means "do not turn, be cowardly, or give up." This parable concerns a needy widow who sought assistance from an unjust judge. The poor widow had no political clout authorizing her appeal to the judge, yet she boldly went to him with her desperate need. We are not told the details of her request, only that it was an appeal to get justice from her adversary.

Herbert Lockyer observes, "Her words were few, eight only, 'I pray thee avenge me of mine adversary.' Her cry was short and explicit. She had nothing to say about her widowhood, her family, or divine judgment upon unjust judges. All she wanted was one thing—justice meted out to her adversary."[5]

The judge in this parable is called unjust because he had a reputation of fearing neither God nor man. In the end, however, the judge granted the woman's request because of her "continual coming."

The unjust judge decided, "This woman is driving me crazy! I am going to grant her request just to get rid of her." He complied, lest she "weary" him. The word for weary in Greek means "to come to blows, to strike under the eyes, or bruise." Literally, the phrase means "give me a black eye," which certainly suggests a rather intense level of persistence. To avoid that, the judge granted her request.

If importunity or shameless asking sways people who are evil, how much more will our righteous, loving heavenly Father be influenced by the prevailing prayers of His children? The greatest evidence of faith at the time of the Lord's return to this earth will be that of persevering prayer. The person who truly believes will be communing with God continually.

The Parables Compared

Both parables of Jesus are similar in design, although they reflect different circumstances. Crisis prompted both petitioners to act, and both went directly to the source of assistance rather than try to get someone else to intercede for them. Both were specific in their requests, one asking for "three loaves" and the other for justice from her adversary. Both petitioners were in desperate circumstances, and when people are desperate, they are persistent or shameless in asking.

The needy host and the widow continued to present their petitions until they were granted. Their strategy is not to be confused with vain repetitions against which Christ cautioned, for those who employ such repetitions believe they will be heard if they keep talking. Persistent petition and vain repetitions involve repeating a request, but the motivation is different. The former is birthed by intense need, the latter by a desire to manipulate.

Both parables stress the principle of importunity or dogged persistence. Curtis Mitchell speaks to this point:

> The concept of importunity and dogged persistence is certainly one of the more emphasized and clearly delineated aspects of Jesus' teaching. Strangely, some men have tried to deny persistence in prayer altogether. They have argued that to ask over and over again for the same thing day after day is actually a demonstration of a lack of faith. It is contended that a person should ask God for something once and then quietly sit back in faith and wait for God to answer. Such thinking may be logical (on a human level), but it is certainly not Biblical.[6]

By this point you may be saying to yourself, Now that I know the basic principles I am ready to prevail in prayer for my answers!

202

The disciples of Jesus, to whom these parables and principles were taught, also thought they were ready. But one dark night, in the stillness of a garden called Gethsemane, they learned that the spirit is willing, but the flesh is weak.

29

The Spirit Is Willing

The deep shadows of darkness were penetrated by thin slivers of moonlight that filtered through the gnarled limbs of the ancient olive trees in Gethsemane. Their soft rays illuminated the kneeling figure of a man who was praying with tremendous intensity while a short distance away His disciples slept with unconcern. "Watch and pray, lest you enter into temptation," Jesus warned when He returned to find them dozing. "The spirit indeed is willing, but the flesh is weak" (Matt. 26:41).

In this brief statement, "The spirit indeed is willing, but the flesh is weak," Jesus summarized both the problem and the solution of prevailing prayer. The enigma is that many people know the principles and have an intense desire to prevail in prayer, but most find it a struggle to do so. Jesus explained that because "the flesh" is weak, its frailty affects spiritual desires. The obvious solution, then, is that the spirit must be allowed to rule the flesh.

The Spirit Versus the Flesh

We all have a carnal or fleshly way of thinking, an inherited nature that can be traced back to Adam and Eve. The Bible declares that in the beginning there was God, who is a Spirit. The Spirit of God moved across the void of this planet, and then the Word came forth proclaiming, "Let there be. . . ." First came the Spirit, then came the Word, and the result was darkness and light, land and waters, plants and animals. God created Adam and Eve in the same way. They were made spirit when God breathed life into them and then they became flesh.

Adam and Eve originally enjoyed perfect relationship with the heavenly Father because their interaction occurred on a Spirit-to-spirit basis when the Lord came to commune with them each evening. At the foot of the tree of the knowledge of good and evil, however, the couple lost the supernatural ability. Satan tempted Eve to partake of the fruit, promising that it would enable her to "know all things." God warned, "Don't eat of the tree, lest you die." When Adam and Eve partook of the forbidden fruit, they did not immediately die physically, although that was an end result of their sin. Instead, they died spiritually and no longer had the divine ability to communicate Spirit-to-spirit with God. The carnal mind ("you will know") dominated the spiritual being.

Several generations later at the Tower of Babel, sinful people effected a diabolical plan to build a tower to reach the dwelling place of God in heaven (Gen. 11:1–9). The people still spoke the language originally given to Adam and Eve, and because they were united by the heavenly tongue, God declared that nothing would be impossible to them. So the Lord confounded their language, and the people eventually scattered across the face of the earth.

Jesus Christ came to earth to restore human fellowship with the Father, and His death and subsequent resurrection effected reconciliation and redemption from the curses of sin. While Jesus was here on earth, He was the divine communication from God to humankind, for He was the Word personified.

Prior to returning to heaven, Jesus promised to send the Holy Spirit in a new dimension to enable the restoration of the Spirit-to-spirit communication that Adam lost. Acts 2 records that when the promise was fulfilled and the Holy Spirit descended upon believers in the Upper Room at Jerusalem, a unique and interesting phenomenon occurred. The believers spoke supernaturally in various languages unknown to their intellect.

Spirit First, Then the Word

From the beginning of time, the divine pattern established by God was Spirit first, then the Word. God's Spirit moved on the earth, then the Word came forth and creation occurred. Re-creation, or the new birth experience, occurs in the same way. First you are drawn by the Spirit, then the Word results in regeneration (John 6:44). Jesus said that we must first worship in spirit, then in truth. The apostle John was "in the Spirit on the Lord's Day," and then he heard behind him "a loud voice" (Rev. 1:10).

This pattern of Spirit, then Word is repeatedly illustrated in the Scriptures, but what generally happens is that we try with the natural mind to do what can be done only in the atmosphere of the Spirit. That was the problem experienced by the disciples in the Garden of Gethsemane when they tried to enter into prevailing prayer.

This tendency of mental domination is not only an inherited aspect of our carnal nature, but it also reflects how many of us have been taught. In Bible school, I was instructed to study the Word to get a message to preach and then ask God to bless it. I have subsequently learned, by observing the pattern revealed in the Bible, that I should receive a message in my spirit and then go to the Word to develop it.

That happened on what has come to be called the day of Pentecost. The Holy Spirit descended in the Upper Room at Jerusalem, and then the word came forth. Peter, who never went to seminary and a short time previously denied and deserted Jesus, experienced the Spirit and preached a powerful word that resulted in the conversion of three thousand people.

When the Holy Spirit came in this new dimension, revelation began to flow from the inside out again rather than from the outside in, from the spirit to the mind rather than the mind to the spirit. This enables the human spirit to be empowered by God's Spirit and dominate the flesh. Much like the reestablishment of contact between an estranged child and an earthly dad, communication was restored with our heavenly Father.

The evidence was that the disciples began to speak in languages unknown to their intellect. The Holy Spirit bypassed their mental faculties, men who previously could not tarry even one hour in prayer became dynamic prayer warriors. They were praying not only with their minds but also with their spirits.

The Door Is Open

Remember my vision of the man knocking on a closed door and receiving no answer? Similar frustration occurs as long as we try to prevail in prayer through our intellect. I experienced this in my prayer life because even though my spirit was willing, my flesh (mind, will, intellect) was weak. Eventually, I discovered that the only way to break through the barrier is to let the spirit take precedence over the flesh.

E. M. Bounds comments that praying from your spirit is more than just habitual or routine prayer: "Prayer must be habitual, but much more than a habit. It is the expression of a relation to God, a yearning for divine communion. It is the outward and upward flow of the inward life toward its original fountain. It is an assertion of the soul's paternity, a claiming of the sonship which links man to the eternal."[1]

The spirit has instant access to your vocal cords just as your mind does. Therefore, a prayer can come out of your spirit, bypass the mind, and use your tongue to communicate directly to God. This is called praying in the Spirit. God's response can then be registered in your mind, enabling you to pray with understanding (1 Cor. 14:13–15).

In essence, to pray without ceasing and prevail in intercession, we, like the disciples, must be willing to go out of our minds.

How to Go Out of
Your Mind

Y ou may smile as you look at this chapter title and think to yourself, *I really don't need anyone to tell me how to go out of my mind. My struggle is to hold on to my sanity!* But I believe that by the time you finish this chapter, you will understand the importance of going out of your mind, and you will be ready to deliberately do it!

Going out of your mind is a whole different way of spiritual life from what most people are used to because, as we learned in the last chapter, the majority of us are ruled by the intellect instead of the spirit. The carnal mind says, "You can't pray without ceasing." The spiritual mind says, "Oh, yes, you can!"

The Bible indicates that as a believer, you have the mind of Christ (1 Cor. 2:16), and the prayer language of the Holy Spirit enables you to release it by circumventing the carnal mind, which is led by logic. Your prayer language triggers the release of the mind of Christ within you and permits you to go out of your carnal mind, so to speak.

Christ's death on the cross broke every curse associated with human sin, including the diversities of tongues imposed at Babel. The baptism of the Holy Spirit with the physical sign of other tongues restores our original heavenly language. When we communicate with God in this heavenly tongue, the Holy Spirit interprets God's message to us.

An excellent example is Rev. Oral Roberts, a Pentecostal healing evangelist who one day walked across an empty stretch of Oklahoma land while communing with God in the prayer language of the Holy Spirit. When he paused to listen, the Holy Spirit spoke God's words to his mind. God said, "Build Me a university on this land." Oral Roberts went out of his mind and prayed with his spirit. My son and some twenty-five thousand other graduates are beneficiaries of the word he received from God.

The Baptism of the Holy Spirit

Receiving this prayer language is an experience called the baptism of the Holy Spirit. The word *baptize* as used in the Bible means to "entirely immerse or submerge in something." The New Testament mentions several baptisms, including Christ's baptism of suffering (Luke 12:50), water baptism (Matt. 3:11–17), and the baptism of the Holy Spirit (Acts 2:1–13).

In the Old Testament, the Holy Spirit came upon men and women of God, but Jesus told His followers that although the Holy Spirit was with them, He would someday be in them (John 14:17). The disciples were instructed to wait in Jerusalem until they received this new dimension of baptism or spiritual immersion in the Holy Spirit.

The Evidence of the Baptism

Jesus compared the Holy Spirit, who is invisible to the natural eye, to the wind (John 3:8). Although the wind is invisible, the effects it produces can be seen and heard. When the wind blows, dust rises from the ground, tree leaves rustle, waves of the sea crash against the shore, and clouds move across the sky.

So it is with the Holy Spirit. Even though He is invisible, the effects of the Holy Spirit can be seen and heard. One of these effects is the prayer language evidenced on the day of Pentecost (Acts 2), at the infilling of Cornelius and his family (Acts 10:44–46), and in the Holy Spirit baptism of the converts at Ephesus (Acts 19:6). As we compare these passages, we see one physical sign common to all three: Those who received the baptism of the Holy Spirit spoke with other tongues.

Types of Tongues

These tongues of the Holy Spirit can be languages known to people as those exhibited on the day of Pentecost: "Then they were all amazed and marveled, saying to one another, 'Look, are not all these who speak Galileans? And how is it that we hear, each in our own language in which we were born?'" (Acts 2:7–8).

The prayer language can also be in a language unknown to people, which is directed to God: "For he who speaks in a tongue does not speak to men but to God, for no one understands him; however, in the spirit he speaks mysteries" (1 Cor. 14:2).

The Spirit Prevails

The importance of the prayer language is revealed in the following passage:

> *Likewise the Spirit also helps in our weaknesses. For we do not know what we should pray for as we ought, but the Spirit Himself makes intercession for us with groanings which cannot be uttered. Now He who searches the hearts knows what the mind of the Spirit is, because He makes intercession for the saints according to the will of God (Rom. 8:26–27).*

Tongues do not make you superior to others, nor do they make you inferior. The experience is not necessary for salvation, and it is not a cure-all for every spiritual malady or a solution to all problems. Tongues are a dynamic tool of spiritual communication.

Although you use the model prayer regularly in personal prayer, there are times when you don't know exactly how to pray about certain things. At these times the Holy Spirit communicates directly to the Father through your prayer language. Because your intellect is bypassed, you make intercession according to the perfect will of God.

Purposes of the Prayer Language

Here are some of the powerful purposes of the prayer language in prevailing prayer:

Exaltation

Jesus said, "When He, the Spirit of truth, has come . . . He will glorify Me" (John 16:13–14). The prayer language of the Holy Spirit enables you to praise God and exalt Jesus Christ. You are able to worship in spirit and truth because you bypass the carnal deception of your mind. When you run out of words in your language and cannot think of anything else to say, release the Holy Spirit to glorify the Lord.

Impartation

After the disciples were baptized in the Holy Spirit and received their prayer language, a tremendous impartation of spiritual gifts and power ensued. The prayer language catapults you into new dimensions of the Spirit you will never otherwise know. It is a trigger to release the impartation of spiritual gifts, and it is the impetus for spiritual power. Jesus said, "You shall receive power when the Holy Spirit has come upon you" (Acts 1:8).

Intercession

When we pray in tongues, the Holy Spirit intercedes according to the will of God, and the Spirit "helps in our weaknesses" (Rom. 8:26). You may have prayed for your marriage so long that you just don't know what to say anymore. Your financial situation may be in such a mess that you don't know what to ask God for, much less how to straighten it out. That is when you need to let the Holy Spirit make intercession according to the will of God.

Are there times in prayer when you could use an advocate, someone to plead with God on your behalf? The Holy Spirit has already been designated to this position. The word *comforter* means "called to one's side for the purpose of giving aid," similar to a legal assistant or counsel for the defense in a court of law. The Holy Spirit intercedes for you here on earth, and Jesus intercedes in your behalf in heaven.

If you are to receive the Holy Spirit's help, you must admit your weaknesses. You will never receive assistance if you are too self-reliant or self-righteous to admit your need. When you come to the place that you admit you don't know, your spirit will bypass your intellect, and the Holy Spirit will intercede because He *does* know. The Spirit knows your background, your shame, your emotional scars and hurts, so He can adequately represent your case before God.

After you pray in the Spirit, pause to listen. The Holy Spirit will testify to your spirit what God says, for the Bible indicates that "when He, the Spirit of truth, has come, He will guide you into all truth; for He will not speak on His own authority, but whatever He hears He will speak" (John 16:13).

Edification

To *edify* means to "build up or to promote spiritual growth." In his brief but poignant message warning of deceptive conditions believers would face, Jude admonished, "Beloved, building yourselves up on your most holy faith, praying in the Holy Spirit, keep yourselves in the love of God" (Jude 20–21). The Bible warns that in the end times iniquity will abound, and many will become cold and uncaring. As we rapidly approach these devastating times, the way to edify your faith and love is to pray in the Holy Spirit.

Revelation

Praying in the Spirit moves you from tracking your life through carnal reasoning into the dimension of being led by the Spirit. Once you learn to release your prayer language fluently in intercession, pray for understanding and learn to interpret what you said to your spirit. When you pray in the Spirit, you are talking to God. After you pray in the Spirit, wait for an interpretation because that is how God speaks to you. The Holy Spirit may quicken a Scripture verse to your mind, give you a mental image, a phrase, one or two words, or a detailed message from God.

Not everything you pray in your prayer language will be interpreted to you. As Harold Horton notes, "It is obviously not necessary that everything we utter in private in other tongues should be clear to our understanding; but in circumstances where an interpretation is necessary or desirable, God will give one, that the understanding might profit as well as the spirit."[1]

Restoration

The prayer language of the Holy Spirit provides spiritual rest and restoration. Isaiah prophesied,

For with stammering lips and another tongue
He will speak to this people,
To whom He said, "This is the rest with which
You may cause the weary to rest,"
And, "This is the refreshing" (Isa. 28:11–12).

We are warned, "Therefore, since a promise remains of entering His rest, let us fear lest any of you seem to have come short of it" (Heb. 4:1).

Objections to Tongues

Many fail to enter into the spiritual rest of the prayer language because they succumb to objections against speaking in tongues. Here are some common objections to prayer language of the Holy Spirit:

"Every Christian Has the Holy Spirit"

Some believe that the Holy Spirit is received at the time of conversion and that no further experience is necessary to receive the baptism of the Holy Spirit. Consider, however, the example of the believers at Samaria who were converted through Philip's ministry (Acts 8:14–17). The people of Samaria heard the gospel, believed, and were baptized in water through the ministry of Philip. Later, they received the baptism of the Holy Spirit through the ministry of Peter and John.

Acts 19:1–6 describes how Paul went to Ephesus and met people described as "disciples." The first question Paul asked was, "Did you receive the Holy Spirit when you believed?" If people automatically received the baptism of the Holy Spirit when they received salvation, it would have been foolish for Paul to ask this question.

"Do All Speak with Tongues?"

Another objection to speaking in tongues results from misunderstanding a question of Paul: "Do all speak with tongues?" (1 Cor. 12:30). The answer to this is, "No, all do not speak with tongues." But in this passage Paul was speaking not of the prayer language of the Holy Spirit but of a spiritual gift of diversities of tongues (1 Cor.

12:4–11). This is a supernatural ability to give special messages to the church in tongues under the power of the Holy Spirit. Although everyone can experience the prayer language of the Holy Spirit, not everyone receives the special gift of diversities of tongues.

"I Am Afraid"

Some believers do not seek the baptism of the Holy Spirit because they are afraid they will receive an experience that is not of God. The Bible teaches, however, that our heavenly Father's goodness surpasses that of earthly fathers and He will not give His children anything that would harm them. The prayer language of the Holy Spirit is a fatherly provision of God for His children (Matt. 7:7–11).

"It Is Just an Emotional Experience"

Another objection to speaking in tongues is that it is an emotional experience. God created you an emotional being. Conversion does not eliminate your emotions; it frees them from the control of sin. The word *joy* in Scripture is closely associated with the Holy Spirit as exemplified in Acts 13:52 where it notes that "the disciples were filled with joy and with the Holy Spirit." Some people react with great joy to the baptism of the Holy Spirit because they are naturally more emotional than others. They may shout, laugh, or exhibit other responses. How one reacts emotionally to this experience is usually related to one's emotional tendencies.

Going Out of Your Mind

On the day of Pentecost, God reinstated the pure language of communication people lost through sin. The Holy Spirit came down from heaven and completely immersed (baptized) believers who were waiting for His coming as they had been commanded by Jesus. Peter said the experience fulfilled the promise of God made through the prophet Joel:

> *And it shall come to pass afterward*
> *That I will pour out My Spirit on all flesh;*
> *Your sons and your daughters shall prophesy,*
> *Your old men shall dream dreams,*

Your young men shall see visions.
And also on My menservants and on My maidservants
I will pour out My Spirit in those days (Joel 2:28–29).

Male and female, young and old are included in this outpouring of the Holy Spirit. They are to prophesy, have dreams, and see visions as they experience continual communion with God.

This communion is called *koinonia*, which means "having in common, partnership, fellowship recognized and enjoyed, a participation in what is derived from the Holy Spirit."[2] Revelation 3:20 expresses this type of fellowship in a picture of two people sitting down and sharing a meal together, getting to know each other, drawing from each other's spirit, and conversing intimately.

On the day of Pentecost, Peter indicated the experience was promised to his listeners, their children, those who were far off, and as many as the Lord God should call (Acts 2:38–39). The baptism of the Holy Spirit is a national promise ("to you"—the Jewish people), a family promise ("to your children"), and a universal promise ("to all who are afar off, as many as the Lord our God will call").

Are you ready to receive this wonderful communication tool that enables you to go out of your mind? You do not have to tarry or beg for it. Just as an earthly father delights to give his children presents, your heavenly Father will give you this gift if you ask for it (Luke 11:13). Just open your mouth and speak out by faith, and your new language will come forth. It will come not from your mind but from your spirit, so don't try to think about what you are saying. You may experience stammering lips first, but if you continue to yield your tongue to the Holy Spirit, He will speak through you words foreign to your understanding (Isa. 28:11). Some people receive a fluent language immediately, while others receive only a few words or phrases at first. Whatever God gives you, speak it forth, for the kingdom principle is that you must use what you have if you are to receive more. Your mind has been accustomed to being in control. Now let the Spirit control you.

It may seem strange to you at first, but praying in the Spirit is not unusual to God. Many of us are so dominated by our minds that if we can't figure it out intellectually, we will refuse it. Yet there are many things—like microwaves and computers—that we use each day without comprehending how they work. Why not in the spiritual world? In the next chapter, we will see how going out of your mind is fundamental to prevailing prayer because it results in an ear to hear what the Spirit is saying.

31

The Hearing Ear

Have you ever tried to carry on a one-sided conversation? Perhaps you were talking to your mate or a friend, but the person was distracted or ignored you. You probably became quite frustrated when no response was forthcoming.

Prayer—the kind that prevails with the anointing you seek—is more than a patterned monologue. Prevailing prayer is a dialogue, and to enter into it, you must learn to hear as well as speak because a one-sided conversation will not last long.

In the Garden of Gethsemane, Jesus prevailed in prayer because He was in intense dialogue with His heavenly Father. The disciples, although willing in spirit, slept and eventually succumbed to temptation because they had not yet entered into the anointing of prevailing prayer. They were more concerned with their tired flesh than with the divine purposes of God. William Barclay comments,

> *The great fault of prayer is that it can so easily become self-centered and self-seeking. We can be so busy thinking of what we want that we have no time to think of what God wants. We can be so concerned with our own desires that we never think of God's will. We can be so busy talking to God that we never give God the chance to talk to us. We can be so busy telling God that we never stop to listen to God.*[1]

Ears to Hear

If you are to dialogue in prevailing prayer and cultivate a Father-child relationship with God, you must develop spiritual ears so you can hear His voice. One time God revealed to a friend of mine that I had big "Mickey Mouse" ears in the spiritual realm. He told my friend, "Larry is able to hear My voice because he has developed his spiritual ears." Jesus said, "My sheep hear My voice, and I know them, and they follow Me" (John 10:27). A healthy sheep has big ears. A sheep knows the voice of the shepherd and is not lured away from the safety of the fold by an enemy.

I want to help you develop your spiritual ears because a thief would come to snatch you away from your Father's care. The secret to remaining safe in the Father's fold is coming to know His voice. Your heavenly Father wants you to develop big, healthy spiritual ears so you can recognize His voice as easily as you do the voice of your earthly dad.

You need to have a hearing ear because in everyday situations, you are constantly making choices that determine whether or not you will continue to function in the perfect will of God and live under the anointing of prevailing prayer. Each minor decision affects your future destiny, so it is vital that you come to know God's voice. If you are to hear God's voice, you must believe four basic things: (1) there is a God; (2) He communicates with human beings; (3) God has something to say; and (4) you can recognize His voice when He speaks.

The Biblical Record

The Bible, which is the inspired written record of our heavenly Father's communication to us, confirms each of these premises.

Open your Bible to the book of Genesis and read chapters 1—3, which record the creation of the world and the first human beings, Adam and Eve. You will note that in the beginning, "God said"—and He hasn't stopped speaking since that time. God created the entire universe through the spoken word, and He gave specific instructions to its first residents, Adam and Eve. They received direct words from God, not just a vague impression. Adam and Eve had no preachers, no organized church to attend, and no written revelation of God's Word. They actually heard the voice of God.

When sin became so rampant on earth that God decided to send judgment through the Flood, He gave specific instructions to Noah on how to build the ark and what animals to take with him.

Read the story of Abraham in Genesis 11—25, and you will note that Abraham had a continual dialogue with God concerning the Promised Land and his promised son. Then there came the day when God told Abraham to offer his son, Isaac, as a burnt sacrifice. Can you imagine how difficult that was for a father?

But Abraham knew God's voice, so he obeyed. As Abraham raised the knife in the air to perform the sacrifice, the angel of the Lord (the preincarnate Christ) spoke to Abraham again and said, "Do not lay your hand on the lad, or do anything to him" (Gen. 22:10–12). Abraham could have declared with dogmatic self-righteousness, "I've already heard God speak, so I am not going to deviate from what I've heard." But Abraham was accustomed to listening to God. He immediately recognized His voice and responded in obedience.

A detailed record of God's dialogue with Moses appears in Exodus 3—4. Moses continued to hear God's voice throughout the wilderness journey, and he received the revelations of the Law and the tabernacle at Mount Sinai.

The entire book of Judges focuses on people raised up and directed by God's voice. Especially significant is the account in Judges 13 where God spoke to Manoah, told him that he would have a son, and provided specific instructions on how to raise him.

The word of the Lord was rare in the days when God first spoke to Samuel (1 Sam. 3:2–10). God was speaking, but no one was paying attention. God found in young Samuel a person who would listen. At first, Samuel assumed Eli or someone else was talking to him. That often happens when you begin to hear God's voice. You assume that another person is speaking or that the voice you hear is your own imagination. But you can easily clear the communication lines when, like Samuel, you declare, "Speak, Lord. Your servant is listening."

God spoke to Job out of a whirlwind. The entire record of King David and his Psalms reveal his intimate communication with God.

Later on David's son, Solomon, received specific directions from God regarding the building of the temple.

The Old Testament includes an extensive record of prophets who received specific and direct messages from God. The word of the Lord came to Jonah (Jonah 1:1–2), to Elijah (1 Kings 17:8–9), to Isaiah (Isa. 38:4–5), and to Jeremiah (Jer. 1:4–5). Ezekiel recorded that he heard "a voice of One speaking" (Ezek. 1:26–28).

If God spoke to people under the old covenant, don't you think that believers under the new covenant should enjoy at least equal privileges? The book of Hebrews declares that we enjoy better privileges. We have a better hope (Heb. 7:19), a better covenant (Heb. 7:22), better promises (Heb. 8:6), better sacrifices (Heb. 9:23), a better possession (Heb. 10:34), and a better resurrection (Heb. 11:35).

The New Testament record opens with God announcing the births of Jesus and John the Baptist. God spoke audibly at the time of Jesus' baptism and on the Mount of Transfiguration. During His earthly ministry, Jesus constantly communicated His Father's words to His disciples, for He was God's voice: "God, who at various times and in various ways spoke in time past to the fathers by the prophets, has in these last days spoken to us by His Son, whom He has appointed heir of all things, through whom also He made the worlds" (Heb. 1:1–2).

Although the religious leaders of the time heard Christ's voice, they did not have a hearing ear. Jesus declared, "And the Father Himself, who sent Me, has testified of Me. You have neither heard His voice at any time, nor seen His form. But you do not have His word abiding in you, because whom He sent, Him you do not believe" (John 5:37–38).

After Jesus returned to heaven and the Holy Spirit was given, God continued to speak to men and women. It was not just apostles who heard God's voice, but laypersons and deacons as well. For example, a deacon named Philip received specific instructions to minister to a man riding in a chariot on a desert road (Acts 8:29–31, 35). God spoke to Paul on the Damascus Road and gave specific instructions to Ananias to go and minister to him (Acts 9). God spoke to Peter and Cornelius simultaneously, preparing one to share His word and the other to hear (Acts 10). Throughout the entire New

Testament record, we find prophetic words from God given by and to various individuals, culminating in the great revelation on Patmos when the apostle John heard "a loud voice, as of a trumpet" (Rev. 1:10).

The Clamor of Voices

The biblical record confirms that God speaks to people, but there are other voices in the world of which we must be aware. These voices are of man, self, and the false father.

The voice of man is easy to recognize because it is the audible voice of another human being. Whenever it conflicts with God's voice, the choice is clear that you must obey God rather than men (Acts 5:29).

The voice of self is you talking to yourself (Jonah 4:8). Be careful when you talk to yourself that you say the right things. Keep in mind the caution given in Jeremiah 10:23: "O LORD, I know the way of man is not in himself; it is not in man who walks to direct his own steps."

The voice of Satan was first heard by people when he spoke to Eve in the Garden of Eden (Gen. 3:1, 4–5). The voice of the false father always lies, deceives, and attempts to lead you into sin and away from God. You can easily recognize this strategy in the temptation of Jesus (Matt. 4:1–13) and in conversations between Satan and God (Job 1:7–12; 2:1–6).

Although Satan sometimes speaks audibly through demonically controlled individuals, most often he speaks in an inaudible voice. As we learned in Part 2 of this study, the false father deceives and contradicts every truth proclaimed by God the Father. You must come to know God's voice because it is vital to the Father-child relationship, and your spiritual survival depends on it to keep you from falling prey to seducing spirits.

In the Bible, believers are compared to sheep, and it is characteristic of sheep not to know where they are going. Jesus said His sheep would know His voice and follow Him instead of the strange voice of man, self, or Satan (John 10:3–5). But how can we distinguish the Father's voice from the clamor of other voices competing for our attention? How can we learn to communicate with the Father in effective dialogue that enables persistent, continual prayer?

Opening the Communication Channel

As you probably discovered in conversing with your earthly father, true communication requires relationship. If you have unresolved feelings toward your dad, communication is difficult. The same is true spiritually. Relationship is the prerequisite for hearing your heavenly Father's voice.

Adam and Eve enjoyed intimate relationship with God. He walked and talked with them daily until they did not heed His warning and they ate from the tree of the knowledge of good and evil. When they realized what they had done, they immediately hid themselves from God: "Then the LORD God called to Adam and said to him, 'Where are you?' So he said, 'I heard Your voice in the garden, and I was afraid because I was naked; and I hid myself'" (Gen. 3:9–10).

Sin and its resulting shame separate us from intimate relationship with God, harden our hearts, and prevent us from hearing the Father's voice. Jesus came to restore right relationship between sinful human beings and a righteous God, so when we are born again, the communication lines are automatically reconnected to our heavenly Father.

Children seem to have an innate ability to recognize Dad's voice at an early age. When you are born again into the family of God, you receive a similar spiritual capacity. God places within you a supernatural ability to hear and know His voice. All you must do is learn how to develop it. Morris Cerullo writes, "There are many Christians who are depending upon other people to give them a 'word from the Lord' to tell them what God is saying. God wants you to know His voice. He wants you to be able to hear when He speaks to you and for you to respond in obedience."[2]

He Is Speaking . . . Are You Listening?

Jesus said, "It is written, 'Man shall not live by bread alone, but by every word that proceeds from the mouth of God'" (Matt. 4:4).

The word *proceeds* speaks of a continuing function. It means something that happened in the past, is happening in the present, and will continue in the future. God spoke, He speaks, and He will continue to speak. The question is, Will we listen and respond?

Jesus identified two main divisions of listeners, those who hear and are unresponsive and those who hear and respond (Matt. 7:24–27). A foolish listener hears the voice of God but does not act upon it. A wise listener hears and acts upon the message of God. One listener is a hearer only. The other is both a hearer and a doer:

> But be doers of the word, and not hearers only, deceiving yourselves. For if anyone is a hearer of the word and not a doer, he is like a man observing his natural face in a mirror; for he observes himself, goes away, and immediately forgets what kind of man he was. But he who looks into the perfect law of liberty and continues in it, and is not a forgetful hearer but a doer of the work, this one will be blessed in what he does (James 1:22–25).

As you hear your heavenly Father's voice and obey, He will continue to speak to you. Disobedience results in a hardened heart and spiritually deaf ears. That is why the Holy Spirit warns,

> Today, if you will hear His voice,
> Do not harden your hearts as in the rebellion,
> In the day of trial in the wilderness,
> Where your fathers tested Me, tried Me,
> And saw My works forty years (Heb. 3:7–9).

The "trial in the wilderness" and the "rebellion" of the fathers mentioned in these verses refer to the sins of the nation Israel who, after being delivered from Egyptian captivity, disobeyed repeatedly when God spoke to them. The people of Israel heard God's voice as they stood at the foot of Mount Sinai and witnessed an awesome manifestation of His power and glory. How is it possible that they would refuse to hear and obey His voice?

As New Testament believers, we have an even greater responsibility to hear and obey God than Israel did because they had limited access to the presence of God due to a thick cloud on the mountain and a veil in the tabernacle. The use of "today" confirms that God still speaks to people in present times just as He did in times past. The warning to "hear" confirms that what He has to say is important. He speaks to strengthen, edify, and encourage. He wants to give you direction, reveal His purposes and will for your life, instruct you, and warn you.

Morris Cerullo asserts, "Hearing the voice of God should be a normal occurrence in your life, not the exception. You should be walking in continual communion with God where you are listening for His voice and are being led and directed by Him."[3]

Do you have an intense desire to enter into a new spiritual dimension where you can hear and know the Father's voice? If so, declare aloud right now the words of the psalmist, "I will hear what God the LORD will speak, for He will speak" (Ps. 85:8).

32

✦

How the Father Speaks

Communication with God is essential to the anointing of prevailing prayer as well as our intimate relationship with Him, so we must learn exactly how the heavenly Father speaks to us. We learned in the last chapter that God speaks in an audible voice, but our Father also uses other methods of communication. These include the written Word, circumstances, angels, miracles, dreams, visions, counselors, and the "still, small voice" in our spirits. God may speak to you through any of these methods as this prayer anointing is released in your life.

The Written Word

God does not need to speak to you in any other manner concerning things already revealed in the Scriptures, but when He does speak in other ways, it will never conflict with His written Word. The Bible reveals God's predetermined plan for the universe, which is known as His sovereign will. It also reveals His moral will, the commandments teaching how we should live. When God speaks to you, it will always be in harmony with the sovereign and moral revelations of His written Word.

When a baby is born, she must attain a certain level of maturity before she recognizes her parents' voices. The same is true in the spiritual world. When you are first born again, you may not readily identify the voice of your heavenly Father, but as you mature spiritually, you will come to recognize it. Spiritual maturity develops by listening to what God has already said in His Word: "For everyone who partakes only of milk is unskilled in the word of righteousness, for he is a babe. But solid food belongs to those who are of full age, that is, those who by reason of use have their senses exercised to discern both good and evil" (Heb. 5:13–14). The "milk" and "solid food" mentioned in these verses refer to the simple truths (milk) and the deeper precepts (solid food) of the Word of God. As you study what God said in His Word, your spiritual senses mature, you learn to discern good and evil, and you are able to recognize God's voice when He speaks to you.

Circumstances

God also communicates through both positive and negative circumstances. An excellent example is Joseph, whose story is recorded in Genesis 37—50. Joseph's brothers sold him into slavery in Egypt, he was falsely accused by Potiphar's wife, and he was unjustly imprisoned. Through difficult circumstances over which Joseph had no personal control, he became the instrument God used to save the lives of thousands of people in a time of severe famine. Joseph viewed his experiences as direction from God and explained to his brothers, "It was not you who sent me here, but God" (Gen. 45:8).

Circumstances result in open and closed doors, and God often speaks to us in this way. Paul told the Corinthians that "a great and effective door" was open to him at Ephesus (1 Cor. 16:8–9). On another occasion Paul desired to minister in Asia, but the doors were closed at the time (Acts 16:6–7).

When you pray, bring the circumstances of your life before the Lord, and ask Him to show you exactly what He is trying to say to you in each situation. Let God open and close the doors of circumstance in your life, and advance or stop accordingly.

Angels

There are numerous biblical records of God speaking through angels. Angels appeared to Abraham and Lot with a message concerning the destruction of Sodom (Gen. 19:12–14). The births of John the Baptist and Jesus were announced by angels (Luke 1), and an angel told Philip to go to the road between Jerusalem and Gaza where he met a spiritually hungry eunuch (Acts 8:26–27). The gentile nations came into the kingdom through an angelic appearance to Peter recorded in Acts 10:9–22, which resulted in his sharing the gospel with Cornelius and his household. The word *angel* means "messenger," and angels are appointed by the Father to minister to all those who are the heirs of salvation (Heb. 1:14). They provide protection and deliverance to all who dwell in the secret place of prayer (Ps. 91).

Miracles

A miracle is a supernatural occurrence, beyond the power of people to perform, through which God communicates His word or will. One example is the event recorded in 1 Kings 18 where the prophet Elijah prepared an altar before the heathen and called down fire from heaven (vv. 36–39). God used this miracle to speak to people who worshiped idols and reveal Himself as the true and living God.

Expect God to perform miracles in and through you when you pray. When you begin to witness miracles in response to your prayers, you will never again experience difficulty in prevailing in prayer.

Dreams

Our heavenly Father desires so much to communicate with us that He even speaks through dreams while we sleep! These are not the dreams experienced by everyone, but supernatural dreams from God that are detailed, specific, and purposeful. God warned Abimelech in a dream about his sin of taking Abraham's wife, Sarah (Gen. 20:3). An angel spoke to Jacob in a dream to remind him of his vow to God (Gen. 31:11–13), and God used dreams to guide Joseph (Gen. 37:5–9). God appeared to Solomon in a dream and gave him the opportunity to ask for whatever he desired (1 Kings 3:5), and a dream directed the wise men to return to their country by a different route because of an evil king (Matt. 2:12–13).

Visions

A vision is similar to a dream because you see visual images, but it differs because you are awake when you experience it. Visions may be seen with spiritual eyes as well as physical eyes, meaning that you may not see a vision with your natural eyes, but God gives you a "picture" in your spirit.

God appeared to Abraham in a vision and gave him prophetic promises (Gen. 15). The book of Daniel is filled with visions that revealed things about the future of the world. God spoke to many other Old Testament prophets in the same way. The New Testament reveals that God gave Peter a vision concerning the need to take the gospel to the gentile nations (Acts 10:9–22) and called Paul to Macedonia (Acts 16:9). The final book in the Bible, Revelation, is based on a vision seen by the apostle John.

Counselors

God communicates through Christian counselors, and there are many biblical examples of people seeking guidance from spiritual leaders. The writer of Proverbs stated,

> *Where there is no counsel, the people fall;*
> *But in the multitude of counselors there is safety (Prov. 11:14).*

> *The way of a fool is right in his own eyes,*
> *But he who heeds counsel is wise (Prov. 12:15).*

We must seek counsel only from mature Christians because the Bible cautions against walking in the counsel of the ungodly (Ps. 1:1). Some people go to a counselor hoping to get the counselor to agree with their opinions, but you will receive little benefit from counseling if this is your attitude. Counseling should be viewed as an avenue for hearing God's voice, not confirming preconceived ideas.

Christian counselors serve an important function in the body of Christ, but remember—your heavenly Father wants you to learn how to hear His voice also.

The Inner Voice of the Holy Spirit

While it is true that God speaks through miracles, dreams, visions, circumstances, and counselors, the Father wants you to experience an even more intimate level of communication in prevailing prayer. Most often, God uses the inner voice of the Holy Spirit to speak to your spirit when you are in prayer. This is called being led by the Spirit, and Romans 8:14 confirms that those who are led by the Spirit of God are children of God.

Being led by the Spirit assumes a spiritual life in those being led. A soul dead in sin with no spiritual life cannot be led by the Holy Spirit. Being led by the Spirit also assumes an inability to lead yourself. When you experience the new birth of salvation, God gives you a new spirit that is receptive to His Spirit: "I will give you a new heart and put a new spirit within you; I will take the heart of stone out of your flesh and give you a heart of flesh. I will put My Spirit within you and cause you to walk in My statutes, and you will keep My judgments and do them" (Ezek. 36:26–27).

The spirit is that "hidden person of the heart" (1 Peter 3:4). When God speaks to the inner person, He speaks to your spirit. The writer of Proverbs said the spirit of someone is the "lamp [or candle] of the LORD" (Prov. 20:27). In the natural world, a candle enables you to see in darkness. In the spiritual world, God uses the candle of your spirit to direct, enlighten, and guide you.

During a journey by ship, the apostle Paul told the captain of the vessel that he "perceived" there would be danger to the ship and its occupants if they continued their voyage (Acts 27:10). Paul did not say that he had a vision or dream or that God had audibly spoken to him. His spirit received a witness from God that proved to be correct.

We must train our spirits to be sensitive to God. Much time is spent on intellectual development through education and physical development through exercise, but usually little time is devoted to spiritual development. Your spirit can be educated and increase in spiritual strength just as your physical mind and body can be developed.

God uses the inner voice of the Holy Spirit to convict your conscience, your inward awareness of right and wrong. *Feeling* is the voice of the body, and because the flesh is an enemy of the spirit, feelings can deceive you. *Reason* is the voice of the mind, and God's ways are often beyond human reason. *Conscience* is the voice of your spirit. The Holy Spirit speaks to your spirit, the spirit convicts your conscience, and you are brought into conformity to the will of God.

Now that you know your heavenly Father wants to communicate with you, and you understand how He speaks, you are ready to allow the Holy Spirit to remove the hindrances to hearing.

33

---✠---

Hindrances to Hearing

When I was growing up, it was difficult for me to converse with my dad during the years he struggled with alcoholism. Only after he was delivered from its debilitating effects did I realize that although Dad and I had talked many times over the years, we had never really communicated. I had the physical capacity to hear and the mental capacity to understand, but it was only when the hindrance of alcohol was eliminated that I was really able to communicate with Dad.

When you were born into this world, you arrived with certain standard physical equipment including your heart, hands, feet, eyes, and ears, all of which enable you to function properly in the natural realm. When you are born again spiritually, you receive similar spiritual equipment. You receive eyes capable of seeing into the spirit world, hands with the ability to receive the things of God, a new heart, and feet that can walk in His ways. You also receive spiritual ears that are capable of hearing God's voice.

Communication with your heavenly Father is not something you must work up or pray down. It results naturally when you learn how to release the life flow of your new nature and use the spiritual abilities received at the time of your new birth. When you learn to function in the spirit instead of the flesh, you cease struggling and striving in prayer, and it becomes as easy as talking with a cherished friend.

But even as there were hindrances that blocked communication between my dad and me, there are spiritual hindrances that have the potential to prevent you from hearing the voice of your heavenly Father. These obstacles must be eliminated if you are to experience an intimate level of communication with your heavenly Father. The five hindrances are (1) an unbelieving heart, (2) an undeveloped spirit, (3) unhearing ears, (4) an unresponsive conscience, and (5) an unconcerned attitude.

1. An Unbelieving Heart

To communicate with God, you must eliminate unbelief and have faith that you *can* hear His voice because everything in the spirit world starts with faith. You became God's child by faith: "For by grace you have been saved through faith, and that not of yourselves; it is the gift of God" (Eph. 2:8). You are sanctified by faith (Acts 26:18), justified by faith (Rom. 5:1), and walk and live by faith (2 Cor. 5:7). The shield of faith is your defense against the enemy (Eph. 6:16), it is faith that establishes you in God (Col. 2:7), and it is through faith that you are healed (Acts 3:16; James 5:15).

Faith makes impossibilities possible: "For assuredly, I say to you, if you have faith as a mustard seed, you will say to this mountain, 'Move from here to there,' and it will move; and nothing will be impossible for you" (Matt. 17:20). Without faith, it is impossible to please God (Heb. 11:6), and the Bible declares that whatever is not of faith is sin (Rom. 14:23).

Because everything in the kingdom of God operates by faith, communication with the Father functions on the same basis. You do not hear in order to believe, but you believe in order to hear.

John 1:14 indicates that "the Word became flesh and dwelt among us." What does a word do? It communicates—and that is exactly what Jesus did when He dwelt among people during His earthly ministry. According to John 14:17, the Holy Spirit now resides within us. It is not an ideology, an ethic, or a philosophy within us, but it is the Spirit of our Father. The anointing of perpetual, prevailing, effective prayer is not us working something up; it is learning to communicate with the One who is constantly with us. In so doing, we become a house of personal, power, and prevailing prayer.

2. An Undeveloped Spirit

The second hindrance to hearing our Father's voice is an undeveloped spirit. Each of us is a spirit being living in a body, not simply a body with a spirit. The spirit is God's place for communing with us. The soul is the place of personality where we receive God's communication. In the scriptural order established in 1 Thessalonians 5:23, Paul claims preservation for the "spirit, soul, and body." The spirit is to be preeminent over the soul and body as it was at the time of original creation.

Many of us are actively involved in developing our physical bodies by swimming, jogging, running, walking, biking, and lifting weights. Most of us exercise our minds through advanced education or the mental stimulation of reading, solving problems and puzzles, participating in discussion groups, or attending lectures. But many of us neglect the development of the spiritual being and as a result have difficulty hearing the Father's voice.

The Word of God combined with prayer provides the spiritual workout that exercises and develops your spiritual nature. The Word tunes you to the right frequency to hear your Father's voice, and prayer is the direct line by which the two-way communication occurs. The Bible is God's primary method of communication, and its purposes are summarized in 2 Timothy 3:16–17: "All Scripture is given by inspiration of God, and is profitable for doctrine, for reproof, for correction, for instruction in righteousness, that the man of God may be complete, thoroughly equipped for every good work."

The Bible develops your spirit because it contains basic instructions, or doctrines, that prevent you from becoming a target for seducing spirits when you pray. These doctrines also help you pray according to God's will and enable you to detect the false father's lies, which we discussed in Part 2. John MacArthur states, "Knowledge gleaned from studying the Bible is what gives birth to a meaningful prayer life. You can't pray in a vacuum. We must know God's Word before we can pray effectively."[1]

The Bible confirms the Spirit's leading. When a voice of uncertain origin speaks to you in prayer telling you to do something, wait until you know by confirmation of God's Word that it is your Father's voice.

The Bible serves as a lamp and light to guide you through the darkness of this world (Prov. 6:23). By the Word of God, you are reminded, illuminated, and instructed. The Word of God cleanses your spiritual being. Just as you need a daily bath to get rid of grime and odor, you need a spiritual bath after being in contact with the pollution of this world (Eph. 5:26–27).

Here are some guidelines for using the Word to develop your spirit being:

Read systematically. Use a reading plan that will enable you to eventually cover the entire Bible. "All Scripture . . . is profitable," so if you want to be mighty in spirit and prevail in prayer, you must develop your inner being through disciplined study of the entire Word of God.

Read expectantly. Believe that God will speak to you through His Word.

Read spiritually. Allow the Holy Spirit to direct you to specific passages and reveal their truths to you.

Read responsively. Ask yourself, How does this passage apply to me? Pray about what God shows you, claiming His promises, repenting of violations, following scriptural commands to praise and worship, and so on.

Read habitually. Form a habit of reading the Bible each day whether you feel like it or not. Having trouble finding time? If you have time to read a daily newspaper, watch television, or listen to the evening news, you have time for the Bible. Just replace one of these activities with Bible study.

The primary reason most of us do not hear God's voice is that we neglect to act upon what He has already said. Luke 16:10 indicates that those who are faithful with what they are given will be trusted with more. You must be faithful with what God has already placed in your hands, His written Word, if you want to foster deeper communication with Him.

Continue to be faithful in reading systematically, expectantly, spiritually, responsively, and habitually whether you feel like it or not. Sometimes you will receive tremendous revelation, and other times it will seem you are not getting much out of it. In the "dry" times continue to read because even when you do not seem to be hearing much from God, you are still tuning your spiritual ears by His Word.

The process works similarly to the small steel two-pronged instrument called a tuning fork used by piano tuners. When struck, this fork vibrates at a fixed, constant, known rate with perfect musical pitch. Keys on a piano or strings on a guitar can be adjusted according to this pitch because it is true and constant. When it is time to perform, the instruments are in tune and harmonize perfectly.

The Word of God is like this tuning fork because when your spiritual ears continually listen to the proper tone, you can distinguish whether other spiritual sounds are sharp or flat. When it is time to perform your ministry, your spiritual execution will be true, constant, and in perfect harmony with your Father's will.

3. Unhearing Ears

Jesus told the Pharisees, "You have ears to hear, but you do not hear." It wasn't the fact that they did not have the capacity to hear God's voice, for Jesus said, "You *have* ears." The Pharisees refused to hear what God was saying, and for that reason Jesus said, "Seeing they do not see, and hearing they do not hear, nor do they understand" (Matt. 13:13).

Christ came to reveal the truth, and those who received it heard God's voice. Jesus declared, "For this cause I was born, and for this cause I have come into the world, that I should bear witness to the truth. Everyone who is of the truth *hears My voice*" (John 18:37, emphasis added).

The Pharisees knew the Scriptures and could quote all the prophecies concerning the Messiah, but they did not have a hearing ear to accept the truth revealed in Christ. They refused to hear when God spoke at Christ's baptism. On one occasion while Jesus was teaching, God spoke again, saying, "I have both glorified it [My name] and will glorify it again" (John 12:28). The people standing nearby heard an audible voice, but they did not comprehend the message because of their unhearing ears (John 12:29).

Jesus told the Pharisees that the Father was speaking, but they refused to hear: "And the Father Himself, who sent Me, has testified of Me. You have neither heard His voice at any time, nor seen His form. But you do not have His word abiding in you, because whom He sent, Him you do not believe" (John 5:37–38). To hear God's voice, you must accept what He has already said in His written Word and have the Living Word (Jesus) resident within you. Because the Pharisees refused God's Word and His messenger, their spiritual ears were deafened. Spiritual deafness results from deliberately refusing to hear what God is saying (Isa. 6:9–10).

4. An Unresponsive Conscience

Your body communicates comfort, distress, pleasure, and pain through feeling. If you don't believe it, just smash your finger with a hammer and you will see how well it communicates! Your soul communicates through the mental capacities of thinking and reasoning and through emotional responses such as joy, anger, hatred, depression, and grief.

Your spirit communicates through your conscience, but the human conscience has the capacity to lead you astray. The popular belief of our times is in relative morality, which claims there are no absolute standards of right and wrong but only what is deemed right or wrong to an individual or society. Our condition parallels that of the time of the judges in Israel when each person did what was right in his or her own eyes. Such ungodly philosophy results in the degradation of conscience described by Paul: "Now the Spirit expressly says that in latter times some will depart from the faith, giving heed to deceiving spirits and doctrines of demons, speaking lies in hypocrisy, having their own conscience seared with a hot iron" (1 Tim. 4:1–2). A "seared" conscience is one that is cauterized, hardened, and insensitive. A conscience becomes "seared" by habitual sin, and Paul stated that a conscience affected in this manner results in shipwrecked faith (1 Tim. 1:19).

If you allow your conscience to become seared by rejecting the commands and principles of God's Word, when you hear a voice, it will most likely be that of human desire and reasoning, the voice of the false father, or a seducing spirit. For example, in personal counseling sessions people have told me,

- "God told me to divorce my wife and marry this woman."
- "God told me it was okay to take the night off and get drunk."
- "I don't care what the Word says. I know God spoke to me!"

God continues to communicate only as you obey what He has already said. When you disobey, further communication is hindered, and your conscience begins to harden. Pretty soon you will be hearing voices, but you won't hear that of your heavenly Father.

In the New Testament, the phrase is reiterated, "He who has an ear, let him hear." As you hear and respond, the voice of God continues to speak. When you fail to respond, the perception of your spiritual ears becomes dull.

Here are some practical steps for recognizing and responding positively to the voice of God. You do not have to go through each of them in a certain order every time you hear a voice speak to you, for you will soon come to know God's voice with certainty. These steps aid in the process of praying and obeying:

Submit to Christ's Lordship. Submit every aspect of your life to the lordship of Jesus Christ. Do not be like the Israelites who insisted on having their own way (Ps. 106:13–15).

Believe God will speak to you. Be confident that His word is on its way to you and that, in His time and way, you *will* hear His voice. Like Daniel, whose answer took twenty-one days to arrive, you will sometimes wrestle against negative spiritual forces, but the secret to prevailing prayer is perseverance.

Receive the message. If you are a born-again, Spirit-filled believer, the Holy Spirit dwells within, and one of His purposes is to transmit God's messages to you (John 16:13–15).

Test the spirits. Satan uses the same inner frequency of your spirit to transmit his messages, but as you tune yourself to the perfect pitch of the Holy Spirit, voices or messages containing error will not ring true. Don't stop listening for God's voice because the false father attempts to deceive. That is like having your telephone taken out because you receive an obscene call. Test the voices you hear by making sure they agree with the written Word of God (1 John 4:1).

Wait for the peace of God. Satan confuses you with voices and impressions, but he cannot counterfeit God's peace. The peace of

God is like an umpire in your spirit, calling "foul" when you head in the wrong direction (Col. 3:15).

Refuse to go when you do not know. If you are not convinced that God has spoken to you and that a certain thing is right for you, don't do it. You must act out of conviction that God has spoken to you, because "whatever is not from faith is sin" (Rom. 14:23).

Wait for God's timing. When you receive a word from God, wait for His timing to implement what you have heard. If God is able to speak to you, He is also able to direct you as to when and how to implement that word in your family, business, or ministry.

Obey immediately and completely. Patience is a positive fruit of the Spirit, while passivity is an apathetic offspring of fear. When you know you have a word from the Lord and it is time to act, step out boldly in faith and obey.

5. An Unconcerned Attitude

Productivity and activity are often equated with spirituality, but that equation is deadly. Many marriages fail because an attitude of unconcern develops between the partners, and they become too busy to spend quality time together.

In Luke 10:38–42, we find Jesus visiting the home of a woman named Martha where Lazarus and Mary, her brother and sister, also lived. Martha was hurrying about, busy and distracted, while her sister, Mary, chose to sit at the feet of Jesus and listen to His every word. Lest we be too critical of Martha, we should be quick to note that she was a courageous person, for it was growing increasingly dangerous to associate with Jesus, and she was hospitable, as evidenced by her consideration for her guests.

Martha's error was an unconcerned attitude. She was more concerned about the cares of life than the words of the Master. Martha was "distracted with much serving." Even though she was serving because of her love for others, Martha lost sight of proper priorities. As a result, she was aggravated and critical.

When Martha complained about Mary, Jesus said, "Martha, Martha, you are worried and troubled about many things. But one thing is needed, and Mary has chosen that good part, which will not be taken away from her" (Luke 10:41–42). Jesus rebuked Martha because she was anxious and troubled about "many things." The word *troubled* means to be "disturbed, agitated, in turmoil, or ruffled." Martha was trying to please the Lord with work, but He really desired for her to hear His words. Her inattentive attitude made her unable to hear His voice above the noise of her frenzied serving. Mary, on the other hand, chose "that good part," meaning she made listening a priority. Mary sat at Christ's feet, which denotes close attention, a readiness to receive, and an attitude of submission to His message.

Jesus told Martha, "One thing is needed." What was that one thing? Making listening a priority. Jesus told Martha it was a matter of choice. Mary chose the good part. Which will you choose? To serve or sit? To work or worship? To choose the "many things" or the "one thing"?

If you have lost an earthly parent through death, as I did my dad, you can readily identify with me when I say that if I had the opportunity to hear my dad's voice speak to me one more time, I would make it my highest priority. I would set aside every appointment and the pressing matters of business—just to hear his voice again.

Should we not give similar priority and attention to hearing our heavenly Father's voice? The question is not whether He wants to speak to us, but whether we will choose to be attentive. Address the five hindrances to hearing we have discussed as you pray this prayer:

Dear heavenly Father, I ask You for a believing heart and in so doing I reject the unbelief that would say I cannot hear from You. I claim a developed, mature spirit and a hearing ear so I can know Your voice. Make my conscience responsive to You and enable me to make listening my highest priority. In Jesus' name, Amen.

34

For This Cause

We see their young, determined faces in faded film footage shot during World War II, and we wonder how it could have ever happened—thousands of young people caught up in the delusion of Hitler's youth movement, pledging allegiance to the diabolical purpose of establishing a "superior" race through ethnic cleansing.

A search for purpose and meaning in life drove many of those young people to join Hitler's ranks, to be deluded by his propaganda, and to fulfill his evil agenda. It seems men and women are ever seeking a cause greater than themselves to which to commit. Each night on the evening news we witness the efforts of those committed to purposes that range in diversity from being pro-life to saving the endangered kangaroo rat. People commit to causes because a sense of purpose gives meaning and direction to life. Purpose provides a reason for being, enables people to set goals and objectives, and motivates them to action.

There is tremendous power in perceived purpose. For this reason God established a divine purpose from the beginning of time, and He revealed it to us. When you learn about this purpose and your part in it, you will never again be defeated in your prayer life.

The Father's Purpose

Paul describes God's purpose in his letter to the Ephesians. He introduces the subject by commenting that in previous times the purpose was not made known to people, but it has now been revealed by the Spirit through the apostles and prophets. Then Paul explains this mystery and his role in it:

> *To me, who am less than the least of all the saints, this grace was given, that I should preach among the Gentiles the unsearchable riches of Christ, and to make all see what is the fellowship of the mystery, which from the beginning of the ages has been hidden in God who created all things through Jesus Christ; to the intent that now the manifold wisdom of God might be made known by the church to the principalities and powers in the heavenly places, according to the eternal purpose which He accomplished in Christ Jesus our Lord (Eph. 3:8–11).*

God commissioned Paul to share with the Gentiles (nations) that through Jesus, they are fellow heirs with the Jews in God's divine plan. The purpose for this church composed of people from all nations is that the manifold wisdom of God our Father is made known through us to the principalities and powers in the heavenly places. We have authority to penetrate the spiritual forces of darkness, which rule men and women, communities, and entire nations, with the light of the gospel. Through us, God desires to work His plan to bring all things into Christ.

Our lives have greater purpose than going to work each day and coming home to crash in front of the television. You have a greater goal than earning your degree, buying a new house, or purchasing the latest model car. God's eternal and timeless purpose of salvation for all was revealed in Jesus, and now *you* are the one through whom God wants to work to penetrate the forces of darkness and make that purpose known. You have been entrusted by your heavenly Father with the family inheritance and the authority to invest and multiply it in the lives of others.

For This Reason

Even if you understand this divine purpose, you may not have applied it to your prayer life. Once you do, you will never again be defeated in prayer, you will not be bored, you will never be at a loss for something to say, and your prayers will always be answered.

Paul connected the purpose of God to prayer in Ephesians 3:14–15 when he stated, *"For this reason* I bow my knees to the Father of our Lord Jesus Christ, from whom the whole family in heaven and earth is named" (emphasis added). Paul was saying, "This is the reason—this is the cause and purpose—that motivates me to bow in prayer."

Paul's prayer had a specific objective, as revealed by the words *for this reason,* which refer to the eternal plan of God. Each time Paul knelt to pray, he acknowledged his responsibility to make known the manifold wisdom of God to principalities and powers in the heavenlies. The cause was so great that it drove Paul to his knees, for bowing reflects desperate need and utter dependence on God.

This sense of divine purpose caused him to literally "explode" in prayer for the Ephesians, claiming

> *that He would grant you, according to the riches of His glory, to be strengthened with might through His Spirit in the inner man, that Christ may dwell in your hearts through faith; that you, being rooted and grounded in love, may be able to comprehend with all the saints what is the width and length and depth and height—to know the love of Christ which passes knowledge; that you may be filled with all the fullness of God (Eph. 3:16–19).*

Paul's prayer was that God's people might be charged with power, rooted and grounded in faith and love, and endued with spiritual understanding. He prayed for Christ to take up permanent residence and abide in them, filling them with the "fullness of God" to empower them to fulfill their destiny.

Paul proclaimed that God "is able to do exceedingly abundantly above all that we ask or think, according to the power that works in us" (Eph. 3:20). What is that "power" at work within? It is the power of God's purpose—the ability to poke holes in the darkness of spiritual powers that hold people and nations in bondage so that the light of the gospel can penetrate. It is for this cause that we pray.

Most of us do not bow before God "for this reason," and we do not prevail in prayer because we pray with lesser purpose. We are concerned with our issues, our problems, and our concerns. We pray for healing, but not so we can accomplish His purpose. We are just tired of hurting.

We pray for strength, but not with the idea of being empowered to accomplish His plan. We ask for more finances to fulfill our carnal desires rather than to enable us to give more to advance His cause.

When your Father's kingdom becomes more important than your ministry, His cause becomes more important than your cause, and His house becomes your focus instead of your house, you will never again be defeated in prayer. You will literally explode with the knowledge of the width, length, depth, and height of God's love, and you will be filled with the fullness of God. Although you may have struggled with bondage for years, when you seek deliverance "for this reason," you will receive it!

God wants to work through your life to accomplish His purposes. That is why Paul admonishes us to yield our "members as instruments of righteousness" (Rom. 6:13). When you yield yourself to become an instrument of righteousness, you bring your life in harmony with your Father's purpose. You become an instrument through which He can work, actually becoming a worker "together with Him" (2 Cor. 6:1).

You align your life with His purpose each time that you bow before Him with the same motivation Paul had—"for this reason." When you are in harmony with God's purpose, there is no way you can ever fail in your prayer life because God declares His purpose will succeed (Isa. 14:24, 26–27).

King David was a man who was in harmony with God's purpose, and the epitaph of his life was that he served the purpose of God in his generation (Acts 13:36). No foe of the enemy—no evil principality or power—can stand against you when you are aligned with your heavenly Father's purpose. Even a Pharisee named Gamaliel recognized that when he commented, "For if this plan or this work is of men, it will come to nothing; but if it is of God, you cannot overthrow it—lest you even be found to fight against God" (Acts 5:38–39).

A Prayer Life of Divine Origin

Do you want a prayer life of divine rather than human origin? Do you want to be able to prevail in prayer so that no force is able to stop you? Do you want to be aligned with God? Then each time you pray, bow "for this reason": That through your life, God may be revealed to the principalities and powers of this world.

Begin right now by praying this prayer:

I receive this word as a revelation to my life. I repent of praying only for my cause, my needs, and my personal comfort. I declare right now to the evil principalities and powers that they have no legal right to conceal Your glory from being manifested through me. I bind and cast out anything that is sapping my spiritual strength. I reject doubt and receive the assurance that Jesus Christ is in my heart. I declare that I am rooted and grounded in love. From this time forth, I bow for Your cause, for this reason! Amen.

35

—✠—

Trigger Points for Prayer

"They are playing our song!" How often have you heard that expression? Or perhaps you said it yourself when a familiar tune elicited fond memories. Images of your childhood may be evoked whenever you smell a fresh-baked apple pie, and perhaps certain perfumes or colors remind you of a loved one. Such sights, sounds, and smells trigger your mind to recall certain people or events that take you back into a different time or place, another dimension of life in your subconscious memory.

In similar manner the Bible reveals there are trigger points for prayer that will catapult you into a supernatural dimension of prevailing prayer. These triggers are the thoughts that come into your mind throughout any given day.

Spend just one day analyzing every thought that comes into your mind and you will find that you can categorize all of them into two major areas: people and problems. Paul addresses both in the book of Philippians and explains how to use them as triggers for perpetual prayer.

People

Paul told the Philippian believers: "I thank my God upon every remembrance of you, always in every prayer of mine making request for you all with joy, for your fellowship in the gospel from the first day until now, being confident of this very thing, that He who has begun a good work in you will complete it until the day of Jesus Christ" (Phil. 1:3–6).

The apostle Paul reveals that he thought often of the believers at Philippi, and whenever they came to his mind, he prayed for them, using his thoughts about them as triggers for prayer in their behalf. Paul prayed that they would be faithful in fulfilling their spiritual destiny, that their love would abound, that their knowledge and discernment would increase, that they would be sincere, without offense, and filled with the fruits of righteousness (Phil. 1:9–11).

Tucked in this brief passage is a powerful spiritual principle of prevailing prayer. During the course of each day, you think about many people with whom you are acquainted or to whom you relate or interact in some way. You also think about individuals you do not know personally, but you have heard about through friends, from prayer requests articulated at church, or in the news media. Each time a person comes to your mind, use this thought as a trigger to fire off a prayer in the person's behalf.

Problems

In addition to people, our thoughts focus on problems, circumstances, or issues. Paul admonished the Philippian believers to "be anxious for nothing, but in everything by prayer and supplication, with thanksgiving, let your requests be made known to God" (Phil. 4:6). The believers at Philippi had every reason to be anxious. They were suffering persecution, experiencing disunity in their church, and wrestling with the challenges of carnal members and false teachers in their fellowship. Yet in the midst of all that, Paul admonished them to avoid anxious thoughts and lift their problems to God in prayer.

Paul says to "be anxious for nothing." The Greek word translated "nothing" (*meden*) means "not one thing!" The four words Paul uses for prayer in this passage reveal how it is to be used as an antidote for anxiety. "Prayer" (*proseuche*) refers to special times of prayer in periods of devotion and worship during which we lift our problems and issues of life to our heavenly Father. "Supplication" (*deesis*) refers to prayers that focus on special needs for which we feel intense burden. "Thanksgiving" (*eucharistia*) means we thank and praise God for all that He is and all that He has done. "Requests" (*aitemata*) denotes specific requests.

Paul's words reveal another tremendous principle that will catapult you into perpetual, prevailing prayer. Each time a perplexing situation, problem, or issue comes to your mind, don't fume and fret over the matter. Instead, use your thoughts to trigger intercession to your heavenly Father. You will soon find yourself in constant dialogue with God, fulfilling the command to "pray without ceasing" (1 Thess. 5:17).

Prayer Triggers

You can devote small segments of time each day to prevailing prayer. You can fire off prayers while showering, driving your car, waiting in line at the store, and exercising. You can use breaks on your job and times when you are doing routine jobs such as ironing, peeling potatoes, and so on. When you are on hold on the telephone, waiting for the copy or fax machine, or waiting for a tardy person to show up, use the time to pray. Curtis Mitchell notes, "Prayer should be such an integral part of our lives that throughout each day we should be carrying on a running conversation with God. Each problem, each decision, each difficulty should occasion a brief prayer."[1]

The Bible reveals that the strength of a prayer does not depend on its length. Consider the impact of the brief prayer of the thief on the cross: "Lord, remember me when You come into Your kingdom." Compare the effectiveness of the publican's cry, "Lord, be merciful to me, a sinner," to the lengthy prayer of the Pharisee. A Bible commentator explains, "Praying continually does not mean some sort of nonstop praying. Rather it implies constantly recurring prayer, growing out of a settled attitude of dependence on God."[2]

The Promise of Peace

When you learn to pray continually in this manner, Paul says that "the peace of God, which surpasses all understanding, will guard your [heart and mind] through Christ Jesus" (Phil. 4:7). "Peace" speaks of a confident assurance that God will guide, strengthen, deliver, and provide.

This peace that passes human understanding is like a soldier, assigned by God, who guards and protects your most precious possessions: your heart and mind. Peace in your spirit permits you to focus your attention on the truly important things of life, things that are noble, just, pure, lovely, of good report, virtuous, and praiseworthy (Phil. 4:8). Thoughts like these will keep your heart and mind safe from every onslaught of the enemy because you are no longer fretting, stewing, and working your emotions up into fevered intensity.

In summary, here is the formula for these two simple, yet dynamic, prayer triggers: People and problems lifted in perpetual prayer = prevailing peace, which protects your heart and mind. E. M. Bounds declares, "What a beautiful conception of prayer we get if we regard it in this light, if we view it as a constant fellowship, an unbroken audience with the king. Prayer then loses every vestige of dread which it may once have possessed; we regard it no longer as a duty which must be performed, but rather as a privilege which is to be enjoyed."[3]

36

Finding Your Personal
Prayer Level

I was preaching a youth revival in Hereford, Texas, in 1976, and each night we were holding the service at a different church. The first night we preached at the Assembly of God church and the second at the Baptist church, and nothing unusual happened either evening. In fact, nothing happened—period! There was no dynamic move of God and no response to the altar calls.

The third night we were at the Methodist church. It was a traditional church with the podium up high to the left at the front, which meant I was far removed from the congregation. I was nervous because the revival was floundering and the service was dead. I noticed two nuns at each previous meeting, and before this service, they came up to ask me to tune their guitar. As I labored with their old, beat-up guitar, one of the nuns said to me, "Don't worry, Larry. We prayed for you for eight hours today."

I said to her, "If you prayed for me eight hours today, then would you please pray for me right now?"

The nun said, "Actually, that was the real reason we came up here. We wanted to lay hands on you and pray." The nuns began to pray for me, speaking in tongues and singing in the Holy Spirit. That continued for about thirty minutes until I became lost in the presence of God. When we stopped praying, one nun said, "It is finished. These are the words that have come to me all day." I was shocked, for they were the exact words I had written down as my sermon text for that night. I preached with a tremendous anointing, and when I gave the closing invitation, one hundred young people walked down the aisle to give their lives to Jesus Christ.

The next night the nuns prayed for me again. "We live our lives in prayer," they explained. Then one of them asked, "Does the Scripture passage about the woman with the issue of blood mean anything to you?" Again—that was the exact message I was planning to preach that evening! That night another one hundred young people responded to the invitation to receive Christ as Savior, and we had to move to a larger facility for the remainder of the revival. At the end of the week we baptized more than five hundred teenagers in water.

As I was en route home from the meeting, the Holy Spirit spoke to me and said, "You had nothing at all to do with this revival. It happened because somebody *prayed* the price." He didn't say they "paid" the price; rather, they "prayed" the price.

God declared in His Word, "Call to Me, and I will answer you, and show you great and mighty things, which you do not know" (Jer. 33:3). The reverse of that is, "If you don't call to Me, I will not answer you." Most of us are not at a level where we pray eight to ten hours a day as did the nuns who had a special gift of intercession, but each of us has an individual prayer level for which each of us is personally responsible. When we "pray" the price, God will move in our behalf (Dan. 9:23).

When Jesus was in the Garden of Gethsemane, He prayed with such intensity that "His sweat became like great drops of blood" falling to the ground. As He waged the battle in prayer, an angel was dispatched from heaven to strengthen Him (Luke 22:39–44). The angel did not come to strengthen Jesus until He prayed to the Father. Angels receive direction through prayers, so if you don't pray, they sit with folded wings without instructions from the Father to execute warfare in your behalf.

Your Personal Prayer Assignment

Each of us has a prayer assignment from God, a personal level of prayer. I believe there are five distinct levels of prayer, and each person functions at one of these levels. You need to determine your personal prayer level and know when you are operating at optimum efficiency at that plane so God can activate His angels to move in your behalf.

1. *Desperation.* Many believers pray only when there is a crisis. Even atheists turn to prayer when their airplane is going down! You will never learn to walk in the Spirit at the desperation level of prayer, but God does hear and answer these prayers because He is a compassionate Father. If you are still operating at this level, you need to move on to the maintenance level by setting an objective to pray the Lord's Prayer each day. This commitment will help you make the transition to the next level of prayer.

2. *Maintenance.* At the maintenance level you use the Lord's Prayer regularly each day to open up the seven arteries of your spirit. As you have learned, these spiritual arteries correspond with the seven major points of the model prayer. As long as your spiritual arteries remain open, the blood keeps pumping through your life, and you can easily maintain this level of prayer. This level is "you"-oriented prayer where you declare, "You are my righteousness, and I need righteousness. You are my provider, and I need provision," and so on. Maintenance prayer focuses on you and your personal needs.

3. *Basic intercession.* This level involves "you and them"–oriented prayers where you are not just focused on your needs, but you demonstrate concern for others. I believe everyone in the body of Christ needs to persevere through the desperation and maintenance stages to arrive at this level.

4. *Warfare prayer.* At the warfare level your prayers are concerned with "them" rather than just "you" or "you and them." The impetus behind prayer at this level is other people. The prophet Daniel was functioning at this level when he prayed for the liberation of the Jews from Babylonian captivity. His prayers and those of his colleagues broke Israel out of bondage in Babylon and returned them to freedom in their own land.

5. *Intimacy.* This level of prayer has to do with "Him" rather than "you" or "them." This is the rarest and highest level where all you care about is ministering to Him. People who function at this level are consumed with an insatiable desire to be with God. In this

sacred environment of intimacy—to these people—God reveals His secrets, and as they pray these secrets, their intercession affects people, powers, and entire nations.

How to Find Your Optimum Prayer Level

Five factors confirm you are operating at your optimum prayer level, whether it be at the first level of desperation or the highest level of intimacy.

1. There Will Be Peace with God and Peace in Your Heart.

If you are not functioning where you should be, there will be holy dissatisfaction with your prayer life. I do not mean condemnation, for there is no condemnation at any prayer level where you are presently functioning. Holy dissatisfaction is a restless unmet desire in your spirit.

I experienced that when God first began calling me to prayer. I was a seminary graduate and had a successful public ministry, but my prayer life was frustrating. I wasn't even praying at the maintenance level, and I certainly was not at a level that satisfied my heart. I was frustrated in prayer until I received the revelation of the seven parts of the Lord's Prayer that helped me break through to the maintenance level.

2. Confusion Will Be Replaced by Revelation.

God does not intend for you to be confused because He is not the author of confusion. If you are still living in a state of confusion, you are not praying at your optimum level. Once you are functioning at the prayer level where God wants you, confusion will cease, and He will speak to you. You will start living your life by knowing, not hoping. (There may be times and seasons when God does not speak, but that is the exception, not the norm, because He wants to reveal things to you.)

3. God Will Become Your Friend.

A few years ago I was at one of the lowest times of my life, my ministry was in shambles about me, and my friends had forsaken me. I didn't want to minister, pray, or play golf. I didn't even want to eat.

One day the Lord said, "Will you let Me in on this?" I answered, "I'm not sure You want in on this mess!" God said, "That's what friends are for."

A major purpose of advancing through these prayer levels is not to show your superior spirituality; rather, it is to move you into relationship with your heavenly Father.

4. Your Prayers Will Start Being Answered.

Considering all the promises Jesus made concerning answered prayer, it would be an exception not to have your prayers answered. God does not honor unfaithfulness, however, so if you are not faithful to your personal, optimum level of prayer, your requests will not be answered. Your intercession will be effective and your prayers consistently answered when you function at your optimum prayer level.

5. Praise Will Become Habitual.

You will not have to work at praising God, but praise will become habitual when you function at your optimum prayer level. Depression and praise cannot dwell together very long because God gives the oil of beauty for ashes and the garment of praise for the spirit of heaviness.

Gain Without Shame

Perhaps your motivation for purchasing this book on releasing the prayer anointing was guilt about the status of your prayer life. One of the major objectives of this book, however, is to free you from shame regarding your prayer life because—as you have learned—prevailing prayer is shameless asking. You cannot receive the prayer anointing and break through to your optimum prayer level until the force of shame is broken in your life.

Take what you have received from this book, and use it. Start praying the Lord's Prayer each day. This is a prayer for disciples, not just something for children to memorize or to recite on special occasions. If you are a disciple, you should be praying this prayer daily.

Do not be frustrated if you cannot immediately attain a higher level of prayer. Begin where you are, and let God move you up to the next level. Do not try to emulate the prayer levels of others because your efforts will only frustrate you. This is true of any gift or calling from God. For example, Billy Graham has the gift of evangelism. When he speaks and gives an altar call, multitudes respond because of his gift. You might say the same words as Billy Graham but have no response. The same is true in prayer. Some are called as intercessors and will be able to function effectively in that realm; others are not. When I was a young minister, I was insecure, and I struggled to find my identity until I discovered that God had a special prayer level just for me and I didn't have to imitate others.

Ask the Lord to fill you with the Holy Spirit daily. Ephesians 5:18 says, "Be filled with the Spirit," and the phrase means to "be continually filled." If you are filled with the Holy Spirit each day of your life, you are continually controlled by the Spirit. Peter Wagner, author of numerous books on prayer and spiritual warfare, said that when he prays for daily bread, he relates it to spiritual bread, asking to be filled with the Spirit for that day.

Have a specific time and place of prayer. When I was in seminary, I had a special chair where I prayed. It seemed that God would draw me to that place by saying, "Come here!" When I pastored in Rockwall, I had a special place in the woods to pray. Now I have a place in my backyard where I meet God regularly in prayer.

Stay in your special place until you are satisfied. (This might be longer than an hour some days, shorter other days.) Something supernatural occurs when you commit yourself to pray regularly.

Pray at your current level without guilt or shame. If you are only at the desperation level, begin right there. Make a fresh commitment to the level where you are now, begin to pray the model prayer each day, and ask God to move you to the next level in His timing. Be faithful to function where you are, and when you are ready to move up a level, God will do it!

How do I know this? Because in the next chapter we will join together to release a supernatural prayer anointing over your life and ministry.

37

Releasing the Prayer Anointing: Impartation

We have traveled a long way together spiritually since starting this study on how to receive the prayer anointing. Along the way I have drawn open the curtains of my life to share with you intimate details of how I received these revelations on prayer. As we come to the end of this book, we are not concluding our spiritual journey together. In reality, this is a new beginning.

Before we proceed, let me make this observation: You may have turned to this chapter first before reading the remainder of this book. If you have done that, be sure to use this chapter as a springboard to go back and read the previous chapters. The prayer anointing released in this final chapter is a superstructure that rests on the foundation built in the remainder of the book. If you read only this chapter, you may end up with emotion without substance, and that will not last.

The foregoing pages of this book have disseminated much information regarding the anointing of personal, power, and prevailing prayer. But we live in an information age, and with the advent of the Internet and the information superhighway most of us are deluged with more knowledge than we can ever absorb or apply. That is why you must move beyond information to impartation. *Information* is learning about prayer while *impartation* occurs when you function under the mantle of the prayer anointing.

Three Settled Issues

We have already discussed three basic issues that must be settled if you are to receive the prayer anointing. The first issue is your past. You cannot boldly access the throne of God with a spirit of shame because persistent prayer is actually shameless asking. Have you released your past to God?

The second issue is to make a commitment to pray each day using the model prayer Jesus taught. When you use this seven-point pattern of prayer, it functions much like the seven major arteries in your natural body, bearing life and health to your spiritual being. If you are to move into the anointing of prevailing prayer, you must make a commitment now—in the present—to pray the model prayer each day. Have you done this?

The third issue concerns the future. You must obey in the future without fear.

If you are faithful in these three areas, you have the proper spiritual foundation to receive the anointing and continue to make the transition from level to level in your prayer life. Don't get frustrated and try to make it happen. Let God do it. Jesus said, "I will build My church." He will build your prayer life, also. You do not have to strive to make it happen. Be faithful to what you know God wants you to do, and watch Him move you to the next level of prayer until you reach your personal prayer capacity.

The Anointing

God revealed He would throw out the mantle of the prayer anointing each time I shared regarding these three issues that open the door to effective prayer. To *anoint* means to "apply oil to a person or thing." To *anoint* is to dedicate or consecrate someone or something by applying oil that is symbolic of the Holy Spirit. It actually means to "rub off," which indicates that anointing can be transferred.

The power in spiritual anointing is not in the oil, the person doing the anointing, or the abilities of the recipient. The power of the anointing flows from the Source, God the Father. Jesus said, "The Spirit of the LORD is upon Me, because He has anointed Me" (Luke

4:18). The apostle Paul confirmed, "Now He who . . . has anointed us is God" (2 Cor. 1:21).

Although men and women are symbolically anointed with oil by people, the true anointing is from God. The prophet Samuel anointed King David, but God proclaimed, "I have found My servant David; with My holy oil I have anointed him" (Ps. 89:20). The source of the prayer anointing is God, not a person, an organization, or a denomination.

The Purposes of Anointing

This new anointing of prayer will enable you to get your needs met, and you will no longer want to sit immobile as a spectator in the back row of some church. This new anointing is for the following purposes:

Ministry

Luke 4:18–19 and Acts 10:38 provide an index of ministry purposes of the anointing. The anointing enables you to preach the gospel, minister to the poor, heal the brokenhearted, heal the physically ill, preach deliverance to those in spiritual bondage, open the eyes of those in spiritual blindness, set free those bruised and wounded by the enemy, preach the acceptable year of the Lord, go about doing good, and deliver people oppressed by the devil.

Regarding the need for the prayer anointing to empower ministry, E. M. Bounds observes,

> What the church needs today is not more machinery or better, not new organizations or more and novel methods, but men whom the Holy Spirit can use—men of prayer, men mighty in prayer. The Holy Spirit does not flow through methods, but through men. He does not come on machinery, but on men. He does not anoint plans, but men—men of prayer.[1]

Instruction

The anointing provides spiritual instruction (1 John 2:27). You may receive scriptural teaching from others because God sets teachers in the church for this purpose (Eph. 4:11). But the anointing within you affirms what is being taught as truth and enables you to hear the Father's voice. He explains truths you do not understand and opens the revelation of His Word to you. Note that the Spirit within you will "[teach] you concerning all things." There is such power available when you come into this prayer anointing that you will be instructed in every area of life as well as ministry.

Security

The anointing enables you to abide securely in God: "But the anointing which you have received from Him abides in you . . . and just as it has taught you, you will abide in Him" (1 John 2:27). Prayer will cement your relationship with your heavenly Father in the same way that intimate interaction bonds a parent and a child together.

Intercession

The anointing releases intercession through you. It enables you to rise up in prevailing prayer and claim God's promises. The intercessor's anointing already abides in you; all you must do is learn to release it.

Liberty

The yoke is destroyed by the anointing (Isa. 10:27). The yokes of sin and shame that bind men and women today will not be destroyed by deep teaching, education, counseling, or better organization. These yokes will be destroyed by the anointing of God on spiritual leaders who learn how to engage in personal, power, and prevailing prayer.

The Three Anointings

Jesus taught personal prayer in the model given in Matthew 6; He engaged in power prayer in behalf of His disciples (John 17); and He travailed under the anointing of prevailing prayer in the Garden of Gethsemane.

There are three ceremonies described in the Old Testament that I believe correlate with these anointings of personal, power, and prevailing prayer demonstrated by Jesus. We must experience each of these spiritually: (1) the leper's anointing for personal prayer, (2) the leader's anointing for power prayer, and (3) the priest's anointing for prevailing prayer.

1. The Leper's Anointing: Personal Prayer

Leprosy is a dreaded disease that slowly consumes the flesh of its victims, causing them to die a slow and painful death. Leprosy is used in the Bible as a "type" of sin, a natural parallel of a spiritual truth. Just as leprosy destroys the body physically, sin destroys a person spiritually.

In the Old Testament law, God gave specific instructions for cleansing a person with leprosy (Lev. 14). A bird was sacrificed in an earthen vessel over running water, and then another bird was dipped in this blood and released to fly away. The ceremony was symbolic of the blood of Jesus shed for our earthen vessels, which carried away our sin and shame. After cleansing by blood, the person with leprosy received the anointing of oil on his ear, thumb, and toe, enabling him to hear God's voice, do His work, and walk in His ways.

In personal prayer, as you received the revelation of the blood of Jesus, you gained access to the throne room of God. There, in His presence, you will develop the Father-child intimacy that enables you to know His voice, serve Him, and walk in His ways. You will never move into the realm of power prayer without first and continually experiencing the intimate anointing of personal prayer.

2. The Leader's Anointing: Power Prayer

The second type of anointing in the Old Testament was the leader's anointing reserved for those who would serve as kings, prophets, captains, and so on. Examples are the anointing of Saul as captain over God's people (1 Sam. 10:1) and the anointing of David to serve as king (1 Sam. 16:12–13).

The leader's anointing imparted the position, power, and authority of the office to which a person was ordained. Through this anointing, the Holy Spirit came upon a person and endued him with special power to fulfill his destiny. The New Testament parallel of this anointing of power is promised in Acts 1:8 and fulfilled in Acts

2 through the coming of the Holy Spirit, who empowers us to fulfill our purpose and finish our appointed course.

Through the anointing of power prayer, you will rise up to fulfill your destiny, expose the lies of the false father, employ spiritual weapons to pull down strongholds, and war effectively against principalities and powers in spiritual places.

3. The Priest's Anointing: Prevailing Prayer

Exodus 29—30 and Leviticus 8 detail the anointing of the priests, which set them apart for service to God. The priests were anointed to stand continually in the presence of the Lord, worshiping, praising, and interceding for the people. This models the anointing of prevailing, persistent, effective prayer.

The New Testament believers' anointing to this position is described in 1 Peter 2:9 as "a chosen generation, a royal priesthood, a holy nation, His own special people, that you may proclaim the praises of Him who called you out of darkness into His marvelous light."

Results of the Prayer Anointing

The prayer anointing is the last great anointing of the Holy Spirit before the return of Jesus Christ. Several major results of this anointing will be manifested in your life:

Acceleration. Prayer becomes an easy yoke when the Holy Spirit takes over your prayer life. This doesn't mean you won't wake up in the morning with your flesh resisting rising up to pray. It means you will tell the flesh to shut up! The prayer anointing makes your will more powerful than your emotions. When you release your past, say yes to the present, and make the commitment to obey God in the future, a new anointing is present that accelerates your prayer life. As you go through the day, the Holy Spirit will call you to prayer repeatedly. He will say, "Pray right now!"

Revelation. Intercession births revelation. As your prayer life is accelerated, you will come to know God more intimately.

Interruption. This new anointing of prayer will interrupt the normal routines of your life. Your sleep habits may be interrupted as the Holy Spirit calls you to prayer. There may be an interruption of friendships and relationships as the Holy Spirit sets you apart to fulfill your God-given destiny.

Suppression. Demonic powers and the forces of darkness will be silenced. The more you pray, the more spiritual light is manifested in your life. Don't be so concerned about the darkness. Turn on the light because the light drives away the darkness.

Resolution. There will be a resolution of the troubling circumstances in your life. The prayer anointing resolves your personal issues according to God's will because you cannot pray out of the will of God when you are under the anointing. The prayer anointing is not a technique; rather, it is a spiritual mechanism that moves God into your circumstances to change them.

Exaltation. The final result of the prayer anointing is that you will be able to exalt God as the One who hears and answers prayer. You will rise up to declare, "To God be the glory, great things He has done."

Releasing the Prayer Anointing

You do not experience the prayer anointing by being ordained by an organization or denomination (although there is nothing wrong in doing this). God does not anoint on the basis of your intelligence, education, experience, or abilities. The anointing is based on your heart attitude.

When Samuel went to the house of Jesse to anoint a new king, he was looking for a man with a great outward appearance, but the Lord told him, "Man looks at the outward appearance, but the LORD looks at the heart." And E. M. Bounds asserts: "Many great men have led and molded the church who have not been great in prayer, but they were great only in their plans, great for their opinions, great for their organization, great by natural gifts, by the force of genius or of character. However, they were not great for God."[2]

To activate this prayer anointing, you cannot focus on your inadequacies. The disciples were men who originally were fearful and unbelieving, they slept in the Garden, deserted Jesus in His time of need, and even denied knowing Him. Yet Jesus entrusted that same group of men with the responsibility of reaching the world with the gospel, and each of them became mighty in prayer.

Jesus did not focus on their inabilities, lack of education, inferior social standing, or past failures. He saw the men as what they would become when they allowed the anointing to change their lives. Stop focusing on yourself, your inabilities, or your previous failures in prayer. Recognize that the "anointing which you have received from Him abides in you" (1 John 2:27). It is not that you are going to "get" an anointing. You have learned how to release the anointing through the revelation shared in this book:

> No man has ever yet desired to pray without ceasing . . . without having obtained it. To suppose such a thing would be manifest absurdity. For who is it who gives you the desire? God, of course. Does He give it to you in order that it may stay unfulfilled? That is impossible. He implants within you a desire for something with the intention of giving you that very thing.[3]

Are You Ready?

In the Old Testament, God told Moses to select elders, and He would take the same spirit that was on him and impart it to them. This book did not fall into your hands by accident. Your heavenly Father heard the cry of your soul for intimacy with Him and saw your desire to pray effectively. I believe you have been chosen to receive the same anointing of prayer that God has imparted to me.

I have inserted a special gift coupon on page 275. Remove this coupon from the book and mail it to me at the address indicated. I will send you a free cassette tape that will permit you to join me in personal prayer as we pray through the model prayer together.

Studies by behavioral scientists have indicated that it takes twenty-one days to impart a new habit or break an old one. You will recall that the prophet Daniel received his spiritual breakthrough in twenty-one days. I challenge you to use this tape every day for twenty-one days. Make a commitment to start in the morning and work through the model prayer each day as I provide personal guidance on the cassette. If you will commit to this for twenty-one days, I guarantee that you will establish a personal prayer life that will release you to experience the deeper anointings of power prayer and prevailing prayer. Prayer becomes a way of life when you find your personal prayer level, not one more thing on your daily list of things to do. It provides continual, intimate communion with your heavenly Father.

As you commit to pray the model prayer daily, the anointing will continue to flow, even as it happened for the widow who drew from the container of oil and the bin of flour (1 Kings 17:2–16). Despite three years of famine and desolation around her, she had constant supply.

Your prayer anointing will overflow to fill empty vessels around you, a spiritual parallel of the widow whose story is recorded in 2 Kings 4:1–7. This woman, who faced devastating circumstances and was in debt to creditors, was asked by the prophet Elisha, "What do you have in the house?" She replied, "Nothing except a jar of oil." Elisha told her to bring every empty vessel she could find, and as she began to pour, the oil multiplied. You have received the prayer anointing, and as you impart it to others, it will continue to flow in and through your life.

As you continually release your past, seek God in the present using the model prayer, and obey without fear in the future, this anointing will saturate your prayer life and enable you to function effectively at your personal prayer level.

When the disciples asked Jesus, "Teach us to pray," they began a course of instruction that was never completed. When you get caught up in the cycle of this anointing, you also will discover that there is no graduation from the school of prayer—there is only commencement.

NOTES

INTRODUCTION
1. Emily Morrison Beck, ed., *Bartlett's Familiar Quotations,* 15th ed. (Boston: Little Brown, 1980), 746.

CHAPTER TWO
1. Philip Harner, *Understanding the Lord's Prayer* (Philadelphia: Fortress, 1975), 3.
2. Taylor Bunch, *The Perfect Prayer* (Takoma Park: Review and Herald Publishing Association, 1939), 12.
3. Larry Lea, outline drawn from *Could You Not Tarry One Hour?* (Altamonte Springs: Creation House, 1987).

CHAPTER THREE
1. Phillip W. Keller, *A Layman Looks at the Lord's Prayer* (Chicago: Moody, 1976), 12.
2. Philip Harner, *Understanding the Lord's Prayer* (Philadelphia: Fortress, 1975), 41.
3. Keller, *A Layman Looks at the Lord's Prayer,* 13.

CHAPTER FIVE
1. Dr. William Gaultiere, *Returning to the Father* (Chicago: Moody, 1993), 131.

CHAPTER SIX
1. Norman H. Wright, *Always Daddy's Girl* (Ventura: Regal, 1989), 16–19.
2. Marcus Mabry, "No Father, No Answers," *Newsweek,* May 4, 1992, 50.
3. Dr. William Gaultiere, *Returning to the Father* (Chicago: Moody, 1993), 95.
4. Unknown Christian, *The Lord's Prayer in Practice* (New York: Revell, 1930), 37.

CHAPTER SEVEN
1. George Dorn, *The Creed of Jesus* (Burlington: Lutheran Literary Board, 1937), 29.

2. Andrew Murray, *The Power of the Blood of Jesus* (London: Marshall, Morgan, and Scott, 1943), 19.
3. David Alsobrook, *The Precious Blood* (Self-published, 1984), 28.
4. Benny Hinn, *The Blood* (Lake Mary: Creation House, 1993), 93.
5. Murray, *The Power of the Blood of Jesus,* 102–103.

CHAPTER EIGHT

1. William Barclay, *The Beatitudes and the Lord's Prayer for Everyman* (New York: Harper and Row, 1968), 176.
2. Unknown Christian, *The Lord's Prayer in Practice* (New York: Revell, 1930), 56.
3. Brad Young, *The Jewish Background to the Lord's Prayer* (Austin: Center for Judaic Christian Studies, 1984), 9.
4. Unknown Christian, *The Lord's Prayer in Practice,* 61–62.
5. Barclay, *The Beatitudes and the Lord's Prayer for Everyman,* 188.
6. Gerhard Ebeling, *The Lord's Prayer in Today's World* (Philadelphia: Fortress, 1963), 24.
7. Phillip W. Keller, *A Layman Looks at the Lord's Prayer* (Chicago: Moody, 1976), 55.
8. Ibid., 45–46.
9. Elmer Towns, *My Father's Names* (Ventura: Regal, 1991), 118.
10. Gary Smalley and John Trent, *The Blessing* (New York: Simon and Schuster, 1990), summary of chapter theses/titles.
11. Keller, *A Layman Looks at the Lord's Prayer,* 54.

CHAPTER NINE

1. Philip Harner, *Understanding the Lord's Prayer* (Philadelphia: Fortress, 1975), 67.
2. Taylor Bunch, *The Perfect Prayer* (Takoma Park: Review and Herald Publishing Association, 1939), 48.
3. Ibid., 49.
4. Ibid., 43.
5. George Dorn, *The Creed of Jesus* (Burlington: Lutheran Literary Board, 1937), 44.
6. Patrick Johnstone, *Operation World* (Waynesboro: STL Books, 1978).

CHAPTER TEN

1. Phillip W. Keller, *A Layman Looks at the Lord's Prayer* (Chicago: Moody, 1976), 87.

2. William Barclay, *The Beatitudes and the Lord's Prayer for Everyman* (New York: Harper and Row, 1968), 210.
3. Keller, *A Layman Looks at the Lord's Prayer*, 89.

CHAPTER ELEVEN

1. Curtis C. Mitchell, *Praying Jesus' Way* (Old Tappan: Revell, 1977), 47.
2. William Barclay, *The Beatitudes and the Lord's Prayer for Everyman* (New York: Harper and Row, 1968), 222.
3. Taylor Bunch, *The Perfect Prayer* (Takoma Park: Review and Herald Publishing Association, 1939), 72.
4. Barclay, *The Beatitudes and the Lord's Prayer for Everyman*, 225.

CHAPTER TWELVE

1. Gerhard Ebeling, *The Lord's Prayer in Today's World* (Philadelphia: Fortress, 1963), 69.
2. John MacArthur, *The Disciple's Prayer* (Chicago: Moody, 1986), 198.
3. Philip Harner, *Understanding the Lord's Prayer* (Philadelphia: Fortress, 1975), 105.
4. Phrases "don't curse it, don't nurse it, don't rehearse it, but disperse it" drawn from message by Dr. Robert Schuller.

CHAPTER THIRTEEN

1. William Barclay, *The Beatitudes and the Lord's Prayer for Everyman* (New York: Harper and Row, 1968), 253.
2. Ibid., 245.
3. George Dorn, *The Creed of Jesus* (Burlington: Lutheran Literary Board, 1937), 80.
4. Henry Bast, *The Lord's Prayer* (Grand Rapids: Church Press, 1957), 67.
5. Larry Lea, *Could You Not Tarry One Hour?* (Study Guide) (Rockwall: Church on the Rock, 1987), 86.

CHAPTER FIFTEEN

1. William Barclay, *The Beatitudes and the Lord's Prayer for Everyman* (New York: Harper and Row, 1968), 256.

CHAPTER SEVENTEEN

1. Robbie Castleman, *David: Man After God's Own Heart* (Wheaton: Harold Shaw, 1981), 11.

2. Ivor Powell, *David: His Life And Times* (Grand Rapids: Kregel, 1990), 25.
3. Charles Swindoll, *David: A Man After God's Own Heart* (Waco: Word Educational Products, 1988), 12–13.

CHAPTER NINETEEN
1. Charles Swindoll, *David: A Man After God's Own Heart* (Waco: Word Educational Products, 1988), 67.
2. Ivor Powell, *David: His Life and Times* (Grand Rapids: Kregel, 1990), 85.
3. Swindoll, *David: A Man After God's Own Heart*, 47.
4. Powell, *David: His Life and Times*, 92.
5. Swindoll, *David: A Man After God's Own Heart*, 46.

CHAPTER TWENTY
1. Ivor Powell, *David: His Life and Times* (Grand Rapids: Kregel, 1990), 144.
2. Matthew Henry, *Commentary on the Whole Bible* (Old Tappan: Revell, n.d.), 2:438.
3. J. Vernon McGee, *Through the Bible* (Nashville: Thomas Nelson, 1983), 2:183.
4. Powell, *David: His Life and Times*, 144.

CHAPTER TWENTY-ONE
1. Charles Swindoll, *David: A Man After God's Own Heart* (Waco: Word Educational Products, 1988), 101–102.
2. Matthew Henry, *Commentary on the Whole Bible* (Old Tappan: Revell, n.d.), 2:494.
3. Ibid., 2:495.
4. Swindoll, *David: A Man After God's Own Heart*, 105.
5. J. Vernon McGee, *Through the Bible* (Nashville: Thomas Nelson, 1983), 2:210.
6. Swindoll, *David: A Man After God's Own Heart*, 110.
7. Ibid., 109–10.
8. Ibid., 119–20.
9. Ibid., 126.
10. Henry, *Commentary on the Whole Bible*, 2:105.

CHAPTER TWENTY-TWO
1. Morris Cerullo, *Forgiven* (Eastbourne, E. Sussex, Great Britain: Kingsway Publications, 1993), 55.

CHAPTER TWENTY-THREE

1. Charles Swindoll, *Demonism* (Portland: Multnomah, 1981), 5.
2. Terry Law, *The Power of Praise and Worship* (Tulsa: Victory House, 1985), 99.
3. A. L. Gill, *Not Made for Defeat* (Fawnskin, Calif.: Powerhouse, 1988), 149.

CHAPTER TWENTY-FOUR

1. A. L. Gill, *Not Made for Defeat* (Fawnskin, Calif.: Powerhouse, 1988), 99.

CHAPTER TWENTY-FIVE

1. *Newsweek,* January 13, 1992, 48–53.

CHAPTER TWENTY-SIX

1. Charles Swindoll, *David: A Man After God's Own Heart* (Waco: Word Educational Products, 1988), 72.
2. Ibid., 74.
3. A. L. Gill, *Not Made for Defeat* (Fawnskin, Calif.: Powerhouse, 1988), 177.
4. F. J. Hugel as quoted by Leonard Ravenhill, *Revival Praying* (Minneapolis: Bethany House, 1961), 14.

CHAPTER TWENTY-SEVEN

1. Charles Spurgeon, *Morning and Evening* (Grand Rapids: Zondervan, 1980), January 15.
2. Samuel Chadwick as quoted by Leonard Ravenhill, *Revival Praying* (Minneapolis: Bethany House, 1961), 44.
3. E. M. Bounds, *The Complete Works of E. M. Bounds on Prayer* (Grand Rapids: Baker, 1992), 35.

CHAPTER TWENTY-EIGHT

1. Charles Spurgeon, *Morning and Evening* (Grand Rapids: Zondervan, 1980), February 5.
2. Matthew Henry, *Commentary on the Whole Bible* (Old Tappan: Revell, n.d.), 5:694.
3. Curtis C. Mitchell, *Praying Jesus' Way,* (Old Tappan: Revell, 1977), 84.
4. Ibid.
5. Herbert Lockyer, *All the Parables of the Bible* (Grand Rapids: Zondervan, 1959), 301.

6. Mitchell, *Praying Jesus' Way*, 136.

CHAPTER TWENTY-NINE
1. E. M. Bounds, *The Complete Works of E.M. Bounds on Prayer* (Grand Rapids: Baker, 1992), 39.

CHAPTER THIRTY
1. Harold Horton, *The Gifts of the Spirit* (Springfield: Gospel Publishing House, 1975), 148–49.
2. W. E. Vine, *Expository Dictionary of New Testament Words* (Peabody, Mass.: Hendrickson), 430.

CHAPTER THIRTY-ONE
1. William Barclay, *The Beatitudes and the Lord's Prayer for Everyman* (New York: Harper and Row, 1968), 157.
2. Morris Cerullo, *Victory Miracle Library* (San Diego: Morris Cerullo World Evangelism, 1995), March 1995, 9.
3. Ibid., 13.

CHAPTER THIRTY-THREE
1. John MacArthur, *The Disciple's Prayer* (Chicago: Moody, 1986), 3.

CHAPTER THIRTY-FIVE
1. Curtis C. Mitchell, *Praying Jesus' Way* (Old Tappan: Revell, 1977), 119.
2. Frank E. Gaebelein, ed., *The Expositor's Bible Commentary* (Grand Rapids: Zondervan, 1978), 2:291.
3. E. M. Bounds, *The Complete Works of E. M. Bounds on Prayer* (Grand Rapids: Baker, 1992), 325.

CHAPTER THIRTY-SEVEN
1. E. M. Bounds, *The Complete Works of E. M. Bounds on Prayer* (Grand Rapids: Baker, 1992), 447.
2. Ibid., 385.
3. Quoting Jean-Nicholas Grou, Leonard Ravenhill, *Revival Praying* (Minneapolis: Bethany House, 1961), 92.

BIBLIOGRAPHY

Alsobrook, David. *The Precious Blood.* Self-published, 1984.

Barclay, William. *The Beatitudes and the Lord's Prayer for Everyman.* New York: Harper and Row, 1968.

Bast, Henry. *The Lord's Prayer.* Grand Rapids: Church Press, 1957.

Beck, Emily Morrison, ed. *Bartlett's Familiar Quotations,* 15th ed. Boston: Little Brown, 1980.

Bounds, E. M. *The Complete Works of E. M. Bounds on Prayer.* Grand Rapids: Baker, 1992.

Bunch, Taylor. *The Perfect Prayer.* Takoma Park: Review and Herald Publishing Association, 1939.

Castleman, Robbie. *David: Man After God's Own Heart.* Vols. 1 and 2. Wheaton: Harold Shaw, 1981.

Cerullo, Morris. *Forgiven.* Eastbourne, E. Sussex, Great Britain: Kingsway Publications, 1993.

———. *Victory Miracle Library.* San Diego: Morris Cerullo World Evangelism, 1995.

Chappell, Clovis G. *Sermons on the Lord's Prayer.* Nashville: Cokesbury, 1934.

Dorn, George. *The Creed of Jesus.* Burlington: Lutheran Literary Board, 1937.

Duffield, Guy P. and Nathaniel Van Cleave. *Foundations of Pentecostal Theology.* Los Angeles: LIFE Bible College, 1983.

Eastman, Dick. *The Hour That Changes the World.* Grand Rapids: Baker, 1987.

Ebeling, Gerhard. *The Lord's Prayer in Today's World.* Philadelphia: Fortress, 1963.

Gaebelein, Frank E., ed. *The Expositor's Bible Commentary.* Grand Rapids: Zondervan, 1978.

Gaultiere, William. *Returning to the Father.* Chicago: Moody, 1993.

Gibson, Noel, and Phyl Gibson. *Evicting Demonic Squatters and Breaking Bondages.* Drummoyne: Freedom in Christ Ministries Trust, 1987.

Gill, A. L. *Not Made for Defeat.* Fawnskin, Calif.: Powerhouse Publishing, 1988.

Harner, Philip. *Understanding the Lord's Prayer.* Philadelphia: Fortress, 1975.

271

Henry, Matthew. *Commentary on the Whole Bible*. Old Tappan: Revell, n.d.

Hinn, Benny. *The Blood*. Lake Mary: Creation House, 1993.

Horton, Harold. *The Gifts of the Spirit*. Springfield: Gospel Publishing House, 1975.

Johnstone, Patrick. *Operation World*. Waynesboro: STL Books, 1978.

Keller, W. Phillip. *A Layman Looks at the Lord's Prayer*. Chicago: Moody, 1976.

Laubach, Frank. *Prayer: The Mightiest Force in the World*. Old Tappan: Revell, 1946.

Law, Terry. *The Power of Praise and Worship*. Tulsa: Victory House, 1985.

Lea, Larry. *Could You Not Tarry One Hour?* Altamonte Springs: Creation House, 1987.

————. *Could You Not Tarry One Hour? (Study Guide)*. Rockwall: Church on the Rock, 1987.

————. *The Hearing Ear*. Lake Mary: Creation House, 1988.

————. *The Weapons of Your Warfare*. Lake Mary: Creation House, 1989.

Lea, Melva. *Desperate Women*. Nashville: Thomas Nelson, 1991.

Lockyer, Herbert. *All the Parables of the Bible*. Grand Rapids: Zondervan, 1959.

Loeks, Mary Foxwell. *The Glorious Names of God*. Grand Rapids: Baker, 1986.

Lohmeyer, Ernst. *Our Father*. New York: Harper and Row, 1965.

Mabry, Marcus. "No Father, No Answers." *Newsweek,* May 4, 1992.

MacArthur, John. *The Disciple's Prayer*. Chicago: Moody, 1986.

McGee, J. Vernon. *Through the Bible*. Nashville: Thomas Nelson, 1983.

Miliclochman, Jan. *The Lord's Prayer*. Grand Rapids: Eerdmans, 1990.

Mitchell, Curtis C. *Praying Jesus' Way*. Old Tappan: Revell, 1977.

Murray, Andrew. *The Power of the Blood of Jesus*. London: Marshall, Morgan, and Scott, 1943.

Newsweek. January 13, 1992.

Powell, Ivor. *David: His Life and Times*. Grand Rapids: Kregel, 1990.

Ravenhill, Leonard. *Revival Praying*. Minneapolis: Bethany House, 1961.

Smalley, Gary, and John Trent. *The Blessing*. New York: Simon and Schuster, 1990.

Spurgeon, Charles. *Morning and Evening*. Grand Rapids: Zondervan, 1980.

Swindoll, Charles. *David: A Man After God's Own Heart*. Waco: Word Educational Products, 1988.

———. *Demonism*. Portland: Multnomah, 1981.

Towns, Elmer. *My Father's Names*. Ventura: Regal, 1991.

Unknown Christian. *The Lord's Prayer in Practice*. New York: Revell, 1930.

Vine, W. E. *Expository Dictionary of New Testament Words*. Peabody, Mass.: Hendrickson, Revell.

Wallis, Arthur. *God's Chosen Fast*. Fort Washington: Christian Literature Crusade, 1977.

Wright, H. Norman. *Always Daddy's Girl*. Ventura: Regal, 1989.

Young, Brad. *The Jewish Background to the Lord's Prayer*. Austin: Center for Judaic Christian Studies, 1984.

About the Author

Dr. Larry Lea is well known to Christians of all denominations as a strong advocate of prayer, having generated a prayer pattern drawn from Matthew 6 that is used daily by literally thousands of people around the world. He has hosted prayer rallies and crusades in Australia, Canada, Great Britain, South Africa, Israel, Colombia, India, Germany, and throughout the United States.

Dr. Lea is the author of several books on prayer and spiritual commitment including *Could You Not Tarry One Hour?*, *The Hearing Ear, Weapons Of Your Warfare,* and *Wisdom—Don't Live Life Without It.*

He holds a B.A. in religion from Dallas Baptist University, a master of divinity from Southwestern Baptist Theological Seminary in Fort Worth, and a divinity degree from Oral Roberts University in Tulsa.

Dr. Lea formerly served as youth pastor at Beverly Hills Baptist Church in Dallas, where he began with fourteen people and increased the group to more than one thousand. He is the founding pastor of Church on the Rock in Rockwall, Texas, and presently serves as senior pastor of San Diego Lighthouse Church, San Diego, California.

Prayer Cassette Coupon

Now you can experience an hour of intimate, personal prayer with Dr. Larry Lea as he guides you through each section of the model prayer. Dr. Lea also includes a special prayer of impartation on the tape, transmitting to you the anointings of personal, power, and prevailing prayer.

Remove this coupon from the book, fill it out, and mail it to Dr. Lea to receive the *free* cassette tape he has prepared as a gift for you.

Complete This Information:

Name_____

Street Address or P.O. Box Number_____

_____

City_____ State_____ Zip Code_____

Country_____

Mail This Coupon To:

Larry Lea Ministries
P.O. Box 81286
San Diego, California 92138 USA

Please allow six weeks for delivery.

(Submit This Original Coupon Only: Due to an agreement with the publisher, we cannot honor facsimiles or copies of this coupon.)

Please Let Me Hear from You . . .

I believe this message will truly transform your life! People from all around the world write to tell me how the prayer anointing has changed and strengthened their lives. Many pastors and ministers have declared their entire ministries were revolutionized through this revelation.

I believe you will be used by God in a mighty, powerful way that will literally astound you because the anointing sets people free. You will experience four things as a result of this revelation:

1. A new exhilaration in your prayer life
2. New revelation from God
3. A new level of intimacy with your Father in heaven
4. A new, dynamic level of power

Please write and tell me how this message has affected your life and ministry. Use the space provided below to share your testimony. I will join you in giving the Lord all the glory!

Pastor Larry Lea

_____

_____

_____

_____

_____

Name _____

Address _____

Mail this response to:

Larry Lea Ministries
P.O. Box 81286
San Diego, California 92138 USA
1-800-895-1700